WORDS OF PRAISE
When Ireland Fell Silent

"Ms. Enis created the family to guide the reader through the turbulent time of one of Ireland's most tragic eras, but the facts of the story are as accurate as historical research allows . . . . the author has cleverly created a family to experience the tragedy and, with gripping narrative, conveys their anxiety, hope, frustration and desperation as they experience the historically accurate hardships. . . . To read this book is to experience An Gorta Mor."

—*The National Hibernian Digest,* September-October, 2010.

<hr />

"May the sun shine on this book that plumbs the joy and despair of days that will never be forgotten. It will stir readers as it stirred the author's heart."

> —Carolyn Hart, award-winning novelist and mystery writer, author of the Death on Demand series, the Henrie O series, and more.

<hr />

"*When Ireland Fell Silent* is compelling historical fiction, rooted in genuine research and an appreciation of the era. It is epic, grand, brimming with life, filled with believable characters. "

> —James A. Percoco, historian, educator, author of *A Passion for the Past*, *Divided We Stand*, and *Summers with Lincoln*.

"The book is not only factual in every detail, but her style of writing put me in the cottage beside the Reilly family . . . . I even welled up tears at her telling of the American Wake . . . . you will find this one easy to read and, more importantly, easy to comprehend, even though it will never be easy to understand the rationale for the Hunger."

—Mike McCormack, AOH National Historian,
    author of *Echoes of Irish History, Profiles in Patriotism,* and
    The Long Voyage Home

<hr>

"I expected to find lots of good history in this book. What surprised me was how engaging the Reilly family story was and how involved I got in learning about the Irish famine through their eyes. It is a much-needed story, well researched and told. This book should be required reading in all school curricula that teach about the Irish Famine, the Jewish Holocaust, and Native American removal."

—Elaine Reed, Executive Director Emeritus of the
    National Council for History Education

<hr>

"I really enjoyed the book . . . couldn't put it down. The story brought to life and reality the unbelievable suffering, oppression, and discrimination the Irish of Famine times endured at the hands of the British. As a Mayo man first, an Irishman, and now an Irish-American, the book confirmed for me the unjust manner in which the Brits treated our fellow Irish and put into perspective the immense tragedy that could quite easily have been prevented with just an ounce of helpfulness from Ireland's worst neighbor. As a person with a degree in the Irish language, I am impressed with your accuracy, except for a few minor glitches."

—Jim Graven, President, Irish Center of Pittsburgh

"I found this book to be a true depiction of "An Gorta Mor," the Great Hunger, told as it was lived at the time. It was indeed not a famine but a forced hunger on the Irish people. I hope that people will read this book to learn what happened."

—Seamus Boyle, National President of the
Ancient Order of Hibernians in America, Inc.

"The book provides details that grip you as you wonder whether the Reilly family can overcome the famine and survive. Toward the end, the meaning [of the title] is revealed through the tragedy and triumph of the Irish people."

—Joe Hight, *The Oklahoman*, October 31, 2010, 7D

"Enis has thoroughly researched the Famine and . . . . skillfully recreates both tenant farmer life and the incomprehensible actions and inactions of the British government and landlords. One of the most memorable parts of the novel is of a wedding . . . from the house-raising to the toasts, to the sharing of the wedding cake. . . . excellent narrative flow . . . . moving and realistic recreation of a society on the brink of destruction."

—Kristin Romano, *Irish America*, August/September, 2011, 75

"A work of fiction grounded in a gritty reality. . . .the first-ever book we would require you to read. . . . No detail escapes her keen eye and everything is explained using concise descriptions and wonderfully contextual references. As reports in the local paper update the travesty taking place in an uncaring and brutal Parliament, you can almost feel the cold and the hunger —and the seething sense of cruelty and injustice. . . ."

—Pete Maher, *Irish Focus*, July / Juil 2011, 16

When Ireland Fell Silent:

A Story of a Family's Struggle Against Famine and Eviction

To Lisa,
with Best Wishes
Harolyn Enis

Harolyn Enis

Rose Rock
PUBLISHERS, LLC

This book is a work of historical fiction.
Except for public figures and their actual
documented incidents and statements, the
names, characters and incidents are products of
the author's imagination or are used fictitiously.

The photographs used on the front cover and in
this book were all taken by the author in County
Mayo, Ireland, 2008.

Published by Rose Rock Publishers, LLC
P.O. Box 20040, Oklahoma City, OK 73156
Email: rose.rock.pub@att.net

Manufactured in the United States of America

ISBN: 978-0-9844821-0-8

FOREWORD

This story was inspired by years of researching historical and eyewitness accounts of the Irish Famine. The actions and attitudes of powerful policy makers and leaders such as Sir Charles Trevelyan, Sir Charles Wood, Daniel O'Connell and others are true to their documented record.

The suffering and injustices endured by the fictional family named Reilly are representative of the millions of nameless persons who shared their experiences and lived, died, or fled this island. Actual events and voices from that time reveal the forces at work as Ireland fell silent.

When Ireland
Fell Silent

PROLOGUE

Ireland Before the Great Famine: A Short History

For centuries before the Great Irish Famine (1845-1852), England made repeated attempts to subjugate neighboring Ireland. As early as 1171, Henry II invaded Ireland to acquire land and power. Although overwhelmed by English armies numerous times, the Irish proved to have a strong spirit and never stopped trying to regain their independence.

By the sixteenth century, religion became embroiled in this struggle. In 1534, the English king Henry VIII asked permission from the Pope to divorce his wife. When denied, the monarch broke with the Catholic Church and made himself head of the church which he now called The Church of England. From that point on, the king assumed those who remained Catholic were disloyal to him and a challenge to his power and authority. Henry VIII repressed not only Catholics but other religions as well and seized churches, monasteries, land, and wealth of the Catholic Church. He executed some otherwise loyal subjects and waged campaigns against Catholics, calling them "Papists." His actions inflamed religious antagonism for centuries.

In 1541, Henry VIII forced Ireland's Parliament to declare him its king, but Catholic Ireland, evangelized by St. Patrick in 433, refused to abandon its religion and resisted English domination. Periodically the Irish mounted revolts, often with the help of Spanish or French allies. But success against the English was difficult because, unlike the American colonies which were separated from England by the Atlantic Ocean, the Irish had only the Irish Sea – 130 miles at its widest point – between them and the most powerful and richest nation on earth.

England's treatment of the Irish became increasingly bloody and brutal. English monarchs, regardless of whether they were Catholic or Protestant, whether they were named James, Elizabeth, or Mary, all practiced the same ruthless tyranny against the Irish. Instead of trying to reduce the causes of Irish discontent, the English decided to punish and crush the Irish once and for all. In 1649, under the leadership of Oliver Cromwell, they landed a huge army on Irish shores. Without mercy they massacred entire towns, destroyed monasteries and churches, and captured 100,000 young Irish whom they shipped as slaves to the West Indies.

Land confiscation, long used by colonial nations to dominate native people, had begun in 1557, and around 1606 King James I seized millions of acres in Ulster (Northern Ireland) and gave large tracts to Scottish landlords. But now throughout Ireland, confiscation of land continued on an even grander scale. Cromwell's army stripped eleven million acres away from their Irish owners and gave them to English landlords.

These Anglo-Irish landlords – English living in Ireland – became an elite minority. As early as 1366, the Statutes of Kilkenny sought to preserve supposed racial purity and separateness by forbidding the Anglo-Irish from adopting local customs, intermarrying, or speaking the language of the natives called Irish or Gaelic. The English government deliberately maintained the gulf between the native Irish and the English overseers as a way to keep landlords loyal to the crown and enforcers of English dictates. The nurturing of religious and racial bigotry was a way to preserve the segregation of the elite. At the top of the social pyramid in both Ireland and England was a prestigious aristocracy that enjoyed power, inherited titles, wealth and land.

The all-powerful English landlord in Ireland could act in any manner toward a tenant without fear of penalty since the tenant had no legal protection in the law. He could increase rent at any time and evict tenants at will. This relationship between landlord and tenant existed well past the years of the famine and changed very slowly.

By the 1690's, Irish Catholics, which included practically all native Irish, were the target of special laws called the Penal Codes. The purpose of the Penal Codes was to take away freedom, human dignity, civil rights, economic options, and to impoverish Irish to the level of serfs, even slaves. These laws forbade education and made it a crime to attend a school, to hire a teacher, or even to instruct one's own children. The government banished school masters, Catholic priests, and monks and trailed them with bloodhounds in order to kill them. They hunted religious leaders for sport and offered bounties for their heads.

Nevertheless, the Irish secretly tried to preserve their learning, culture, and religion. Although the Penal Codes outlawed Catholic worship, many Irish attended religious services in remote countryside locations, risking their own lives and those of the priests who hid amidst them. Long steeped in traditions of scholarship and learning, the Irish clandestinely pursued education in the bogs, forests, and hedges while posting a lookout for soldiers. The English also tried to stamp out Irish culture by outlawing traditions, dance, and music. But as with their religion, the Irish kept much of their rich cultural heritage alive by secret performances and an indomitable spirit that refused to succumb.

Economically, the Penal Codes denied Irish Catholics the right to purchase, inherit, or lease land, enter a profession, or engage in trade or commerce. Having no civil rights, they could not vote, hold public office, or serve on juries. They were not permitted to live in a corporate town or within five miles of one, nor could they own a horse worth more than five pounds or a wagon.

As a result of these laws, the Irish became the poorest population in Europe with most living in one room, stone huts covered in stucco. The government levied an extra tax when they had a window or a chimney. To enforce these laws and its will, the English dictators occupied the island with a large army.

According to the colonial or imperial philosophy, the so-called "mother country" was entitled to exploit all conquered lands for her benefit, and thus, England made it unlawful for Ireland to have commerce with the colonies or other nations whenever it competed with English merchants. At various times the English passed laws to inhibit Irish manufacture of cloth, glass, or crafts for export. In 1571 Queen Elizabeth declared that all products brought into Ireland must be carried in English ships with most of the crew being English. All cargo going to or from Ireland had to be unloaded in England first and charged fees. These policies trapped the native Irish in poverty with few options.

In 1776 the American Revolution began and stretched British resources for the next seven years, keeping much of her army across the ocean. During this revolt, England feared that France might invade Ireland, and so it organized the Protestant Volunteer Army in Northern Ireland which trained itself and purchased its own equipment.

At the end of the American Revolution, the British government's grip on Ireland was at its weakest point in centuries. It had squandered money and prestige in a failed attempt to control the Americans, and the ideas of rights, republics, and revolution were taking root everywhere. Slowly and grudgingly, the English rulers eased some laws against Catholic Irish. In 1778 they permitted Catholics to lease land, and in 1782 they openly allowed them to have Catholic schools.

About this same time, the English finally let Catholic priests legally return to Ireland and Catholics could again build places of worship. Catholic priests and monks had been banished from Ireland for almost a hundred years, but some had hidden among the people. However, Catholics were still forced to pay the hated tax to support the Church of Ireland, as the monarch's church in Ireland was called, even though these churches were generally empty and many originally had been Catholic cathedrals.

The British were not in a position to subdue easily the capable Irish Protestant Army which still existed at this time, so they made concessions rather than challenge the army. The Protestants of Northern Ireland under the leadership of Henry Grattan demanded trade concessions, some of which the English granted as early as 1779.

In 1782 the Irish Parliament, which met in Dublin, won partial independence when a new constitution gave it permission to make some decisions with only the monarch's approval. The English still had control of the executives in Ireland whom they appointed, but Grattan dreamed of greater autonomy and saw Ireland and England as equal nations under the same king. Irish Catholics were still excluded from the Irish Parliament and could not vote for its members who were limited to Anglo-Irish aristocrats. Yet, this Irish Parliament generally showed more concern for Ireland's welfare than did officials in London.

In 1789 the French revolted against their king. Their battle cry was "liberty, equality, fraternity, and democracy," and British rulers rightly feared that the concepts of democracy and representative government might "infect" the Irish. In 1792 to appease the Irish at its "back door," they allowed Catholics to vote for candidates to the Irish Parliament and to become lawyers. This period of fragile independence on the part of the Irish Parliament lasted approximately eighteen years.

But when another Irish rebellion occurred with the assistance of French troops in Mayo in 1798, the English decided it was time to clamp down on Ireland again. No longer did they trust the Irish Parliament to rule in the interest of England, and they demanded that the Irish law-making body be dissolved in favor of a union of Ireland and Britain as one nation. At first the Irish Parliament refused the demand, and only after a year of bribery and inducements with pensions and peerage did it accept the Act of Union. Huge sums of money were paid out to members of the Irish Parliament before the Union Jack Flag flew over both Ireland and England in 1801.

However, it was not a true marriage or union, and in many respects Ireland was still treated like a lowly colony. English law did not extend to Ireland, nor did it accord to Irish the same rights as British citizens. In Ireland for the next fifty years, special coercive legislation such as the suspension of *habeas corpus* was in effect for all but five of these years. Their treasuries remained separate, with Ireland expected to contribute 2/17 of the expense of the United Kingdom. Landlords, who were mainly English and Protestants, still discriminated against and exploited the Irish Catholic farmers.

Seeing what had happened with the Act of Union and hating the result, the Irish longed to be free of the British yoke and concluded that if they could obtain even a measure of self-government, perhaps they could eventually reform things. Responding to this yearning for fair treatment and rights was one of the few Irish Catholic landlords, a lawyer named Daniel O'Connell, who in 1823 began agitating and organizing for peaceful change. Despite the fact that it was illegal for a Catholic to sit in the House of Commons, he ran for this body in 1828, and to the amazement of English leaders, he won the election. O'Connell challenged authorities by going to London to take his seat.

Fearful of making the Irish angry, the King made a concession. He reluctantly signed a law, the Catholic Emancipation Act of 1829, which permitted Catholics to sit in Parliament. However, this law made it more difficult for Catholics to win such seats in the future and made it even harder for native Irish to vote. The king even refused to allow O'Connell to take his seat until he had been re-elected from Clare, so not until 1830 did O'Connell finally become the first Catholic in modern times to sit in the British Parliament.

In 1834, O'Connell introduced debate on repealing the union and later founded the Repeal Association. His tactics used political pressure and moral force in a nonviolent manner and worked within the system. His goals were to gain legislative independence and some degree of home rule. Repeal rallies, which the London *Times* dubbed "monster meetings," were held all over Ireland, attracting crowds in the hundreds of thousands which stretched over the hillsides for miles. They hoped such dramatic demonstrations of public opinion would pressure authorities into concessions. In order to show their unity, Irish would attend the gatherings, even when they stood too far away to hear the speakers. Repeal wardens or patrols made certain that no violence discredited the movement in the British press.

Two men riding in a cart often led the procession to the rallies and dramatized the Irish desire for freedom. A man wearing a black face and a sign "now free" represented the slaves of the West Indies who had been emancipated fourteen years earlier. Beside him, a white man in chains represented the Irish, who still longed for real freedom. People carried banners in red on green which said "Ireland for the Irish," and parallel meetings were often held in New York.

The idealism and language of the American and French Revolutions had inspired and raised the hopes of these barefoot peasants, and now each month they sacrificed to pay "repeal rent" after Mass to local association wardens. These monies paid administrative costs and promoted repeal ideas in both Ireland and England. The native Irish had great faith in the eloquent and charismatic Daniel O'Connell to secure some self government for the Irish.

However, British leaders became nervous when his rallies became larger and his following greater. In 1843 O'Connell scheduled a monster meeting at Clontarf, but the British banned the gathering and brought in troops and artillery to the site as a threat. To avoid bloodshed, O'Connell canceled the rally, but despite his compliance, the government imprisoned O'Connell, his son, and seven assistants.

This action dealt a serious blow to the hopes of the Irish Catholic majority, and the movement was never the same. Although the British released O'Connell in September, 1844, the seventy-year-old suffered from failing health and was disheartened. Within the movement the leaders disagreed about goals, with O'Connell advocating that Ireland become a self governing unit within a federal Great Britain and others wanting more independence.

As 1845 dawned, Irish were still wretchedly poor and without basic human rights. While the government had relaxed most of the Penal Codes, vestiges still persisted in practice and habit. Life for the native Irish was rife with inequality, racial and religious prejudice, and economic exploitation. Rents for tenants in Ireland had steadily increased until they were almost twice as high as those in England. Landlords lived in luxury and took the grain crops and other foods the Irish produced as rent to sell in England or abroad for cash. This forced the Irish to depend mainly on the prolific potato for their food and denied them any opportunity to profit from their own labor.

Despite injustice, eighteen-year-old Liam Reilly, the central character of this novel, still hoped that someday he and his countrymen would win rights. County Mayo was home and his roots ran deep. He could not foresee that the worst human tragedy of the nineteenth century was about to unfold – the Great Irish Famine.

I
At The Edge

Alone in the cottage, young Liam Reilly felt uneasy but did not know why. A damp draft blew in like an unwelcome spirit and made peat smoke swirl around the room, irritating his eyes. The clammy air made his shirt stick to his ribs and the atmosphere oppressive . . . close. This weather . . . so strange for October in County Mayo. The year was 1845.

Shuffling over to the water pail, he gulped from the ladle, dripping on the flagstone. Seeking fresh air, he leaned his long, lanky frame on his elbows out the half-door and glanced up at the dense, gray clouds which made it seem later than early afternoon. Above him, a skylark rustled in the thatch, tilted its head, and peered down but denied him its usual melodious call. It seemed to share the sense of gloom, and he studied it quizzically.

As Liam gazed out over the stone walls which enclosed their small yard to the eight acres of stubble left from summer's harvest, his eyes followed the winding lane that connected them to neighbors. Someone was coming.

Bareheaded, Uncle Padraig was lumbering down the path, with his thick brown and gray hair standing up like a stiff brush. Grown men never left home without a hat, and as he got closer,

Liam saw that his lined face was ashen and worried.

Even before reaching the yard, he yelled, "Liam! Where's Seamus! Is he home?"

Liam opened the bottom half of the door. "No one's here but me. Father took the family berry picking at Lough Carra, and I stayed here to do the milking. What's happened?"

"Heaven help us! The black scourge . . . it's *here* . . . in the Partry Hills!" His voice cracked. Uncle Padraig bent over, hands on his knees, and sucked in air. "It's the . . . devil's work!" he gasped between breaths. "Go to the Sullivans! We're taking what food we can, or they'll starve!"

Liam frowned. "The black scourge?"

"The blight, that's what!" His bulging eyes alarmed Liam. What would terrify a strong man like Uncle?

Padraig's eyes stared ahead at something only he could see, and his voice became husky. "If it spreads, we're doomed." He shook himself. "Got to tell Cousin Eamon!" A bear of a man, he loped away, huffing.

Liam gawked after him, stunned by Uncle's stark fear. Tossing some potatoes in a basket, he sprinted out, and taking a short cut, skirted his own family's recently dug potato beds and bounded over the stile. Without breaking stride, he crossed the mossy log that spanned the brook and trotted down the well-worn path, his bare feet pounding the soft earth.

When he reached the Sullivan cottage, a solemn crowd roamed the side yard as though attending a wake. Neighbors he had known all his life offered no greetings, and Liam felt an eerie foreboding. People wandered about, dazed, while others formed tight circles around the potato pits, several persons deep, and stared into them with wide-eyed horror. Their expressions unnerved Liam who stood at the back and stepped aside when people wanted out.

Women put shawls over their noses, and even a curious dog, slinking away from the hole, whined and whimpered.

Then Liam caught a whiff of the nauseating stench and stretched his long body to get a glimpse over their heads. When one woman in front retched and was pulled aside, he inched forward. Deep in the pit, the potatoes were oozing a black, sticky slime and had collapsed into a putrid mush, decomposing like a dead thing. With his arm over his mouth, Liam retreated from the revolting odor and gagged.

He realized the alarm had spread when grave farmers from surrounding villages clambered into the yard and went directly to the pits. When they wandered away, they stood in knots on the perimeter, and Liam overheard their murmurings.

"Will this rot travel to us . . . one pit to another?"

"It is a curse, it is!"

"My potatoes . . . sound this morning."

A child's voice. "What will happen to us, Da?" Dread of the answers showed in their eyes.

Liam recalled Uncle's words: "If it spreads, we're doomed!"

Through the crowd, he saw Mrs. Sullivan's tear-streaked face and heard her moan between sobs while her whimpering children clung to her skirt.

Nearby, her husband, with red-rimmed eyes, swallowed hard and shook his head. "They were fine when I lifted them . . . now all ruined!" Deep furrows creased his forehead as people filed by, muttering condolences, and promising to share what food they could. Some, like Liam, left baskets at his door.

Liam had always known that the worst fear of an Irish farmer was that some disease would take his potatoes. He eyed the oats piled high beside Sullivan's cottage – part of the best oat harvest Ireland had produced in ten years – but the oats would all go to the landlord to pay the rent. Even if Sullivan's children cried in hunger, he dared not let them eat this grain, for if he did, the landlord would evict them, bringing on a sure death from starvation and disease.

Liam shuddered. What could the Sullivans do? His own family augmented their diet with eggs, cabbage from the garden, and milk from the cow, but nothing could replace the potato. Every family member ate many pounds every day and to lose this staple would force them to the edge.

After a while, people drifted away and only relatives remained. Liam left too and ran back to tell his father about the mysterious, death-dealing rot, only a half-mile away. He met him in the yard where he was contentedly smoking his pipe, but when Father heard the word blight, his face blanched and eyes widened. Tossing his pipe on the stone wall, he rushed to their potato pits, with Liam following.

Beads of perspiration appeared on his temples, and his wavy, auburn forelock fell over his eyes as he threw off chunks of sod and dug under the straw and peat moss with his bare hands. Although the pit looked unchanged, he reached down to the deep corners and pulled up several potatoes, turning them over and over with trembling fingers. Then he exhaled. "Seem to be fine . . . so far." He ran to the other pit, tore off the dome of dirt and sod, and grabbed potatoes from the center, a foot deep. He pressed them for soft spots, but when they were firm, his posture relaxed. "Yes, still all right." He carefully covered them again and shaped the dome so water would run off.

When they told the family the shocking news, Mother and the grandparents gasped and wrung their hands, but the others were too young to have seen blight and needed an explanation. Not even Liam, in his eighteen years, remembered such a rot, and climbing to the corner of the loft with his parents, he watched as they checked potatoes stored under straw. They found them still sound, yet no one felt relief and dreaded what the next hour or day might bring.

That night when the Reilly family gathered around the hearth, the crackling flames seemed loud in the quiet room, and the light flickered on their somber faces. Liam stared into the fire and grimly mused at how quickly things had changed in the course of only one day.

Niall, Liam's older brother, looked perplexed. "This mysterious blight . . . what causes it, Da?"

Father sat in his customary wall seat next to the arched fireplace. "Some neighbors say the dampness is causing it." He drew on his curved pipe. "So I'm thinking that maybe we should uncover the potatoes and stack them in ways to circulate more air."

Grandmother cleared her scratchy voice. "Well . . . my mother once told of a time when blight came to plants still in the field. She laid laundry on the potato stalks over night so the clothes could dry, and the next day, a fuzzy powder covered all except where the clothes had been."

Mother sat up. "If it's a thing borne on the wind, more air would make things worse!"

In the wall seat on the opposite side of the fireplace, Grandda, with his back in a permanent hunch, leaned out of the shadow. "If it's the wind that's bringing it, we best store more potatoes in the loft and leave the pits unopened as long as we can."

As Father inhaled pipe smoke, the tobacco glowed momentarily. "Maybe so . . . Maybe we should pile more straw on the potatoes in the loft . . . blankets too." Liam knew they were only guessing, but he hoped it would help.

Grandmother nodded her snowy head. "Everyday I'll say special prayers for deliverance from our troubles."

Father reached for an ember to relight his pipe. "And I'll

make a pilgrimage to the sacred mountain, Croagh Patrick, and ask the great Saint to pray for us."

Liam's younger brother Sean leaned forward on his stool. "I'll go with ya, Da."

Caitlin's copper braids fell forward as she climbed onto her big sister Aine's lap. "Will we *die* if that blight stuff comes here?" she asked with eyes wide.

Sitting on the flagstone, a troubled Brighid rose to her knees. "We're scared! I'm just eight years old so far, and Cait is only six."

Father was quick to reassure. "Don't be afraid. To survive the bad times, neighbors will share food with each other . . . like we Irish always do."

Liam admired Da's reply, and it was almost true. Neighbors would be generous, but if much food was destroyed . . . if blight was wide-spread . . . .

In the three months that followed, Mother and Grandmother wrapped themselves in their shawls and walked to church in Partry, even when it was not Sunday. In the afternoons the family knelt in a semi-circle on the hard, stone floor in front of the picture of the holy family and recited the rosary. No one could explain why some pits were missed and others were hit as the blight hopped in checker-board fashion across the country. Each week they mourned with another neighbor or relative who brought heart-breaking news of decay, and eventually, half the potatoes in Ireland were destroyed. In every county, starvation cast a long shadow.

Ignoring the disaster, landlords sent their agents all over the island to collect the grain harvest. A mood of dread and worry hung over the family, and Liam slept fitfully. But as the months dragged by, the Reilly's potatoes, and even Uncle Padraig's, continued to escape the cruel rot, and they all thanked God.

When the calendar turned to 1846, their nagging fear abated

and life gradually returned to normal. Gathering for the family's evening meal around the heavy oak table, a grateful Liam watched steam rise from the wicker basket of boiled potatoes draining in its center and smelled their familiar aroma. After they recited grace in unison, hands – large and small, old and young – made the sign of the cross before they reached into the basket.

Father peeled off a skin and put it in his bowl. "*Next* harvest, the potatoes will be plentiful because, like the proverb says – Good fortune always follows bad." He dipped his potato in butter and salt and took another bite. "But we'll not be leaving anything to chance, and we'll fertilize more this year for stronger plants. Some say seagull droppings are better than pig manure, so we'll use both. Tomorrow, you three sons will go with me to the coast. We'll take the cart and scrape up a load."

In March, it was again time for the family project of preparing the potato beds, and as usual, they saved the best fields for the landlord's grain and used slopes with thin soil for their potatoes. Liam and his brothers scooped up dirt from the surrounding hillside and mounded it in ridges, each four feet wide and separated by trenches. The trenches drained away rain and provided a place to stand when they tended the plants. They mixed in gull droppings with the usual pig manure until the ridges stood a foot high.

Liam leaned on his spade and wiped his moist brow with his sleeve. "Da, this is backbreaking work. So tell me . . . why do the English call our potato beds lazy beds?"

Father kept digging from the bottom layer to mix the manure. "They see us using a spade, rather than a traditional plow, and ignore the labor it takes to make these plots. They call them lazy beds to insult us, but in truth," he smirked, "we Irish have devised a clever solution to the thin, rocky soil that they force us to use for our own food. 'Tis amazing how many potatoes this plot will produce, and nothing else can match them. Potatoes feed five times as many people as grain!"

As Liam moved down a trench, his young sisters stood in his path, watching and waiting. Brighid, whose flaxen hair gleamed silvery like the moon, was agreeable and content. Yet, Caitlin, with hair red as a glowing sunset, swung her basket back and forth impatiently. "When can we play the planting game? Is it time yet? . . . Now can we?"

Mother pounded and firmed up the sides of the first ridge. "Yes, now! Start over here."

They scurried up the trench with baskets full of cut-up potatoes, while Aine, age fourteen, dug holes into which they placed a potato eye. "Put it to bed and cover with a blanket of dirt," she instructed.

In the days that followed, the family wandered up to the potato beds both in the morning and the evening to watch for any change, and when the first tiny shoots pushed through, they rejoiced. Cait, with eyes sparkling, summed it up best. "I guess the plants decided to wake up." Amused, Liam smiled down at her and hoped the threat of bad times had finally passed.

Aine, who had not gone to the seacoast earlier with her brothers, persuaded Liam to return with her for limpets and dillisk, an edible seaweed. Caitlin and Brighid begged Father to let them go along, and he consented, but as they were leaving, he grabbed Liam's arm.

"Above all, Son, watch your little sisters. And another thing . . . be alert and cease gathering seaweed if you're observed by English of any kind – sheriffs, soldiers, or land agents. Their courts have ruled that seaweed below the high water line is property of the landlord and claim we're stealing if we take it."

Liam scowled. "Is there nothing of value in Ireland permitted to us?" Father just shrugged.

At dawn as they trooped out, Mother handed them a pail full of potatoes whipped in buttermilk for a mid-day meal. Once his sisters' excited chatter had subsided, Liam enjoyed the peace and beauty of the countryside. Beside the road, spider webs coated with dew shimmered in the early light, and bees buzzed between clumps of light blue gentians and snapdragons. White cottages with smoking chimneys nestled in the valleys and perched on the hillsides. In the sunshine, the new spring grass seemed to glow green, and as he breathed in its fresh scent, he felt confident that 1846 would be a better year without blight.

They had skirted around their favorite village of Ballinglass to save time and steps, but by late morning, a weary Caitlin, who had been lagging behind, abruptly flopped on the ground. "I'm too tired to go!" But hearing a low roar in the distance, rising and falling, she perked up. "Is that the ocean?" Without waiting for the others, Cait and Brighid squealed and scampered ahead with an empty tin pail clattering and braids bobbing.

Aine and Liam jogged past them and stood at the edge of the cliff, taking in the immense sweep of the horizon. The cool, salty wind whipped Liam's hair, and his thick frieze jacket of wool felt good as he scanned the purple mountains and slivers of emerald land which thrust out into the sea. Ocean swells rolled in, collided with cliffs, and sent spray high into the air. "Aine, look at that!" Liam sighed.

She stood facing the endless blue, and as the air lifted her wavy mane, it glistened in the sun with bright, gold streaks. Though his sister had Mother's same large, green eyes and blond hair, he noticed that she was going to be taller. She gazed out for several minutes before looking down over the edge. "Yes, it's beautiful but a bit rough today."

"Yeh, they can surprise you, those waves." Liam smacked his fist into his palm.

Caitlin swung her empty pail and skipped toward the cliff. "Let's go down there."

"Wait." Aine, the self-appointed guardian, grabbed her arm. "Follow Liam and watch for loose rocks." Single file, they slid along an eroded gully to the narrow strip between cliff and ocean. Weary from hours of walking, they lost no time finding a rock on which to rest. In contented wonder, they sat watching and listening to the surf surge and bubble around boulders, wetting the sand before it retreated.

As Liam squinted up at gulls that squawked and glided overhead, his stomach growled. "Hey, let's eat." They gathered around while Aine lifted the lid off the pail of whipped potatoes. Liam splashed his hands in the water, wiped them dry on his shirt, and dipped two fingers into the bucket. The others joined, and soon they scraped it clean.

Caitlin studied the ocean. "Aine, where do we find the dillisk?"

"It's those weeds growing in deeper water, so leave them to me." Aine rapped her fingers on the now empty bucket. "Take this pail and hunt for limpets here in more shallow water."

Crouching, Liam crept forward. "There's a limpet right there!" He plucked the shelled creature from under a rock and tossed it in the pail. As its head peeped out of the shell's opening, Caitlin wrinkled her tiny nose in distaste.

"Brighid, you be the one to grab them in case they bite!" Though just two years older, the gentle Brighid was protective of her little sister and did not object.

For the little girls, Liam made a game of the search, and Caitlin squealed with each discovery. "We're gonna find the most, Liam!"

After several hours, his pail was full, and he sat down to admire the seascape. He figured that if a lad had a boat and sailed straight west, he'd hit Americay. But that's not for me. My roots run deep . . . close family, good neighbors, shared faith. Ireland is home, and I'll live and die here in County Mayo, God willing.

Remembering Father's warning about English spies, he gazed up at the cliffs, but they were deserted. Aine, still stooped over and pulling up seaweed, was in water past her hips. She must be cold and stiff, he mused. Leaning against a boulder, Liam relaxed, slumped over, and dozed off. Suddenly Caitlin's shrill squall startled him awake.

Opening his eyes, he saw Brighid sprawled in the water. A wave rushed in, pushed her about, and dragged her away from shore. The surf's tug was too strong, and when she tried to stand, it thrashed her about like a helpless doll and drew her into deeper water. Liam hurried down the slope, plunged in, and felt the powerful undertow with alarm.

"Brighid!" Aine yelled. "Grab the rocks!" Frantic, Aine struggled to move through the waist-high water, but her heavy, wet skirt held her back. Liam saw that a cross-current was pushing against her and realized that he was Brighid's only chance. For a moment, as the tide shifted back to shore, the billow of Brighid's skirt slowed her drifting, but her small hands slid off the wet boulders, and the next wave sucked her toward the open sea!

With his heart pounding, Liam drove through the surf and lunged forward, digging the fingers of one hand into her slippery arm. He labored to find a footing in the neck-high waves as the undertow swept them both seaward. As Brighid breathed in water and convulsed with violent coughing, her small, wet arm slipped through his fingers, and she was gone. Churning in the surging sea, Liam was caught in a valley between heaving waves and lost sight of her in the choppy water.

"Bridgid! Bridgid! . . . Bridgid!" Panicked, he thrashed this way and that, treading water. When a wave momentarily lifted him high, he spied her, bobbing nearby like floating debris. With four hard strokes, Liam reached her, pulled her against him, and lifted her chin. Limp and with eyes closed, her wet head flopped onto his shoulder, and her body felt cold from the frigid ocean. Kicking, he propelled them toward shore, waded through knee-deep water, and stumbled onto the sand.

Laying her on her stomach, he turned Brighid's head to one side. After pushing her wet, flaxen hair away from her mouth and nose, he slapped her back repeatedly and with each blow, water dribbled from her blue lips. Trembling, Brighid took several labored breaths, and as the small body shook with forceful choking, her eyes fluttered open.

"She's . . . coming around!" Liam yelled. Caitlin crouched next to her, whimpering.

Having scrambled out of the water, Aine hurried to cradle her sister. "Thank God! Thank God!" she whispered over and over as she rocked her. Then she glared at Liam, exasperated. "Weren't you watching them?"

Liam, hearing the sharp edge in her voice, ignored her anger and tried to cheer Bridgid, smiling into her face. "Ah, you . . . you almost floated off to Americay. Look at your legs . . . scraped . . . and bloody." He washed her wounds with salt water and went to fetch his jacket. Both Aine and Brighid shivered as Liam draped his coat around them.

Exhausted, he slumped on the sand, his thigh muscles aching. Emotionally he was shaken, and in his head he heard father's words . . . "Above all, watch your little sisters" . . . how could I have been looking away for so *long* . . . even dozing off! He shuddered as he imagined telling his parents such tragic news and then having to *live* with such a loss. He clamped his teeth shut to control powerful feelings.

Caitlin, still sniffling, sat beside him. "If that mean ocean had swallowed up my sister, I would have been really mad!"

Liam also felt anger, but at himself. He looked over at Bridgid, still cradled in Aine's arms . . . so small, fragile, and in need of protection. He had a new respect for the swells and currents of western Ireland's rough coastal seas which had taken many a fisherman to the depths and today, had almost claimed his precious little sister. Scanning the ocean, he was surprised that waves, once magnificent and shimmering, now seemed menacing as they moved in closer and licked their feet.

"Hey Aine . . . it's time to go! The surf is about to reclaim this sandy stretch. "Brighid, we'll carry everything. You just walk." He gave Cait the basket of dillisk, while he and Aine carried the limpets, but as they climbed up the gully, these heavy pails of shellfish cut into their palms, forcing Liam to stop at the top and wrap the handles with seaweed.

He studied Brighid whose angelic face normally had ruddy cheeks that glowed with health, but now she appeared pale and weary. "Keep my jacket. Are you warmer now?" She nodded weakly, looking lost in his coat which hid her hands and hung to the ankles.

"Why is the way home always longer?" Caitlin whined.

"Don't think about it," Aine said. "Just keep moving." They trudged down the road for perhaps an hour before they heard a faint cry coming from some distance. As they got closer, it became louder and more urgent.

Liam stopped. "Is that an infant's cry? . . . out here with no cottage near?" As they walked around the next bend in the road, they saw a cave-like hideout dug into the hillside. "Someone's carved out a scalp," he said. "The baby's in there . . . sick probably."

Sitting in front of the dugout, two ragged children with distended stomachs and wrinkled, yellow skin stared at them. Their lids drooped over eyes, expressionless and dull, and their hair stood out like a halo of dry straw.

Liam avoided looking at them and herded his sisters to the far side of the road. "Walk around because you can catch fevers from starving people."

Caitlin's eyes were fixed on them. "You mean they're hungry?" Liam reached down and held her hand, but as soon as they had passed, she tore away from his grip and wheeling around, she laid the basket of seaweed at the children's feet.

"Give it to your Mamai and Daidi! / Mom and Dad. They'll fix it so you can eat it." Then she ran back.

Liam scowled at her. "Caitlin! Now you may get a sickness, and it took a lot of walking to get that dillisk . . . with Brighid almost drowning!"

"But they looked so sad!"

"It's all right, Cait," Aine said. "You didn't get that close, and Mother says we always give to beggars because it might be Christ himself."

Caitlin's face brightened. "Our Mamai says that? Then I'll go to heaven, for sure! Since none of you gave anything, I'll put in a good word for ya."

Amused, Liam smiled. "That's good of you, Cait, but you're too young to be getting there ahead of *us*!" Despite his complaints, he was glad to see that the children and basket had disappeared into the scalp.

"Aine, what are they like – those fevers?" Bridgid asked.

"Tell them," Liam said, "then maybe they'll stay away from starving people!"

"Well . . . without a home, you usually get sick. With the

black fever, your skin turns dark, and there's a terrible smell. You can lose toes, feet, and fingers, if you don't die first. Our priest Father Mullen said the English call it typha . . . typhus . . . or something like that."

Caitlin looked at her stubby little fingers. "That sounds baaad!"

"It killed Father Foley." Liam said. "Lots of priests catch it when they go to bless the dying!"

Caitlin frowned. "Who made those children live in a hole anyway? That was mean."

"The landlord." Liam shifted the heavy pail to his other hand. "He has the power to force out any family, and with the blight, more people are getting evicted every day."

Aine lifted her pail into her arms. "Ask Grandfather about the big battles that happened a long time ago. The English won, took our land, and gave it to English landlords. Now we farm for them as tenants and pay high rents."

Brighid stopped walking. "You mean the landlord could put us out of our house, too?"

Aine shrugged off the question. "Don't worry. Father pays the rent – no matter what." At the top of the next hill, she found a way to distract them. "Look down on this patchwork of small fields divided by stone fences and imagine that it's a giant puzzle, already put together. And there off the road and on that hill, you can see a landlord's manor house. Isn't it grand?"

Caitlin squinted. "That building with three stacks of windows?"

"You mean three stories," Aine laughed. "Let's pretend we live there."

Brighid got excited. "We could all sleep in separate rooms and still have more for playing hide and seek!"

Caitlin sighed, "I'd always be lost."

Liam counted the chimneys on the slate roof. "Quite a job to keep so many fires going."

A long curving drive led to the gray stone mansion, and a gatehouse stood midway between the road and a cobblestone courtyard. Liam could see gardens with fountains and footpaths, but no people. The contrast between the deserted mansion and the scalp of the evicted rankled him, but Caitlin interrupted his pondering.

"Hey!" She pointed down the road. "Someone is coming!"

A man, walking beside a donkey and cart, was still far away, but as he drew closer, Aine recognized his round torso. "I think that's Mr. Murphy . . . from Ballinglass."

When he got nearer, he called to them. "Well now! Is this the young Reillys out here on a country road? And a fine lookin' bunch, they are, too!" As he approached with a jaunty walk, a broad smile creased his cheeks and deepened laugh lines at the corners of his blue eyes. He had only two expressions: happy and happier.

"Who do we have here!" He looked down at Caitlin and Brighid. "Two little cherubs with blue-green eyes and roses in their cheeks, and it's not yet spring!" The little girls giggled. "And Aine! More green eyes! You're prettier with each passing day, and that's a fact my sons are noticing, by the way!" Aine blushed at the mention of the Murphy sons.

"How did this Reilly clan get hair laced with sunshine!" he observed. "Cait's is aglow like red coals in a peat fire!" Snatching off the wool hat, he stroked his bald head, encircled by a fringe of hair. "I would have jumped for joy if me hair had turned gray, but instead it turned *loose!*" Their laughter encouraged Murphy. "And Liam," he resumed. "You're a tall, handsome lad, helping your dear parents put food on the table, are ya now! I'm proud to know ya!"

He vigorously pumped Liam's hand.

"Mr. Murphy, do you know who lives in that big house back there?" asked Bridgid.

"Uh...oh yes. That's the estate of Mrs. Gerrard, the landlord of our village and all this land hereabouts." He gestured with a great sweep of his arm. "She usually spends time at her Dublin and London houses - like a *proper* landlord," he added with a touch of sarcasm. Murphy put his palms together as if praying, and with exaggerated piety, he looked up and beseeched heaven: "Dear old Mrs. Gerrard, may God send down his angels to keep ya safe and . . . in London town, far away from *us!*" The Reillys chuckled.

"I wish our Da was rich like her!" Brighid sighed.

"You saw the great house, now did ya? Well, Mrs. Dolan from our village is a cleaning servant there. She tells of a curving, marble staircase that goes up three stories with a dome at the top. It has rose stained glass which lets pink light filter down on those below. The place is a palace, it is, with furniture painted gold, satin drapes, and huge paintings of herself and her ancestors. Irish servants pass through a tunnel that goes from the gate house to the basement kitchens so the fine lady of the house won't have to look upon their faces."

"Really!" Caitlin said. "Is Mrs. Dolan *that* ugly?"

"Oh no!" Murphy laughed. "The tunnel makes it so her highness, Mrs. Gerrard, won't ever see her *lowly* Irish servants. She might discover that they're human beings, don't ya know!" Imitating his landlord, he struck a pose of pompous arrogance — nose up, eyes half closed, and mouth turned down.

They all laughed but Caitlin, who scowled and put her hands on her hips. "Is she the one who made those children live in the ground in a dirt house?"

"What children?" Murphy raised his thick, bushy eyebrows.

Liam told him about the homeless family, and Murphy promised to give them some of his seed potatoes from his cart. In the meantime, he urged the Reillys to stop at his cottage for his wife's soda bread on the way home.

As they ambled down the road, Liam glanced back. "He's a jolly one!"

"Yes," Aine agreed. "He reminds me of Grandmamai's favorite proverb: Good humor is like a feather pillow, filled with what's easy to get but gives great comfort."

"I don't want to sleep! I want to eat," Brighid whined. "Ballinglass can't be *this* far."

Liam stopped. "Here, little sis, you're looking pale. Put your arms around my neck and let me carry you." Aine prodded small Caitlin, and they picked up the pace.

Around the bend, they saw Ballinglass with over sixty well kept cottages lining the road through the hamlet and along side lanes. The thick, stone walls, white-washed with lime, gleamed a bright white, and the steeply pitched roofs of heavy thatch were in good repair. They heard children playing and mothers calling instructions. Barking dogs announced their arrival, and white curtains parted as eyes checked for the cause of the commotion.

From many open half-doors came greetings in Irish, the language spoken by the native people: "*Dia dhaoibh* / Good day and God with you!" When they came to the Murphy cottage, Liam slipped Brighid off his back. Above the door someone had scrawled on the wood frame: "*Céad Míle Fáilte.*"

Caitlin, who had not yet learned to read, studied it. "What does it say, Liam?"

"It says a hundred thousand welcomes." He peered through the open door into the shadowy room and smelled fragrant traces of peat smoke rising from a glowing fire.

"Liam, my lad! Come in! And your sisters, too!" called Mrs. Murphy as she tended something at the fireplace. When his eyes adjusted to the darker cottage, he spotted soda bread, his favorite, and it was hard to wait while it cooked on the flat, suspended griddle.

Kneading fistfuls of dough in a bowl, she nodded toward the table. "Sit yourselves down. I'm betting that you're tired after walking clear to the coast today."

Brighid gave her a sly look. "Now, how would you be knowing that?"

"I have my ways, child. Special elves bring me reports. Just ask my children. Can't get away with anything! Now help yourselves to hot bread." She motioned toward the griddle. In his eagerness, Liam jostled the others aside and, being the first to scoop up a mound, he tossed it hand to hand until it cooled.

Once her bread was half eaten, Brighid continued her questioning. "Mrs. Murphy! Now how did you know we went to the coast?"

Dropping more batter on the griddle, she laughed a hearty contagious laugh that made her large abdomen shake. "All right, I'll tell you me secret. Your father's at Kelly's pub, playing cards. I reckon he came to fetch you, and you'll be glad to know that he brought the cart to save what is left of your feet!"

A group of Murphys entered and filled the cabin with happy noise. Brian Murphy nodded at Liam. "Hello. What's in the pail?" But his eyes were focused across the table on Aine.

"Just some limpets from the coast." Liam opened the pail to show his harvest, but Brian did not give it a glance.

"That's good," Brian said, still admiring Aine. "Liam, is your family coming this Sunday for my sister's wedding?"

Mrs. Murphy overheard. "Yes, I've already spoken to their father. There will be dancing, games, and a wedding cottage to build." Liam observed Aine, and though she was aware of Brian's intent gaze, she was too shy to return it.

Mom Murphy, smiling broadly, looked toward the doorway. "Seamus Reilly, welcome to this house!"

Liam turned and saw his father's silhouette at the threshold. When Caitlin rushed to hug his legs, he picked her up with eyes bright at the sight of her. "Looks like everyone knows where to find good soda bread."

Caitlin felt something squirming under his coat and peeked inside. "What's in there?"

"I wonder! Let me see." He set her down and pulled out a tiny, black kitten with white feet, downy fur, and a tail held straight up. Caitlin squealed with delight, and as everyone pressed forward to pet it, the kitten mewed and retreated into Father's coat.

"Mrs. Connolly gave it to us," he said. "Well, thank Mrs. Murphy for her hospitality and load up, Reilly clan. We don't want British patrols to arrest us for being on the road after sunset!"

After a chorus of thank you's and promises to return Sunday, they climbed into the cart. Father flicked the donkey's reins, and the two wheels ground into the gravel. Sitting in the back behind Liam and Father, the girls tussled over who should hold the kitten. Liam was glad that the new pet distracted them from telling Father about Brighid's close call, and soon the youngest sisters fell asleep.

When Aine leaned forward and described the rough sea, Liam gave her a sharp look and hurriedly added, "So we kept a close eye on the girls." Steering the conversation away, he asked, "By the way, did Shelby have her lamb today?"

"Not unless it happened this afternoon."

When the cart turned into their lane, the lime-washed walls reflected pink from the setting sun, and chickens clucked softly on their way to roost. Smoke rose from the chimney, and Liam knew a meal was in progress. He winced to think someday their landlord could destroy it all.

2

A Soft Morning

Liam awakened to the familiar sounds of morning: a rooster crowed in the yard, and on the thatch just above him, a bird chirped and clawed in the straw. As he lay in the loft on his feather mat, he looked up at the roof which steeply sloped to the loft's floor in a great upside-down V. A massive beam supported the center with smaller oak logs on the sides and stone gables at each end. As he breathed in the earthy scent of sod which was layered under the thatch for insulation, he savored this quiet moment in the cottage he loved. He knew every corner so well that he could find his way in darkness. With walls over two feet thick, it would keep his family warm and shelter them another hundred years. From the room below, he heard the occasional clank of iron pot on flagstone floor and the muffled voices of his parents.

Propping himself up on his elbows, Liam glanced over at his sleeping brothers – the older, nineteen year-old Niall was on one side and on the other, his younger brother Sean, sixteen, his face half buried in his feather pillow. His three sisters had not stirred on their side of the heavy quilt which divided the loft, so Liam lay back and pulled up his blanket. Then he remembered Shelby.

Throwing off the cover, he descended the wooden ladder and smelled potatoes simmering in the black pot hanging from the crane over the fire. As Mother stood on tiptoes and poured water into a second pot, she looked over her shoulder. "*Día dhuit*, Liam. / Good morning, God with you. 'Tis a bit before breakfast."

"That's all right." Liam ran his fingers through his sandy hair and stretched. "Da, I'm thinking we might have a new-born lamb. Last night Shelby was showing all the signs."

Father placed a peat brick on the fire. "We might, at that." From the shelf, he retrieved his clay pipe with its curved stem. "Let's go see," he muttered, clenching it in his teeth. Behind the cottage, they lowered their heads to enter the stone shed, and on the straw Shelby licked her pink lamb clean for his first showing. "You're right, Liam! A fine one, it is!"

Liam crouched beside the ewe, his boyhood pet, and scratched her head affectionately. "He's perfect, ole gal."

Outside the shed, they heard wings flapping as excited chickens clucked and scattered before someone's feet. Grandfather's grinning face peered through the doorway, unmindful of several missing teeth. Being thin and stooped, he shuffled in with ease.

"The lamb's a born, I see! If we don't have to give him as rent, we can eat him someday."

"Eat him!" Liam bristled. "Grandda, the pigs pay the rent, and all we need is his wool."

Father chuckled. "It'll be a long time before he's big enough to make much dinner for *this* family."

Outside they could hear the sisters talking and chickens squawking. Da put his hand on Grandda's shoulder. "I hear the girls so we'll leave and give them some room, but come to breakfast soon, Liam."

Brighid clambered in first, edging around Grandda, but

Caitlin nudged her over and began to pat the lamb energetically.

"Easy, Caitlin. Not so rough," Liam cautioned.

Aine glanced at the lamb but continued stroking the cuddly kitten – black with bright button eyes. "Liam, since the kitten has white fur on all four feet, don't you think Mittens is the best name?"

Caitlin shook her head. "Nooo! Name him Fluffy because he *is*."

Brighid jumped up and felt its fur. "It won't be this fluffy when it's a cat so Perky is a better name. Don't you think so, Liam?"

He gave a hearty laugh. "So you're wanting me to decide this, are you now? Well, I say that henceforth this cat shall be called . . . Mittens! Yes, Mittens, it is! Now with that settled, this lamb needs some sleep and we need breakfast!" The sisters accepted his authority and followed him to the cottage.

Inside, the family gathered on benches along the dark, oak table with Father on a stool at one end and mother at the other. Milk filled the clay pitcher, and the wicker basket of steaming potatoes in their skins rested in the center. On the griddle suspended over the fire, eggs sizzled, and by the time Grandmother scooped the boiled limpets onto a platter, Liam had an appetite.

When Father called for prayer, heads bowed, and since all knew the grace by heart, they recited it in unison. "*Beannaigh sinn, a Thiarna* / Bless us, O Lord, *Agus na bronntanais seo uait* / And these thy gifts . . . ." They hummed the prayer to its end with a cadence so familiar that the voices rose and fell, paused and continued as one. Afterwards, the table became a beehive of eating and chatter.

Father poured himself a cup of buttermilk. "Lads, after breakfast we'll go to the glen and gather stones for the Murphy's wedding cottage."

Mother slid a fried egg into each clay bowl. "Before you go,

I need four buckets of water for the wash tub."

Grandmother nodded toward the trunk in the corner. "We should take a look at Aine's dancing dress and make sure it's ready."

At the mention of dancing, Grandfather stopped eating. "When I was young, I was one of the best step dancers in County Mayo . . . and my five sisters too!"

Grandmother gathered empty limpet shells. "Tomorrow we'll have to hold him down or that toe-tappin' music may take him over."

"Grandda dance?" Caitlin, with dimples deepening in her cheeks, looked squarely at the stooped little man.

Seeing her doubt, Grandfather left the bench. "Watch this, Cait!" He began shuffling his right foot, followed by a sideways leap which lifted the clump of white hair atop his head. "Now that's pretty good for me age!" He sighed and resumed his seat.

Liam nodded approval. "Not bad, Grandda! Many men half your age can't hop that high."

Sean scooped out a limpet. "No one enjoys weddings and fairs more than Grandda! He loves it all . . . music, dancing, arguing politics, and always insists on one more toast while he keeps *us* waiting at the cart."

Mother lifted the trunk lid, held the dancing dress up to herself, and fondly caressed the Celtic design made of ribbon and embroidery. "Aine, keep in mind that your great grandmother's beautiful handwork is on this skirt! I wore it myself as a girl, and in turn, my sisters."

Father leaned back on his stool. "I remember you well in that dress, Erin."

"Of course, you do." Grandfather winked. "Yes, she was a pretty lass, she was!"

"Is," Father corrected as he reached for another potato.

Grandfather grinned mischievously. "You'd watch her

dance like she was the only girl in the line . . . just like Sean watches Maire Murphy."

Caitlin set her milk cup down with a clunk. "That reminds me! I saw Sean kissing Maire Murphy behind the shed!"

All the family chuckled except Sean. "So? . . . what of it, I say!" His blue eyes challenged her, and he shook his wavy auburn mane as he reached for another limpet.

Amused at the exchange, Father had a glint in his eye as he pushed back his bowl, heaped with potato skins. "Well, after Cait's report on happenings behind the shed, let's be off to the glen."

"I'll go," Grandfather volunteered, "And show you lads what to load."

The male Reillys kept up the banter as they filed out, and Sean draped his arm around Grandfather's narrow shoulders. "It's great being the driver with all us slaves, aye, Grandda?"

Grandfather lifted his arms and inhaled deeply as a fine mist cleansed the air. "Ah, 'tis a soft morning and a pleasure to breathe."

While Liam and Niall went to the well to fill the water jug and pails, Sean jumped into the cart and occupied most of the space, and with a smug expression, he waited for Liam's reaction which was not long coming.

"Sean, why is it now that the *one* of you is taking up the space of *three*?" Hearing water slosh in the jug, he decided to lay a cold spray over Sean.

"Yow!" Sean yelped while Liam and Niall howled with laughter. With Grandda at his side, Father clucked to the donkey, and the brothers had to leap into the cart as it started to roll.

Liam sighed contentedly as he gazed out at the endless expanse of green that stretched to the bluish-gray mountains in the distance. This carpet of brilliant green, interrupted by only an occasional tree, piqued his curiosity. "Grandda, didn't Ireland ever have more trees?"

Grandfather, the family historian, glanced back. "Long ago the English stripped away great forests here to build their fleet of ships and to get rid of our hiding places, but maybe we can plant trees here again someday."

Niall looked skeptical. "And when would that be, Grandda, since the English own all our land and run the government? You think we Irish have a voice, do you?"

Grandfather smacked his lips. "That needs to change – if not in my lifetime, yours. Our leader, Daniel O'Connell, is still working to repeal this union that the English forced on us and get some self-government here in Ireland . . . even though, unfortunately, we would *still* be subjects of their English king."

Niall scoffed. "What can you be thinking? Whenever O'Connell rallies our people and seems powerful, the government just throws him into prison for a while."

Grandfather became cross. "But just the same, these English are listening to his arguments and might be persuaded someday. You sound like there's no hope!"

Niall kept shaking his head and his pessimism irritated Liam.

Father tugged on the reins, and the donkey clopped to a stop. "Sean, it's your turn to set aside the stones." When the fence opening was wide enough for the cart to pass through, the wheels made a grinding noise as the cart shook and shifted before it rolled to a stop. They got out on the flinty slope where even purple heather had to fight for a foothold.

Liam picked up a handful of pebbles and threw them as far as he could. "In this part of Ireland, it must have taken a hundred years just to clear enough rocks for farming."

"Generations," Father said. "But we put them to use in

fences and houses. Before Cromwell and the English seized the land owned by Catholics, our ancestors had a fertile farm in County Longford where it wasn't so stony. But Cromwell gave our farm to an English army captain and forced our forefathers and other landowners to move west of the River Shannon to rocky ground here in Mayo. Hey lads, only get the flat stones . . . better to make their floor.

"In fact, all over Ireland, the English seized land and handed it over to English or Scottish Protestants. Fifty years earlier, they grabbed a lot of Irish land in Ulster . . . north of us . . . and gave it to Scots. In a speech, O'Connell said that today only a seventh of our island is in Irish Catholic hands, and here I am – still a tenant of Lord Sligo!"

Sean carried a flat stone to the cart. "Grandda, tell us again about that devil Cromwell so we can teach our own children someday."

Grandfather, always the instructor, climbed onto a boulder and cleared his throat. "Well, 'twas 1649. Oliver Cromwell landed on Irish soil with huge armies and massacred the town of Drogheda, butchering defenseless old people and children as well as the men until the gutters ran red with blood. No one was spared, not even women with babes who hid in church basements or prayed at the altar steps. After the town was taken, Cromwell allowed his men to rampage for three days without mercy, committing every outrage that you can imagine in endless orgy and slaughter. Then he moved to Wexford where he did the same and bragged to the English Parliament in London that thousands had been killed, with none escaping. For eight months he continued through the land, using a new and powerful cannon that crumbled ancient walls and overcame our defenses.

"After all resistance ceased, they sold many thousands of

young Irish as slaves to British landlords in the West Indies, and for more than ten years, Cromwell's son, that rotten Henry, kidnapped our lads and lasses, even out of their homes at night! The British Governor of Galway got rich selling many young Irish to British planters on the island of Barbados."

Niall took a spade and pried up a half-buried rock. "The British didn't just capture slaves from *here*! They also took slaves from Africa, and Father Mullen said the royal family made a fortune in the slave trade . . . set up their own slave trading company and branded slaves with DY for the Duke of York. Can you imagine? Branding!"

Grandfather looked aggravated. "Yes, I know all that! They were the world's biggest dealers of African slaves and sold them all over the world, but stop interrupting!"

Liam worried that this recital of British sins would only make Niall's attitude worse and watched for his chance. "Grandda! That was then, and this is now. A body can't always be thinking the worst about his life! You talk about Cromwell's deeds like they happened yesterday, not two hundred years ago!"

Grandfather's eyes flashed. "Liam! We're still living with what Cromwell did . . . took our land, our rights, everything. For generations we hid in fields and caves to worship in the Catholic faith, and if surprised by soldiers, we were slaughtered. They passed laws forbidding us to teach our own children and hunted down our priests and school masters. To hear a teacher, children had to crouch behind the hedges in secret with a lookout, but we did it, just the same!"

Father chimed in. "They *still* keep us powerless and poor while the landlords live in luxury off high rents. Most Irish are worse off than English beggars!"

Liam raised his voice and tried to drown them out. "But things are better now, I tell ya! We can worship in our own churches, allowed to have schools, and some Irish can vote, yes?"

Niall propped his arms on his spade. "We can't *really* vote! To qualify by English rules, we have to have a lease worth ten pounds with a tax stamp on it. Hardly any of us are even given a lease, and if we are, it's not worth that much. So not one in a hundred Irishmen can vote."

"'Tis the truth!" Father shouted. "'Twas in our newspaper." In his excitement, he jerked on the donkey's reins, and the animal brayed in protest. "The English have built some schools, but those national schools try to undermine our religion, suppress the Irish language, ignore our history and culture, and teach only the most elementary subjects to train us to be lowly servants. And we're still taxed to support the government's church even though we don't go there. They stole our great Catholic cathedrals and made them their own. What kind of a religion would steal a *church,* tell me that!"

Liam scowled. "But you're forgetting that Grandda's hero, O'Connell, got that Catholic Emancipation Act passed . . . was it fifteen years ago? . . . that let Catholics sit in Parliament."

Grandfather got out his handkerchief and blew his nose. "Liam's right about O'Connell being a great man! He's one of the few Irish Catholic landlords and even had a seat in the House of Commons for a while. That's a start, sure is!"

Liam felt encouraged. "Maybe O'Connell can get our fertile land in County Longford back someday."

Grandda clapped his hands. "Now that's an idea! Me father wrote a will that tells you exactly where the land is so you can reclaim it. It should be ours!"

Sean shook his head grimly. "We'll never get it back."

Niall tossed a stone into the cart with a clatter. "The truth is that not much has changed in 200 years, and the smart ones in Ireland are boarding ships for Americay."

"Niall! Don't even think about it!" Liam yelled.

Father raised his brows. "Easy now, lad. He's just talking about the state of things. You two go down by the stream and see if you can find some fallen logs."

Liam felt troubled, and as they walked under the trees, Niall acted distant. To lose his older brother would be a crushing blow like a death. Could he really leave Ireland? As Liam wandered, moss and shamrocks felt soft underfoot, and in high branches, birds called in short bursts of song. Since boyhood, he, Niall, and Sean had played here with cousins, waded barefoot over stones worn smooth by the stream, and made this glen their sanctuary to fish, to think, and to dream.

How could Niall give up on Ireland, leave home, and go around the world to a place strange and unfriendly? Didn't he realize how lucky they were? Their family had two rooms, a loft, and even a window, while many Irish Catholics lived in one room cabins with only piles of straw for bedding, a dirt floor, no window and just a smoke hole.

He walked over to him. "Niall, instead of leaving, stay and try to change things!"

Surprised, Niall looked up. "You're still worrying about that? I couldn't leave the family, and besides, I hear passage on a ship is close to a year's wages, if you can even find a wage in Ireland."

Liam was relieved, but before he could say more, Father called them back. Along the road home, they met a mound of hay on four donkey legs, prodded by a boy with a stick. Father doffed his hat. "Top o' the morning to you."

"And you," the lad nodded.

When their stucco cottage came into view, Liam loped ahead. The high-pitched voices of his little sisters in the distance as they fed table scraps to the pigs sounded like lively chirping. The chickens strutted about the yard with jerky movements, while Aine, with the kitten under one arm, led the cow to the shed for milking. Shelby grazed on the short grass of the yard while her lamb tried to take milk, but seeing Liam, she bleated for his attention, and he paused to stroke her head affectionately.

Mother, sitting on the stone fence beside the potato beds, waved and called to him. "Liam! Come see." He ran up the hill and hopped on the wall next to her. "Look how lush and green the sprouts are. The seagull droppings made the plants vigorous and strong, and everything will be fine. *Ná bíodh imní ort.* / Don't worry." Liam was not sure whom she was trying to reassure – him or herself.

His gaze drifted past the field to the lane where stooped figures limped along, and trailing behind was a woman with a lump on her back . . . a baby, tied in her shawl.

Mother's face fell. "At least I can give them well water, potatoes, and a kind word." She slid off the wall and walked to the cottage.

Watching this family make its way to their door, Liam wondered how many more would come begging before these small potato sprouts finally produced a much needed crop. He studied the plants and lingered a moment, haunted by the memory of the Sullivan's pits. Then he forced himself to repeat the proverb – "Good fortune always follows bad." This year it *has* to.

3

The Celebration

Since dawn the cottage had hummed with preparations. Father milked the cow and harnessed the donkey to the cart while Mother arranged the girls' hair, prepared colcannon for the wedding dinner, and cleared away breakfast. Since Niall was tuning his mandolin and Sean was keeping out of sight, the task came to Liam – "Take these potato skins to the pigs" – and though he grumbled, she ignored him.

Aine tied a crocheted lace collar around her neck and pleaded for Grandmother's assistance in hooking the dance dress which was snug at the waist. Brighid, though young, seemed impatient for the day when she would wear it and admired the Celtic design made with ribbons embroidered onto the fabric. Once dressed, Aine practiced the traditional steps and instructed the eager Brighid who copied her every move like a shadow.

Competition for the only mirror was intense, but Liam grabbed a quick glance and was satisfied. Restless, he pulled up a stool and balanced on the back legs . . . a certain pretty face filled his head, and he wanted to meet her again. He had thought of her often since seeing her at the fair in Ballinglass weeks ago and had asked

Brian Murphy, "*Cé hí sin?* / Who is she?"

"When are we leaving?" he shouted.

Grandfather shuffled over and sat next to him. "What's the hold up? We should be on our way." His bellow sent Aine scurrying to conclude last-minute primping. Grandmother tied her small bonnet trimmed in crochet under her chin and stood near the door, holding a gift of lace she had made for the bride.

When Father brought the cart to the yard, Liam was the first out. Only the grandparents and the little girls rode, but the pace remained slow enough that those walking could converse with those in the cart. The donkey's head bobbed with the heavy load.

A neighbor, Nicolas Flannery, had taken his cow across the road to graze and was re-stacking the stones in the fence. When he saw them, he graciously doffed his well-worn hat and bowed. "Top o' the morning to you, Seamus."

Father nodded and smiled. "And the rest of the day to you, Nic. It's fine weather we're having, glory be to God."

"Aye, it is indeed."

Early morning fog still hung in the valleys, and dew glistened on the grass. The road, bounded by stone fences, branched off in many directions to numerous communities, and small signs directed travelers through the maze. Liam watched for his favorite: the arrow pointing to *Kiltharsechaune,* the Village of Doorsteps. Because its landlord had confined it to such a small area, its cottages were nestled together like a tangle of roots with doorsteps that touched and sometimes overlapped.

When the holy well of St. Brighid came into view, Father reined in the donkey, and Liam and Niall helped their grandparents and young sisters out of the cart. The water seeped up naturally and was encased in stone, and before taking a drink, the Reillys knelt in prayer and crossed themselves. Nearby, a thorn tree had medals and scraps of cloth tied to it by prayerful visitors who wished to leave something of themselves behind. Liam noticed that since the blight, the tree was almost covered by remembrances. After resting in the thick grass, they continued on.

Just outside the village, Father stopped again. "I want you to see what the villagers of Ballinglass have done! All this land here, some 400 acres, used to be a bog, but they drained it, filled it in, and now it can be farmed. It took years."

Grandfather took off his hat. "Should make a landlord happy, if anything will."

"Yes, it enriches the landlord," Father explained, "but with young families needing their own plots to grow potatoes and farm, it's a great thing to add land, instead of more subdividing." After a thoughtful pause, he clucked to the donkey, and they soon reached the village's edge.

The sounds of celebration lifted Liam's spirits: dogs barking, voices and laughter, fiddles being tuned in a minor key. A group of men was playing a spirited game of hurling, with cheers when goals were won and moans when they were missed. The smell of burning peat mingled with the aroma of a pig roasting. Men in black coats and patched pants argued about politics and the causes of last fall's potato blight while women, draped in dark shawls, discussed children, basket-making, and handwork. The hem of a red petticoat could be glimpsed now and then.

As the Reilly cart rolled into the village center, grinning faces came forward and delighted welcomes rang out: *Día dhaoibh* / God be with you. A pleasant woman took Mother's pot of colcannon with an affectionate hug. "Many blessing to you, Erin Reilly, and thank you for this."

Several men directed Father to the cabin raising, and Liam was surprised to see how much was already built. His sisters hopped off the cart to join a throng of girls fluttering around them, and they went off in two giggling packs – one for the younger girls and another for Aine's age. Indifferent to the warm smiles which several lassies cast his way, Liam looked for the one named Colleen O'Neill.

Niall took his mandolin and blended in with a group already playing fast-paced tunes. Joining the violin, harp, tin whistle, and the bodhran was a dulcimer whose melodies were tapped out by special hammers. An old Irish bag pipe, the uilleann, squawked and puffed as air was pumped through the bellows operated by the man's right elbow, but soon it was making beautiful, full tones. Between songs, the musicians conferred briefly to decide which song would be next, as an appreciative crowd gathered around to sing along or nod to the rhythms.

When Liam asked Sean about a new wooden platform for dancing set up on a side lane, he explained: "That traveling dance master who gives lessons in Ballinglass every year suggested they build it in time for the wedding."

Together the brothers meandered about until they found Brian Murphy and his friends, idling near the bridge. Jovial and laughing, the lads warmly greeted Sean and Liam, but the joking stopped and all became alert when the group of older girls began strolling their way. Liam smoothed his tousled hair and adjusted his jacket. Although the girls lingered nearby, they seemed completely absorbed in their own animated conversations.

"What could be that interesting?" Liam mumbled to Sean. Even his own sister, Aine, seemed unaware of Brian Murphy who admired her from afar.

Then Liam caught a furtive side-ways glance from blue eyes, pale as the sky and fringed by thick, black lashes. Was she looking his way? Yes! It was Colleen and she was even more beautiful than he remembered. A delicate blush made her cheeks glow, and long, dark hair contrasted with a complexion fair as porcelain. Entranced, Liam continued to stare until Sean brought him back with a jab in the ribs and a grin.

Although the lads nodded, the girls acted oblivious to their interest and slowly passed by. Casting resigned looks their way, the young men turned to the stream for amusement, and leaning over the rail, they competed to see whose stone would skip farther on the water's surface.

A popular priest wandered up, and out of respect, those who wore hats yanked them off. Since he had been born and raised in Ballinglass, every lad knew him, and as the uncle of the bride, Liam guessed that he would conduct the marriage ceremony. Seeing Liam and Sean, the priest draped his arms around their shoulders. "Glad you're here! These fine fellows are from my own church in Partry." Turning back to the group, he crossed his arms, and his eyes crinkled at the corners with suppressed amusement. "You're enjoying yourselves, are you now?"

"Yes, Father Mullen," they answered almost in unison.

"It's about time for the wedding! Then after dinner, maybe . . . just maybe, we can talk those pretty young lasses who just passed into dancing! But you wouldn't be carin' about that, now would you?" The boys chuckled and knew that he understood. As the friendly priest strolled toward the church, Liam noticed how warmly he greeted everyone.

Soon a strong, sustained note from two Irish bag pipes vibrated the air and signaled that the wedding procession was beginning. With the mellow sound of the bodhran, a broad drum, setting the pace, tin whistles, harps, mandolins and fiddles joined in a dignified hymn. As the groom and his relatives led the way to the bride's house, Liam and the lads fell in line with other villagers.

The crowd waited outside while the couple ate the traditional three mouthfuls of oatmeal and salt for good luck.

Then on her groom's arm, the bride, a radiant Patricia Murphy, emerged in the same white, lace-trimmed dress worn by her mother and two earlier generations of brides. The throng hummed with loving approval, and plump, grandmotherly neighbors whispered among themselves. "She's a lovely bride, she is."

"I remember them as children at my hearth," chubby cheeked Mrs. Conway recalled, dabbing her eyes with her shawl.

As the bride passed among them, she looked into each face and squeezed the extended hands. Surrounded by the whole village on this special day, she was the child of them all, and her lower lip began to quiver. Overcome with emotion, tears trickled down her cheeks, even as she smiled, but the groom supported her with gentle strength as they paraded to the church.

After Liam and the other lads selected a bench in the back, the older girls chose one directly in front of them, and not by accident, he guessed. From here, he easily observed Colleen's very appealing profile, her reverence in prayer, and her gentle patience with the questions of young twin sisters who crowded in beside her.

At the end of the ceremony, Father Mullen blessed the happy couple and signaled the groom to kiss the bride while the congregation clapped. When this subsided, he asked everyone to be seated for a special announcement.

"My dear people . . . despite the happiness of this occasion, I urge you to remember in your prayers those who are starving in Ireland this day. As you know, last year's blight destroyed half the potato crop, and as usual, other crops and livestock have been taken as rent. In the city of Cork, famine is so great that the living can't find the strength to bury the dead. In Limerick, Clare, parts of our own counties Galway and Mayo, the situation is also desperate. The

Irish Relief Committee has collected almost £85,000 from people like you who have given from the little that they have. This is the greatest outpouring of relief ever in Irish history, so please be as generous as you can." As they passed the basket, Liam heard coins jingle and saw expressions of concern.

Yet, once outside the chapel, a festive mood returned. In front of Kelly's Pub and the dry goods store were long tables loaded with food. The Murphys provided the roast pig, and villagers added dishes of colcannon, stew, soda bread, and cottage cheese curdled with nettle juice. There were berries in cream and roast chicken with freshly picked mushrooms. Liam and the lads headed straight for the tables, heaped their bowls full, and stood eating near a group of men who were drinking stout in front of Kelly's.

Liam's father, Seamus, stood in their midst and looked up at the shuttered pub next door. "How long has Mahoney's tavern been closed?"

"About a month, I guess," Denis Murphy replied. "It's due to Father Mathew's temperance crusade, don't ya know. The movement has spread from Cork to Ballinglass and all over Ireland, and now it's even spread to the Irish in America, I hear! They say whiskey drinking in Ireland has been cut in half since 1841. 'Tis amazing that all these people are taking an oath of total abstinence and sticking to it!"

"I suppose it's generally a good thing since many can't resist the lure of it," commented Mr. Ross, as he swirled the stout in his mug. Then with a twinkle in his eye, he added, "Like our proverb says – Drink is the curse of the land. It makes you fight with your neighbor; it makes you shoot at your landlord; and it makes you *miss*!"

Everyone chuckled. Having never heard that proverb, Liam laughed too hard and choked on his food.

"Well, here's to us!" Murphy lifted his mug. "May the good

Lord take a lik'in to ya but not too much and not too soon!" They mumbled and clacked their mugs.

"And may we all get to heaven an hour before the devil finds out we're dead!" said Felic Dowling. Another clack of mugs and jovial camaraderie.

"And may Patricia and Peter live to see their children's children's children," Seamus toasted. "Indeed! *Sláinte* / Health," they answered. Father eyed Liam's plate. "Now let's try Murphy's roast pig! The aromas are stirring my appetite."

"Maureen McGuinness has put out her stew!" reminded Mr. Moore. "Ahh" they sighed in appreciation and shuffled to the tables. Liam was following his friends back when Caitlin tugged on his coat.

"Liam, come with me!" She pulled him into the dry goods store and pointed to a small, colored picture of St. Patrick. "Can you buy this? Can you get it for me?"

"I haven't any money, Caitlin, and I'm sure our parents gave all their coins to the relief collection. It's no use." Frowning, he turned to leave.

Caitlin began to whimper. "I'll be extra good! Can't you find a way?" She grabbed his sleeve and her voice quivered, "Pleeease, Liam."

Behind the counter was an old, toothless woman whose nose almost met her chin. White, wavy hair framed a kind face with bright eyes and an up-turned mouth. "Now child, what are these tears about!" She leaned over the counter to give her dimming eyes a closer look at Caitlin. "What do you want, love?" With that, she reached into the cabinet and took out the little picture. "Here! You can have it on me."

Caitlin was overjoyed and after thanking and hugging the lady, she skipped away to show her picture to Grandmother. When Liam protested, the white-haired lady just smiled and waved off his concerns, and he left the store, feeling warmed by her generosity.

He found his friends at the dance platform where a crowd was gathering. The elders were urging the young people to perform, and their reluctance was more for show, than for real. The lilting music and rhythm were so infectious that it defied anyone to stand still.

Liam admired the skill necessary to play the complicated, fast-paced melodies and noticed how the music affected the crowd. Their faces went from smiling contentedly, to broad grins, to laughter. Spirits soared as heads nodded, toes tapped, and shoulders moved.

Twenty girls ranging in age from fourteen to sixteen years formed two rows in the longways formation, and like Aine, most wore dancing dresses passed down in their families. As if controlled by an invisible puppeteer, their small feet performed the prescribed steps in perfect unison with their arms at their sides and looking straight ahead. At his side, Liam observed Brian Murphy admiring Aine, while only Maire, Brian's sister, held Sean's interest. Once Liam spied Colleen on the back row, he could see no one else. He felt drawn to her and knew this wedding was his chance to know her.

Next, the lads danced with less grace, but more energy and stamina. The drumming and shuffling of rawhide shoes with wooden heels on the wood floor beat out a complicated rhythm of clicks, clacks, and stomps that invigorated dancers and spectators alike. Liam managed to take a position in the back row behind his brother Sean, and to his relief, made no errors. After the exertion, they gasped for air while the responsive audience cheered.

"Sean Reilly alone!" someone shouted, and when others joined the call, they gave the platform to Sean whose athletic ability was well known. The band picked up the beat to give him a challenge. His feet rapidly battered the floor with an elaborate pattern, creating a kind of music of the shoes with a variety of tones. As the brother of the best step dancer, a proud Liam enjoyed reflected glory as everyone thrilled to Sean's high leaps, fast stepping, and loud stomps on beat. He had the crowd clapping till their palms burned, and finally after two encores, he breathlessly retreated to the sideline, his ruddy complexion flushed. Liam had often heard that Sean resembled their father, and in the sun, his hair had the same glint of burnished red.

Then a voice called out, "Father Mullen! It's your turn!" Dressed in his black, priestly garb, he moved to the center of the platform and surprised everyone with his quickness and skill.

"Father Mullen is dancing the jig!" Caitlin squealed. Though his dance was short, it was spirited and made old ladies cackle with fun.

The music now called for the wedding guests to dance, and they merrily ticked off the steps of a reel with great flourishes of heel and toe. Brian asked Aine to dance, Sean approached Maire, but as Liam looked about for Colleen, he was distracted by dust rising in the distance.

Soon others pointed in its direction, questioning, mumbling, "What is it?" The music gradually ground to a halt as both dancers and musicians studied the horizon. As the cloud became larger and the rumble louder, people began to mutter and offer explanations.

"Is it soldiers? What is happening down the road!"

"Who is coming? Why?"

"Horses traveling at great speed!" shouted Mr. Reagan.

Noise and dust filled the main road as five coaches with ornate, gold decorations on their doors entered the town. As the villagers stood in awe, the powerful steeds thundered through, and their coachmen, flourishing whips, pressed the teams to a full gallop. The first coach rumbled by and then another, and through the windows, Liam could see passengers dressed in shiny coats, looking straight ahead. The pounding of many hooves and the sound of the huge wheels grinding into the gravel was now deafening and had everyone standing like stunned statues.

Liam caught sight of a little girl, transfixed by the gray horses and noisy clatter. When the second coach passed, she looked after it in fascination and stepped into the path of the third which was coming on hard. As its large wheels bore down on her, women began screaming!

"My baby!" someone screeched.

Liam was closest to the child and lunged for her. As he snatched her small body with one arm, the passing coach grazed his sleeve.

People gasped and then exploded in relief. "Praise God! Thanks to the prayers of St. Patrick and Mary!" they said over and over. Liam felt hands patting his back and shoulders.

The mother ran towards him and reached for her trembling child. "May all your days be blessed, Liam Reilly!" Despite the joy over the child being saved, he and others gawked after the coaches as they continued west, trailing dust.

"Did they not see all these children?" a woman muttered in disbelief and anger.

"They saw them well enough!" Mr. Connolly said with a bitter tone.

"Who? Who were those people?" Liam asked.

"That's our landlord, Mrs. Gerrard herself, that's who!" croaked a bewhiskered Mr. Martin. "She's come back from England for a brief spell, I reckon."

"And bringing back some of her fancy friends for parties and hunting, no doubt!" Mrs. McDonnell surmised. No one voiced a fear of her return, yet they acted uneasy.

"For the past five years only her agents have been around

to collect the rent, and that is fine with us," explained Mrs. Dennis. "I guess all the lights will be on in the great manor house tonight!" Liam imagined the deserted mansion on the country road as it would soon be transformed by people and elegant parties.

"But they'll not be having as much good music as we're having, to be sure!" said Mr. Murphy, trying to recover the festive mood. "And that reminds me! It's time to bless the wedding cake! Where's Father Mullen?" he shouted and called for the bride and groom.

The coaches were now only a distant dust cloud on the horizon, but Liam could not stop watching till even this had vanished. He shivered as he felt a chill wind blow through the village. What kind of person was this Mrs. Gerrard . . . that she would so recklessly instruct her coachmen to pass through a crowded village without slowing and why? His pondering was interrupted by a young girl's voice.

"'Twas a wonder you reached my little cousin in time! We're so grateful to you!"

"Colleen . . . your relative?" Liam felt his face grow warm. "Anyone standing nearby would have done the same, but I'm glad I was quick enough," he muttered, feeling strangely awkward and speechless under the gaze of the pale eyes with black lashes. He just wanted to stare and memorize each aspect of her exquisite face.

As they walked toward the crowd that was gathering around the wedding cake, he reached for her hand and held it firmly. It felt right, and she responded with a warm clasp in return. When it was time for the toasts, a choice of milk, primrose wine, and tea was passed around to reflect the ingredients of the good life. Everyone encircled the happy couple as the groom's father stood to recite a popular wedding toast:

"Health and long life to you;

Land without rent to you;

A child every year to you;

And death in Old Ireland"

Everyone clicked their cups together amid cries of *sláinte*. Liam wondered about the last and realized that parents must fear their children will emigrate away from them. Liam took a cup of tea, gave Colleen a sip, and passed it on.

Then Mr. Murphy, being short, stood on a stool and dramatically recited his favorite Irish blessing with the skill of a fine orator:

"May there always be work for your hands to do;

May your purse always hold a coin or two;

May the sun always shine on your window pane;

May a rainbow be certain to follow each rain;

May the hand of a friend always be near you;

May God fill your heart with gladness to cheer you!"

Again the gathering toasted with whatever was in their cup and called "*Sláinte mhaith* / good health to you."

Father Mullen blessed the wedding cake and cut a piece for the happy couple. Portions were passed to friends nearby, and those who received cake broke it with good humor, sharing it until many had a taste. Colleen received a small portion and offered it to Liam, but he had lost interest in eating.

When the musicians began their merrymaking once again with a lively fiddle taking the melody and tin whistles playing a lilting counter melody, the crowd began singing, requesting their favorites, and dancing. Liam felt connected to Colleen in heart and palm, as if something special flowed between them, and he never wanted to let her go.

Strolling away from the crowd and down a side lane, Colleen told him about her family. "I also have a brother, Ryan, but government agents came to Ballinglass and forced him and others to leave with them for the British army. My family worries that he will be killed, trying to conquer more lands for their empire. They make a soldier sign up for life, and I wish he could take it back . . . that pledge!"

Liam nodded. "My Grandda says that over a third of the army is Irish so Ryan has lots of company from home. I wish more of our soldiers were stationed here, but they usually send them far away. But don't worry." He patted her hand. "Your brother will be a lucky one, will grow old as a soldier, and *then* they'll let him out!"

They wandered over to the new home where the groom's father was painting the half-doors red. The cottage already had a lace curtain in the window, and the freshly white-washed walls glistened with moisture. Before leaving for Partry, Father Mullen blessed the home and prayed that it would hold every happiness and many children.

Da, standing nearby, motioned to Liam and Sean. "Lads, find Grandfather. I'll round up the family and meet you at the cart."

With their companions, the brothers began a half-hearted search, but unfortunately, Grandda was easily found. They heard him even before they saw him as he and old Mr. Martin shouted back and forth in a heated argument over the Irish patriot, Daniel O'Connell. Nose to nose, they glowered at each other with Grandfather bellowing the loudest.

"I tell you, he's the wisest leader in our time! The British army is too strong for us to take them on, and his idea of using moral persuasion to reform things peacefully is the best way. When he called that big meeting at Clontarf, the British brought in soldiers, artillery, and had a battleship in the bay! What else could he do but cancel the meeting!" Grandfather yelled.

"There you have it!" Martin slapped his thigh. "O'Connell backed down, and they *still* threw him in prison. He says 'Freedom is too dearly purchased if at the price of a single drop of blood.' Well, it's going to take a lot of blood to get free from these tyrants. He relies on just talk, and all he gets is a few tokens and no real changes. His so-called Catholic Emancipation Act is just a bunch of chicken feathers!" Martin stepped closer, staring Grandda down like a charging bull. "Fewer of us can vote now than before it was passed, and based on our population, we should have twice as many seats in the House of Commons as they gave us!" he croaked.

Liam warily approached and touched Grandfather's arm. "Time to go, Father says." Seeing Liam, Grandfather grabbed him and thrust him into Martin's space. "And here is me own grandson, Liam Daniel Reilly, named for the honorable O'Connell! I'll support him till me death, I will!" Grandfather struck a belligerent pose as if about to strike old Martin if he continued to disagree.

But Martin growled back, not backing down an inch. "And your boy here, if we keep doing things O'Connell's way, will have fewer rights than we have when he's old! I walked for two days to reach one of O'Connell's monster meetings with a hundred thousand people stretched over the hillsides! Oh, 'twas quite a sight! All of us Irish standing together. He stirred us up with a powerful speech, but then ended with cheers for Queen Victoria! Whose side is he on anyway?"

Grandfather frowned. "O'Connell's a good politician and knows the English are listening! Can't you see that?"

With Colleen at his side, Liam finally wedged between them. "Hey, don't fight each other! Save it for the British!"

The sight of the beautiful young girl suddenly mellowed Grandfather, and his stormy expression changed to sunshine, showing the gaps in his teeth as he grinned. "Well, Isn't this a pretty sight! Is everyone ready? Don't come for me till everyone's waiting!"

"They are, Grandfather, they are!" Sean assured him, and together the boys shuffled him down the lane.

Bag pipes filled the late afternoon air with their magical, haunting vibrations, and even as men were putting tables back into the cottages, music floated over the hamlet. The dancing, led by the bride and groom, would continue another two hours, and Liam wanted to stay but knew he could not. He hated that damn British curfew – a curfew that interfered with social times and the joy of new-found love.

He held Colleen's soft hand as long as he could until he had to say goodbye. Then he opened his arms, and she slipped into his embrace for one precious moment. The scent of her hair, her warm cheek next to his, her soft curves – all made his head whirl. He kissed her gently on the lips, then again more firmly. It was hard to leave her . . . *so* hard. "Early next Sunday I'll walk back to Ballinglass in time for Mass, and we'll have the entire day. My brother Sean always comes to see Maire and I'll come with him."

Her face glowed. "Good. My family will want to know you, and on Sundays our village has music and dancing. Until then."

He squeezed her hand and turned away. Da had clicked to the donkey, and the cart was moving down the road. As he jogged to catch up, he looked back and waved. Still standing and watching, she broke into a smile that made his steps light.

At the edge of the village, a chill wind began to blow like the one Liam had felt after the coaches thundered through, and he hoped that it did not mean a storm was brewing. He glanced to the west where the dust cloud had disappeared into the horizon, but all seemed well. This fine day he had found the girl of his dreams, so why did he feel apprehensive? It was strange.

4
On March 13, 1846

Liam was sleeping in the loft when urgent pounding on the door startled him awake. He heard his parents stirring below and his father call out, "We're getting a light."

Trying to listen, Liam crouched next to the loft's opening, and Niall, too, sat up on his mat. Dimly lit by the fire's last embers, the room brightened with the addition of a candle. When Father pulled open the door, Mr. Murphy stumbled in and collapsed on the bench, like his news was too terrible to tell.

"Denis Murphy! What's happened!"

"Oh my Lord . . . what am I . . . to do?" Murphy sat hunched like a broken man, and his shoulders began to heave with deep and tortured sighs. Finally, he regained some composure and in a hoarse voice he began.

"About an hour after you left, a Captain Brown and . . . many soldiers from the Forty-ninth British Infantry . . . rode into the village. The sheriff, police . . . wreckers, too. Mrs. Gerrard sent them. The whole village . . . evicted!"

"Oh God! No!" Father groaned.

In the hushed cottage, Liam, Niall, Sean, and Aine quietly

descended the ladder and looked on, motionless and sad. The grandparents had crept from their bed in the second room and stood nearby.

Murphy's voice cracked but he continued. "They drove us from our cottages, tore off the roofs . . . pulled down the walls, and lashed us with whips. Our men cursed, children cried, women keened. It was terrible!" Murphy closed his eyes and shuddered. "We begged for an explanation, but they just told us to leave . . . to get out! When Kevin O'Neill tried to stop a British soldier from entering his home, the soldier bayoneted him, opening his side. 'Twas no use to resist. Too many soldiers and armed police.

"I would swear on my deathbed that I always worked hard for Mrs. Gerrard. I was born and reared in Ballinglass . . . and my father before me, and everyone for generations! From our labor, her family built fine houses and acquired great wealth. Now to be thrown off the land to die!" He buried his face in his rough hands.

Grandfather's face turned red. "We're given no rights at all and treated worse than slaves, we are! The landlords would care if slaves died because they're property!"

Liam frowned. "But what about the 400 acre bog they drained? Doesn't Mrs. Gerrard at least have to pay the villagers for that?"

"No, Son," Father said. "According to British law, all improvements go to the landlord. If you improve things on the land or your cottage, they usually raise your rent."

"Their Parliament in London makes the law for Ireland," Grandfather roared, "and it favors them – enforced by their army of oppression!"

Murphy breathed deeply. "After the soldiers and . . . police left, it started to rain and the chill went to our bones so most of us crept back into the ruins for the night. My family is still hiding. What . . . what am I . . . to do?"

Mother kept shaking her head. "Denis, I don't understand this. Ballinglass was one of the best villages in northwest Ireland! How can we help, Seamus?"

Pacing the floor, Father grabbed his pipe and lit it. He looked at Liam. "Go and harness the donkey to the cart. It will be dawn soon, Denis, and we'll bring your family back here."

"No! I can't let you!" Murphy protested. "If ye own landlord finds you hiding an evicted family, he'll make it hell for you, too!"

"Don't worry. We'll salvage some wood and thatch from your cottage and dig out a scalp down in the glen. We'll share the food we have."

"God bless ya, Seamus. Maybe we can keep body and soul together . . . for at least a while. I'll give you me two chickens and cow, if we can get them here." Murphy stood up, anxious to leave.

The night was chilly and damp with a light mist falling. The hazy moon made the landscape ghostly gray but shed sufficient light for the journey. The only sounds were the clopping of the donkey hooves and the grinding of cart wheels into the gravel. Hoping the British cavalry enforcing the curfew was in bed, the Reilly men stared ahead nervously while Murphy bowed his head.

The violence inflicted on the O'Neill family had stunned Liam and left him despondent. He realized that eviction, more often than not, was a death sentence and that most of the people in Ballinglass would perish, but with Colleen's father mortally wounded, her family was in the gravest of danger. What would they do? Worried and anxious, he wanted to help them, but how? Since yesterday, he had thought of her constantly. She *can't die now.*

White cottages along the road stood dark and still since these neighbors knew nothing of the tragedy that had befallen Ballinglass, but by day they would be besieged by its people, begging for food and water. With a plan for a temporary rescue, Murphy leaned forward in the seat, as if to hasten the pace. Slowly the soft pink glow of morning came over the hills from the east. Just outside the village, Liam scanned the 400 acre bog reclaimed by the villagers, and a strong indignation stirred in him as he recalled Father's words: "all improvements go to the landlord."

Then there, straight ahead, was Ballinglass, silent and lifeless, as fatigue and despair had overwhelmed its people. The neat, well-kept village of yesterday now looked like a hurricane had blown through with roofs ripped off and doors yanked from their hinges. Belongings were strewn all over the ground – lace-trimmed curtains trampled in mud, an intricately carved Celtic cross atop a heap of feather mats, and even baby clothing with elaborate embroidery. The wedding cottage, with whitewash still damp, had gaping holes in its thatch and its red door was splintered by an ax. Liam felt profound pity for these humble and faithful people.

Then an old woman, sitting alone on a stool beside the road, caught his eye. It was the kind lady who gave Caitlin the picture of St. Patrick. With her black shawl pulled around white hair, she stared into space – motionless, in shock.

Liam hopped off the cart to see if he could help and touched her shoulder. "Is there something I can do for you? Where is your family?" Unresponsive, she did not even blink or acknowledge his presence so he jogged back to the cart, puzzled.

Many families had left their cottages as demanded, crawled into ditches on either side of the road, and covered themselves with thatch or blankets to repel the wind's sting. But the sound of the cart and donkey caused some to stir, and faces began peering from under blankets, out broken windows, and over partial walls. It was worse than he imagined, and Liam felt a tightening in his chest.

As soon as the cart halted in front of his demolished home, Denis jumped off and rushed in. Donal, the youngest, came out first, rubbing his eyes which were still swollen from much crying, and others followed, looking lost. Sean rushed over to Maire and enfolded her in his arms.

"Colleen's father . . . he's hurt . . . bad!" she sobbed.

Sean's eyes turned steely. "Murderers they are, and may they burn in hell!"

Brian Murphy came over to Liam. "Ryan O'Neill and other lads from our village are fighting in India at Aliwal - trying to be good 'citizens of the empire!'" His voice was heavy with sarcasm. "Better they die there than return to this!"

Maire struggled for control, biting her lip, but it was no use, and as she clung to Sean, her tears wet his shirt. Father left him free to support the devastated Maire, and motioned to Liam and Niall to lift a section of thatch onto the cart.

"Lads, be quick and gather mats and blankets." He handed Liam a large basket. "Fill this creel with potatoes." Murphy put a chicken under each arm of his five-year-old son, Donal, who gripped them with all his might. Niall brought out an iron pot filled with clay bowls and spoons, while Murphy tied his milk cow to the back of the cart.

Mom Murphy showed Liam a lock of curls tied with a ribbon. "My baby . . . Bláth . . . buried here in the churchyard." She touched the cradle tipped over on the grass and turned her face away to grieve alone.

Most families, lacking a plan or a hiding place, appeared dazed and confused. Bewildered, they sifted through their belongings, dusted them off, and set them aside as if they would soon put them back on the shelf . . . a shelf that was no more . . . a reality they could not accept.

Liam ached for a glimpse of Colleen, but she and her family were inside the partial walls with her father, while relatives mourned outside. Liam loaded the cart and tried to keep moving, but when he heard a low rumbling in the distance, he squinted down the road and saw an ominous dust cloud moving toward Ballinglass. The entire village was frozen in place, listening and watching.

"Soldiers are coming!" Father shouted. "Grab your children!" People screamed as the sound of pounding hooves sent terror through the crowd, and the smell of sweating horseflesh permeated the air as sheriff, police, soldiers and cavalry officers shouted orders in English. Horses at full gallop pulled clattering wagons filled with wreckers to the center of the village.

These barefoot and ragged wreckers knew their purpose: to finish the job they started yesterday and raze everything to the ground. With glum expressions and resignation, they got out and worked like brute animals without minds, trying to avoid the weeping and accusing eyes of the villagers. They took crowbars to the wall plates and with great blows tore at the remaining foundations, but the thick walls of stone and stucco resisted destruction as if in protest. Where part of a roof was stubborn and refused to fall in, they used saws to weaken the beam, while men on the ground pulled it with ropes until it crashed down with a ripping noise and billowing dust.

Liam gritted his teeth. How could these poor Irish do this work of ruin against their own countrymen, even for pay? Yet, he sensed that, despite their own desperation, they were disgusted with themselves and ashamed. Beside the loaded cart, Liam stood watching, dismayed, helpless, and angry.

Amid the chaos, the sheriff passed in his wagon, and Mr. Kelly chased him on foot. Kelly tried to climb on, slipped off, and ran after him with rent money in outstretched hands. "Take this! Why can't we stay here?" he shouted. "Can't you speak Irish? Why are you doing this?" The sheriff rode on and left him standing in the road.

Then a barefoot man in tattered clothes, wielding a crow bar, paused and looked at him with obvious sympathy and sadness. "Mrs. Gerrard . . . she's turning it all to grazing . . . no farms, no people, just sheep and cattle," he explained in Irish. Incredulous, Kelly could only stand with his mouth gaping open.

As infantry tore blankets and thatch off roadside ditches, they cursed and shouted, "Get out! Leave now! Away with you!" Knots of people clung to each other as cavalry cracked whips and lashed at them, but the villagers resisted leaving and delayed because they did not know where to go and were afraid. Soldiers struck them with the butts of their rifles, and the women shrieked in pain, children cried in fear and confusion.

As the land agent and bailiff sat in their saddles and surveyed the scene, a mother threw herself at the feet of the two men's horses. Kneeling, she swayed her body, brushing the ground with her hair and gesturing with her arms. With a voice full of anguish, she beseeched them in eloquent Irish.

"We beg you to stay this eviction. It will doom our children to wretched suffering and a death that is slower than a crucifixion, but no less cruel. The end will be so terrible that we swoon with dread. Remember His words: Blessed are the merciful for they shall see God."

The indifference of the officials mystified Liam because even if they did not understand Irish, could they not see her agony? Then he realized . . . aye . . . they had done this many times before and knew what to expect. Hatred welled up inside him.

Another woman groveled on the ground before Captain Brown, who was riding a powerful, chestnut horse. With a face contorted with woe, she weakly raised her arms toward him and pleaded. "Have you no pity? . . . Have you no mother, no sister? . . .

Open your heart . . . Please, let us stay here! These are our *homes*."
When the Captain kept walking his horse and ignored her, she rose
and stumbled after him, touching his boot in the stirrup.

He reacted with disdain and kicked at her. "Away with you!"
His horse snorted and neighed with wild eyes, and as it reared up,
sharp hooves clawed the air. Someone yelled as the heavy steed
struck her shoulder with a cracking sound. Neighbors ran into
the road and pulled her back while she groaned on the ground and
writhed with pain. With contempt, the Captain scowled and rode
away. Liam gritted his teeth, his breathing was hard and rough, and
a surging fury flowed through his body.

When a soldier came to the remains of the O'Neill cottage,
the wife clutched the door posts, blocked his way, and spoke to him
in Irish. Deaf to her pleas, he pried her hands away, flung her aside,
and motioned for foot soldiers to drag her husband out. As they
carried his blood-soaked and moaning body to the road, Colleen
and his other children followed, crying and imploring.

Enraged and with eyes bulging, Liam's temples pounded
and he clinched his fists. He felt like he was going to explode and
wanted to fight these English with his bare hands. Lunging for the
soldier, he leaped on his back and tried to force him to the ground,
but Father jumped on Liam and seized both arms in an iron grip.
Niall saw the situation, rushed over, and both father and brother
struggled to pull him away and hold him.

"It's no use, Son!" Father shouted. "There are too many
of them, and they have guns!" The soldier glared and waited. His
bayonet was already fixed to the barrel and ready to use should
they fail to subdue him. After the two men overpowered Liam, the
soldier returned to his work of evictions.

As Colleen's father lay bleeding on the ground, Colleen
stood near him, crying and wringing her hands. Maire, realizing

she would never see her best friend again, ran to hug her, to say goodbye, but could only sob uncontrollably. When Sean led the distraught Maire away, Liam stepped up to Colleen.

When filled with tears, her pale, blue eyes looked like ice. He put his arms around her, but she seemed beyond consolation, broken. "Let me know where you are . . . where you go," he murmured. She stood drained of hope, and when he reached for her hand, it was limp. Her young, twin sisters clung to her legs and wailed in fright. Powerless to help, Liam's composure was slipping, and words seemed empty. What could he do? What could he say?

As Father climbed onto the seat and flicked the reins, the heavily loaded cart slowly rolled down the road. "Liam, come on! We have to get out of here!" he yelled.

Reluctantly, Liam walked backwards and called to her, "Colleen, somehow . . . I'll find you! I swear it." The milling crowd soon came between them, engulfed her, and she was gone. Liam wanted to shout her name, but his throat was tight . . . to beg her to follow him, but how could she? Numb, he kept walking backwards, staring her way.

Murphy tried to herd his family to follow the cart, but his wife resisted and hugged each neighbor, weeping. Friends who had shared each other's lives since childhood were scattering like leaves in the wind. Swept along by the same calamity, Liam feared he had lost his special love forever and could not conceive of feeling the same for anyone else.

Passing into the countryside, he seethed with outrage that this village, with only traces remaining, would be erased from the map and in time forgotten. The British should not be allowed to hide their crime, to conceal their cruelty in the weeds of a rural pasture. If only I could erect a signpost here – carved in stone: "Ballinglass, County Galway, was razed to the ground on March 13,

1846, by the 49th British Infantry." It would stand as an indictment
of English oppression. He clinched his jaw and vowed to mark the
place someday.

Over and over Liam asked himself how the government
could allow evictions when they resulted in such terrible destruction
and death and even to use British soldiers to accomplish them!
From now on, whenever Grandfather talked about rights, he would
listen.

The military assault on their village and the wrenching
goodbyes with loved ones had all but sapped the Murphys' will to
live, but they plodded on, each carrying something, not caring where
they were going. Niall decided to put little Donal on his shoulders,
but when he tried to relieve him of the chickens under each arm,
Donal's grip on them only tightened. He shook his mop of tousled,
red hair in an emphatic "no," and the mouth beneath the up-turned
nose was in a pout, so Niall carried both child and chickens aloft
together.

Sitting beside Father in the cart, Mom Murphy rocked back
and forth, groaning. "What will happen to us? What will happen
to us?" Liam understood. "Us" had always included the village and
neighbors, and he wished they could take the whole village to the
glen, especially the O'Neills.

Because they were traumatized, the walk seemed short.
His grandparents, Mother, and sisters were waiting in the yard to
embrace the family, but the Murphys could only manage a weak nod
and were in shock, crest-fallen. The Reillys ushered them into the
cottage and offered the best they had, but Mom Murphy and her
younger children were too stressed to eat, and after taking a cup of
warm milk, they fell asleep, exhausted.

Eating at the table, Liam overheard Maire talking to Aine.
"My Grandmamai used to quote the proverb '*Ar scáth a chéile a*

mhaireas na daoine / People live in the shelter of each other' and that's how it was in Ballinglass. Friendship bound all the hearts together, and in good times and bad, we shared and gave support. So what will we do now?" Aine could only shake her head.

Liam left them whispering and went with the men to prepare a scalp. Outside, he loaded peat into a sturdy, wicker basket worn on the back and followed the loaded cart to the glen. Denis Murphy rallied his sons and chose the area next to the stream for the scalp since trees hid it from the road. Because Da feared a heavy rain might flood them out, Brian and his brother Mick took spades, diverted the creek several feet, and dammed the sides with rock and mud.

Liam and Sean were assigned the heavy work of digging out a cave-like place in the embankment. Da and Denis Murphy used wood from the old door frame to fashion an opening and anchored overlapping thatch on the top and sides. A blanket would have to serve as a door, and in front, they placed the iron pot in a circle of stones. While this was better than most scalps, spring was chilly, and only a few blankets, straw, and mats would shield them from the dampness and cold.

Liam worried that the hovel was too small for this large family, and Murphy read his thoughts. "Well, we're a family of eight and that generates a lot of warmth!" He stooped under the opening and stuck his head inside for a look. "It will be snug, but I think we can all fit in."

Liam marveled at his optimism when the situation was full of peril. The landlords' parks were reserved for sport hunting and fishing of the landlord and his guests, and tenants were not allowed to take as much as a stick for their own use. Irish had to hunt along roads, scavenge where they could, and not get caught when they strayed into forbidden territory.

Father gave a warning. "The agents will be hunting for scalps, so be careful about smoke in daylight."

Murphy nodded grimly. "But thank God for the likes of you, my friend! At least we're not without any shelter tonight, as are my neighbors." They realized that, sooner or later, most of the villagers would die, but Liam hoped if it was later, maybe some could find a way to survive. After placing a stool inside, the tired men returned to the Reilly hearth two miles away.

When they arrived, the young children were playing in the yard. Murphy messed up little Don's hair. "Well, me little ones! I'm glad to see ya scampering about! Is this a game of catch the lamb, I'm seein'? Ah. Be gentle with the kitten, Don. He's still a wee one." To Liam's amazement, Murphy presented a persistent example of cheerfulness and hope to his family.

The smell of a stewed chicken greeted their nose as they entered the cottage. "I told your Erin to add one of my chickens to her pot tonight!"

"You should have saved it for hungry days ahead, Denis! We have potatoes," Father said.

"The children need the lift, the show of confidence, ya know. It's the right time to have it," Murphy said. "I was saving it for Christmas, but who knows by then. I want you to keep me cow with you and we'll come and take milk each day."

Weary, Liam slouched on the bench and listened to Mother's attempts to buoy spirits. "Denis, you and your family should all stay here tonight. Best to go to the glen in the morning light." Murphy knew she was right and nodded in appreciation.

Shouting came from the children in the yard, and Brighid's face appeared over the half door. "Father Mullen is coming!" Everyone flowed out, led the priest inside to Da's seat at the hearth, and crowding around, they listened to the latest report.

Downcast, Mullen took off his hat, and sat looking into the fire as if seeing it all again. "When I heard about the tragedy, I returned to Ballinglass. By then, the soldiers had left and the village was in rubble. Families, carrying what they could, were straggling away to find a ditch for the night. The children were the saddest to me . . . scared, hungry, cold."

"And Father, what of our Patricia?" Mother Murphy asked. "Is she coming here?"

"Ah – Now I can ease your mind on that! They'll be walking here sometime tonight so leave a candle in the window! Peter's elderly grandfather was having strong pains in his chest and unable to walk so the family was gathered around him when I left."

Da pulled up a stool next to the priest. "Father, I can't understand it. Why! Why has Mrs. Gerrard done this terrible thing? Ballinglass always had their rent ready and produced good crops, yet a wrecker said she just wants to graze sheep and cattle!"

Mullen lit his pipe with an ember. "Well, all over Ireland this has been happening more and more often. For the past sixteen years, since around 1829, Lord Carlisle and others, speaking for the British government, have given speeches promoting this idea . . . telling the landlords that they can make more money raising livestock, than from growing grain. Grain can be shipped rather cheaply to England from distant colonies like British Canada. But only Ireland and Scotland are close enough to ship meat on the hoof to England," Father explained. "If landlords decide to create ranches to raise livestock, they must evict tenant farmers to free up land for pasture. I guess Mrs. Gerrard and her agent must have been persuaded by the promise of more profit."

Tears stood in Murphy's eyes. "But our village was not even hit by the potato blight last year! It was a wonderful village, and we drained the bog. Is there no gratitude?"

"The sheep will thank you for the extra pasture," Father smirked, his tone bitter. "Mrs. Gerrard was heartless to destroy the village. In fact, the whole movement is ruthless, with callous disregard for the Irish people. Now that the potato blight has hit so many farmers, I'm afraid we will see more land cleared and people swept away! Those farmers, being hungry and weak, are even less able to cope and survive eviction than you are, Denis."

Murphy gestured excitedly. "But we cannot survive for *long*! We'll slowly sink, don't ya know. What do you think I should do?"

Always the adviser to his flock, Father sighed. "I hate to say this . . . but I think you should consider exile. Much as it will sadden me to see you go and take my sister away . . . ." He cleared his throat. "Go to Boston or New York now while you still have your health, and no fever is upon you."

Murphy looked astonished. "But I don't have enough money to pay passage for my whole family!"

Father Mullen thought a minute and took a draw on his pipe. "How would it be to take your rent money and go to England? Leave Meg here to tend your little children and daughters while you and your older sons go work in English fields. The money you earn there might be enough since children are half fare."

"Ah . . . I don't know." Murphy's eyes were wide and fearful. "I've never been more than ten miles from Ballinglass in me whole life! I speak no English, only Irish and . . . ."

Niall interrupted. "I'll go with you, Mr. Murphy. I've learned English from our traveling teacher, Mr. Barrett . . . enough to read a lot and speak some."

Murphy's expression changed. "Well, that's an idea you have there. Mr. Barrett comes to Ballinglass, too, and 'twas he who said that you're one of the cleverest lads around. With you, we might have a chance." Liam hated the idea of his brother leaving, but he could see that Niall's help was necessary if Murphy was to consider the priest's plan.

"You should leave tomorrow to be there for spring farm work." Father Mullen explained.

"Tomorrow!" Murphy's fears returned. "But how could Meg get by with these little children . . . with babes and no one to protect them?"

"The Reillys will be here to help," Mullen reminded.

"We will, of course!" Grandfather assured him.

"Leave Ireland?" Meg Murphy slumped and put her hands over her face. "No! I won't be an exile . . . with no place . . . banished from my homeland!" Grandmother patted her back sympathetically.

Liam leaned forward. "We *Irish* should not be forced out of Ireland."

Sean looked disturbed by the plan. "I hear America does not welcome us, and the cities are bleak. 'Tis a great injustice to be driven out of our own country."

Brian glanced at Aine and then back to his Mother. "No one *wants* to leave, but it's our only chance. We are fortunate, compared to the poor O'Neill family!"

Father Mullen nodded and sighed. "Ah, yes. Kevin O'Neill is being dragged to the workhouse in a wicker pull car because he is dying. They had no choice so I suggested they go to Castlebar because I knew it wasn't full, but once inside, the family will never see him again or each other. Clearly, exile is better than the workhouse!"

A pall fell over the group. Liam shuddered. Poor Colleen! May God give her strength.

Then Caitlin broke the silence. "Why . . . why can't they ever see each other again if they are all in the workhouse *together*?"

Mother tried to explain. "The English have rules for the workhouses which separate mothers from fathers, parents from their children, brothers from sisters. They make them eat, sleep, and work apart – never able to see or comfort one another. The English masters treat them harshly and make even the children work and never play."

"That's mean! Why would anyone ever go there!" Brighid asked.

"People only enter if they have no hope of surviving on the outside," Mother said. "Once in, it's very hard to get out. They're supposed to give you a bed, a roof, and some food each day in return for your labor, but I'm not sure they always do."

"And they'll bury you, if you die," Father Mullen added, "And many die."

With gloom settling like a fog, Mother intervened. "Let's be having some dinner! Gather at the table, and we'll serve up colcannon and Murphy's fine stew hen." Needing no further urging, the families nudged into standing places and crowded onto the benches. During the grace, Father Mullen prayed for the O'Neills and all the wandering people of Ballinglass.

The minute prayer was concluded, Caitlin asked about her friend. "What's happened to that nice old lady in the dry goods store? The one who gave me the picture?"

"Oh, you must mean Mrs. Donovan," Father Mullen answered. "Since she's a widow and her sons are fighting in India, the O'Neills took her with them to the workhouse."

Forlorn but resigned, Meg Murphy finally conceded that exile was their only option. Tomorrow she would take her children to the scalp, while her husband and older sons left for England. Putting a candle in the window as a beacon to Patricia and Peter, she watched the moonlit lane for their shadowy figures.

After dinner, the two families gathered in close around the flickering light of the fire as flames projected gold and dark shadows on the thick, stucco walls. The cottage was warm and for tonight, at least, the Murphys were safe.

Da took down the old fiddle from the hook above the mantel, while Father Mullen, Sean, and Brian pulled out their tin whistles. Accompanied by Niall's mandolin, they played a hauntingly beautiful melody, "Music of Inishvickillane," a song that reminded Liam of the sigh of the wind. When Father Mullen and Sean played a duet, their skill made the tin whistle as pure of tone as the finest flute and with a clarity that touched the soul.

Although Liam was soothed by the music, he felt anxious, and when he closed his eyes, he could see the faces and terrible misery of the families, wandering without shelter in the darkness. The thought of Colleen – trapped in the workhouse, her father dying, separated from family, surrounded by harsh task masters – was chilling. If only he could rescue her and bring her here. And it was unsettling to think of Niall, going on a long and dangerous journey to a country unfriendly to Irish. Liam's spirits were low, but when Mother's clear soprano voice sang the old song "Deep Peace," sleep finally came . . . there on the hard flagstone.

5

To Castlebar

A dull thumping from the oak table jarred Liam awake as Grandmother pounded oat cakes for the travelers. He had fallen asleep against the stucco wall in a half-seated position, and now he paid for it with a stiff neck. Before he opened his eyes, Mittens had jumped on his chest and purred so loudly that he sat up, stroked the kitten, and looked around. Father was arguing with Niall about taking the mandolin to England, but in the end, Liam knew nothing could separate his brother from his music.

Mother was draining boiled potatoes into a wicker basket to cool. "Carry these in their jackets," she instructed, although no one seemed to be listening.

Denis Murphy tried to comfort his wife who became more distressed the more he talked. "Meg, we'll be back again in just a few weeks, God willin'!"

She gave a deep sigh and looked to Niall. "We've never been apart since our wedding day so take good care of him." The lines of her face drooped with dejection.

Denis gave her ample torso a reassuring bear hug. "We'll all watch out for each other!" Then he whispered, "Be strong for the children, Meg." Liam was amazed that this man, so fearful last night, seemed confident today.

The newlyweds stood with arms around each other in a gentle embrace. "What if you can't make enough passage money for the two of us? I should go and work, too," Patricia fretted.

"They won't treat us well so it's better for you to be here," Peter replied.

When Mother announced that breakfast was ready, Father Mullen rose from the wall seat which served as a bed for guests and took a place on a bench. "Denis, take your rent money, but hide it in different places. I'll go with you as far as Castlebar, and escort you to my fellow priest, Father Henry, who can tell you which port has a ship for England at its dock."

Castlebar . . . Colleen! Liam stopped eating. "Da, let me go as far as Castlebar, and then I can report which route they took."

Father paused, his face quizzical at Liam's sudden interest in going to the town to the north. "Maybe so . . . all right, but don't attract the attention of soldiers."

"True, indeed!" Father Mullen reached for another potato. "The landlords have demanded that Parliament send more troops to protect their food shipments to England and their property here in Ireland. So the government passed that coercion act last month, and now police and soldiers can arrest us on mere *suspicion* and jail us without a charge."

"I don't know why the landlords are so worried," Grandda complained. "We're not allowed to have guns, and our pitchforks aren't much of a threat."

After Liam finished breakfast, he bolted up the ladder to fetch his frieze jacket, and when he got down from the loft, the travelers were gathering their bundles and saying goodbye.

Mom Murphy hid her face in her apron, and her shoulders

shook with sobbing so hard she could not speak.

Denis Murphy was persuaded to reconsider. "Tell me now! What have I been thinking? Just too many troubles for her to bear all at once! Brian, your mother needs you more than I do so you're staying here."

Brian went over and put his arm around her. "Ya hear that, Mamai? You won't be alone now." Comforted by her husband's concession, Mom Murphy dabbed her eyes with her apron and sniffed.

Brian whispered gently. "Can't you give Da a smile to see him off?" With head bowed, she sniffed again, gave Denis a grateful look, and finally a tentative hug, but still could not muster a smile.

The goodbyes moved outside and in the bright light of a fair day, things seemed more optimistic. The lilac bush near the front door emitted a sweet fragrance, and in the side yard, pigs oinked and chickens clucked over the feast of potato skins. After embraces and calls of "*Go raiabh maith agat* / May it go well with you," the men strode down the lane.

Even before they reached the road, Liam asked Mr. Murphy the question that was nagging him. "What if you don't make enough money for passage after you pay for travel to and from England? You have such a large family!"

Murphy hoisted his heavy cloth bag higher on his back, and his mouth became a straight, determined line. "We can't return until we have the passage money, however long it takes! So Liam, I'm counting on you to help Brian keep the family safe! Truth is, it will be months before we can come back, and we may well have to work three, four farms."

With bushy eyebrows raised, Denis Murphy stopped in mid-road. "Father, you always know what's happening. Last year we heard that Prime Minister Peel imported maize from Americay to help feed the starving here in Ireland. So why haven't they turned loose of it?"

"They're supposed to sell it from special depots, sometime this May. There won't be nearly enough to feed all who need it, but it should help."

"Well, they better stop stalling," Murphy said. "The blight hit last October, and by May, half the hungry will be dead! Most Irish tenants have no money to buy maize anyway, so they should just give it to us or let us eat some of what we're growing right here in Ireland."

Father Mullen's eyes lit up. "You are right, Denis, and plenty of Irish leaders agree with you, too. Daniel O'Connell and a committee of important citizens have gone to the Lord-Lieutenant, Lord Heytesbury, with a plan . . . a good plan, I think. They say we should stop using grain to make ale and should reduce the food exported to England until this famine crisis is passed. There are countries like the United States who want to send foods to us directly but, as it is now, their gifts of food have to go first to England, pay a duty there, and then reload into English boats. The English make money off the American aid to us, and it delays the arrival of the food."

"Do you think the government will do any of those things?" Murphy asked.

"Surely England will finally do something for Ireland," Father Mullen replied. "That's what most people think."

Liam remembered one of Grandfather's history lessons. "Grandda says that once before when Ireland was threatened with famine, we stopped food from leaving and starvation was avoided."

"Yes . . . in 1782, I believe, was it not?" Father Mullen asked.

Niall frowned. "If it was that far back, it was when England let the Irish Parliament in Dublin make some decisions. The Anglo landlords in the Parliament didn't want their tenants to starve so they cut back on food shipments to England. But now, since the English forced that union on us, all decisions are made in London, and it bodes ill, I tell ya!"

Father disagreed. "But union with England *should* mean that Ireland receives some help, if we are truly citizens now. Belgium, France, Germany, and the Netherlands were also hit by potato blight, but there has been no mass starvation in those countries because their governments stopped exporting food. We can only hope the British will be merciful to us and do the same here so . . ."

Niall interrupted. "Or else they'll prove, once and for all, that the so called 'union' of Ireland and England is just a sham."

Liam turned on his brother. "Niall, Father Mullen is wise and deserves respect! I admit we didn't see much English mercy in Ballinglass, but things have never been this bad before so surely they'll help us now."

They let the argument rest since they were approaching a small cluster of one room, stucco huts. Liam knew these very poor hamlets called clachans made everything they used, ate potatoes, took milk from a village cow, and shared their fields. The grain they grew and pigs they raised paid the rent. Because the London government levied an extra tax for each window or chimney, this village had none. But as they got closer, he was bothered by an eerie stillness – no barking dogs, no children playing, no people stirring, not even a skylark's song.

Father Mullen shaded his eyes against the sun with his hand. "I'm afraid this is a blight-stricken clachan, and this terrible silence betrays its condition." Liam wondered if the community was deserted since no smoke rose from the roof holes. Whatever the landlord had not seized as rent must have been eaten long ago so maybe the people had fled.

Then, a mother, who must have heard them coming, slowly

crept out of her cabin, carrying her baby whose legs swung loosely like a doll's. The woman's head was skull-like with eyeballs resting in dark, deep sockets and coarsened hair that stood out like tangled brush. Liam could not help but stare at her hands whose bones protruded like spokes, barely covered by skin and at enormous knees over wasted limbs. The travelers stood in the road, sad and still.

The woman whispered in a raspy voice, "The hunger is upon us. Can you spare us something?" Other ghostly figures in rags emerged from the dark doorways as if from the grave and surrounded them, their words merging like a groan. "Help us . . . please . . . please . . . help us . . . please . . . in God's name . . . please" they murmured over and over. With drooping eyelids and mask-like faces, they stood listlessly with skin strangely white as if it had no blood. Green stains around the mouths hinted that they had eaten grass in their desperate craving for food.

"My dear people!" Father Mullen gasped. Tears stood in his eyes as he handed over all the bits of food he had. The men were anguished, torn between pity for the villagers and fear that if they gave potatoes away, they would have nothing for the journey, but Liam saw their dilemma.

"Don't," he said. "Let me give *my* potatoes since I'm going back home." When he opened his bag onto the road, the villagers lunged at them, yet no one fought for more than his share, and some even divided with those who were too weak to scramble.

As the travelers drifted down the road, one man hobbled after them and stroked Liam's arm. "May you be blessed with a long life and eternity with God," he croaked.

Liam was shaken. He realized that very soon this man would be in eternity for these few potatoes could only delay their deaths, not prevent them. Out amid growing fields, his frustration erupted. "How strange to have people starving when harvests are good, and last year's Irish oat crop was the best in ten years! It's not a *real* famine where there is no food, but a *false* famine."

"Ah, some are starting to call it that!" Father Mullen said. "There's plenty of food but the landlords are taking the crops to sell in England for a high price. That's how they pay for their wealthy life style and luxuries . . . spending large sums on horses, hounds, ostentatious mansions, opera boxes, and the like. With such high rent, everything that small clachan grew, except potatoes, went to the landlord . . . the pigs, too. Those farmers probably never tasted meat in their whole lives, so when blight took the potatoes, they starved."

Liam's jaw muscles tightened, and his voice had an edge. "Why won't the landlords let them keep some of the grain to eat so they can survive to farm for them another year?"

Father Mullen pursed his lips. "Yes, they could reduce the rent until better times, *if* they wanted to. But they probably figure they can just replace these tenants or turn the land to pasture, like Mrs. Gerrard is doing in Ballinglass. Another thing, Liam, most of the landlords in Ireland – they say 70 out of 100 – are absentee and live in England most of the time. They send their agents to collect the rent and don't see this suffering first hand or know their tenants as people."

Murphy flushed with rage. "That's no excuse! Mrs. Gerrard did not have to know our children's names to realize we are people and would die if she turned us out! She knew these things and did it anyway . . . just to try and get even richer!"

"Well, one thing for sure," Father said. "No one escapes death, and at that moment, the mighty are judged the same as the poor and weak. Just as the rich man was held accountable by God for ignoring the beggar Lazarus at his gate, we'll all have to answer."

Liam recalled that Gospel and took comfort, but the Irish

needed justice now, here on earth. He remembered passing the fine mansion of Mrs. Gerrard in the country and hearing that she had others in Dublin and London. Father Mullen and Murphy were both right about the cause of the suffering. It was greed without mercy.

About a half mile away, a huge dust cloud arose from the road, and once over the hill, they saw a long convoy of pack animals pulling wagons toward Westport. After they got closer, Liam was astonished to see that about seventy foot soldiers, thirty cavalry, and two small cannon were leading the procession. To have such a large military escort, Liam surmised they must be worried that in desperation, the hungry Irish might try to steal some of the food they had grown.

"Step aside, there! Off the road!" the gruff officer ordered in English. Despite the language barrier, there was no misunderstanding his command, and the travelers leaned on the stone wall beside the road as the wagon train inched along. They squinted into the sunlight and acted nonchalant, except for Liam who glared with resentment. Wanting to calculate the extent of the exports, he sat in the grass and scratched numbers in the dirt.

As they passed, he made notations. He gauged that there were about two hundred wagons loaded with casks of ham, bags of oats and wheat, bales of feathers, a hundred firkins of butter, and packages that he could not tell the contents. Then one open bag revealed a wool jacket, and he realized that pawned clothing must be in many of them. There were enough crates of eggs and rounds of cheese to feed a small city. Then came livestock with about seventy lambs and a hundred noisy piglets.

It took over two hours for the convoy to pass, and Liam was amazed. With all of this in just one wagon train, clearly Ireland could feed herself and many in England at the same time. The committee in Dublin was right: keeping some food at home could save Ireland.

Finally, twenty cows straggled past with more cavalry taking up the rear. One haughty soldier on a black horse looked down at Liam with a contemptuous stare and singled him out with his dark eyes like he would enjoy a confrontation. Liam stood up and without blinking, he looked back at the soldier, refusing to lower his eyes in subordination.

Father Mullen, seeing the interaction, took off his hat and bowed in a friendly show of deference to the officer. "And a fine day to you, sir!" The smiling priest tried to dispel the tension, and as the military horse clomped past, the distracted soldier gave Father Mullen a sullen nod.

When they had passed, the priest turned to Liam and spoke in Irish, "Look away and don't return a stare. Give no hint of defiance, my son, or they'll put you in prison or worse – transport you like a slave to work in a distant colony. Don't tempt them because they run the courts and don't have to justify their arrests. They have imprisoned people for seven years for merely protesting or not being home before curfew," he warned.

Murphy raised his bushy eyebrows and widened his eyes. "Best we all be remembering that, lads. Be humble and tolerate insults. Let Niall here do the talking in English, and you be guarding your tongue!"

Niall looked back at the large number of mounted cavalry. "In our newspaper, I read that the British government provides ten pounds of oats every day for each military horse. The newspaper said that if they reduced that to five pounds per day, they could give 60,000 pounds a day to feed people, and the horses would not suffer."

"So why don't they?" Murphy asked. "Are British horses more important than Irish people?"

No one dared to answer him but plodded on in grim silence. Though the question made Liam cringe, he was intrigued with the idea. "That newspaper is on to something. Maybe the English just haven't thought of that yet, and now someone will tell them."

When they arrived in Castlebar, the mood of the town was subdued. Beggars in various stages of starvation moved slowly through the lanes, weak and in a stupor. They held out thin arms for a crust of bread, anything, and it was hard to pass them with only a prayer and an apology.

Father Mullen led them though the streets to the cottage of Father Richard Henry, who invited them in for a cup of tea. He was shocked to hear about the destruction of Ballinglass. "Such a lovely and prosperous village!" He suggested the travelers go to Westport because he'd heard that a ship was there loading. "The lower decks carry animals and food, and on the top deck, there is standing room for passengers, but prepare yourselves for a damp and cold journey."

Father Mullen set his cup in the saucer. "And how are your parishioners? Much hunger amongst them?"

Father Henry's expression became pained. "It's a terrible thing to see your flock in such dire straits and be unable to help them! Every day some come and beg me to get them relief work for a few pence a day. I do my best, but the number chosen is small." Father Henry hunched over his tea cup. "I have witnessed tears gushing from the eyes of once hardy men. Starvation and despair combine to enfeeble them and break their spirits. Without an opportunity to work or get food or a reason to hope, they stay in their cabins, and I fear they will die there unknown . . . forgotten . . . their deaths unrecorded . . . their bodies unburied."

The priest put his face in his hands, tormented by the heart-rending scenes in his head. The room was still. At last he heaved a sigh and lifted his head. "I've written to my brother in Brooklyn and my cousin in Baltimore to ask their parish priests to make a collection for us, but nothing has come."

Father Mullen gripped Henry's shoulder. "I think they'll respond. In Galway a convent is managing to feed 1,000 orphans breakfast each day with money sent by Catholic churches in America and Europe. But I understand your frustration. I give away as much of my own food as I can, but it's only a drop in an ocean of needy. I fear that with so many deaths, I will not be there to give them the last sacrament. Hopefully, the next potato crop will ease the suffering, if they can just survive till then, but clearly many won't." He turned to Murphy. "So you see, bad as it is, things could be worse for your family."

"True, 'tis true." Murphy sighed. "If only there are no further troubles, and we can make enough for passage."

Liam watched for an opening: "Father, some families from Ballinglass went to the Castlebar workhouse, and I'm wondering how they might be getting along?"

"I serve on the Board of Guardians for the workhouse, and the landlord is not paying his share for its maintenance. Lord Lucan, the wealthiest landlord in our area with many thousands of tenants, is badly in arrears and owes more than anyone. He forces his tenants to give payments for the workhouse but doesn't always pay his own part. The place is low on turf for heat and provides only one small meal each day. The unfortunates sleep on straw without blankets, and conditions are miserable. At least a fourth who enter, die."

Liam felt his heart sink. "And where is the workhouse?"

"It's several miles north of town . . . fine buildings paid for by the poor tax. I really think Lord Lucan hopes to acquire the buildings for himself someday. He talks more about closing the workhouse than supporting it."

Liam gritted his teeth. Here it was again . . . greed without mercy. "Father Mullen, will you go there with me? We have to try and do something for our friends from Ballinglass."

"I'll go, Liam, but don't get your hopes up."

Murphy rose from his stool. "Ya best be going there, if ya are. And we should start toward Westport, I'm thinking. I don't want any boat leaving without us on board!"

The group told Father Henry goodbye and started down the road with a determined gait. Liam and Father Mullen watched until the road turned and the Murphys were out of sight before they headed north to the workhouse.

"When we get there, I'll do the talking," Father said. "It's a gloomy place, you know. Like Father Henry told us, workhouses in Ireland are not funded properly to give even the bare necessities. English rules say what food they receive must be eaten in silence and families separated from each other. Because Irish families are so close, the idea of never seeing each other again is a choice they delay till they're face to face with death."

"The more reason to rescue them, Father."

"'Tis doubtful we can because the rules make it difficult to get out. The bishop who follows debates in Parliament says the English build workhouses for two reasons: to punish the paupers and to get them off the streets. This is true even in England, but in the case of Ireland, they have a third reason: to keep the poor Irish here and prevent them from migrating to England. To accomplish this, they make it almost impossible for anyone to leave the workhouse."

Liam frowned. "By locking up the poor, they are treating them like criminals!"

"Yes, there's truth in what you say. English laws make it a crime to be a vagrant and police arrest them. We Irish think it's our duty to relieve the suffering of the unfortunate and feel guilty if we pass them by and give them nothing. But the English upper classes consider poverty a moral failing and disapprove of giving alms, saying it encourages begging."

Straight ahead was a large complex of two-story, gray stone buildings on flat, treeless land. Enclosed by a thick, ten-foot wall and iron gate, the workhouse resembled both a prison and a fortress. There were no sounds or signs of life, and Liam felt uneasy, like the place was evil and haunted.

Next to the large, iron double gate was a small gate for deliveries and visitors. The guard allowed them to enter only after Father Mullen introduced himself and claimed to have an appointment with the master. Once inside, they guessed that the center building housed the administrative offices because it looked more important with five pointed gables and a decorative stone arch over the main door. Liam was glad to have the priest at his side and felt jittery as Father Mullen pounded the heavy, metal knocker.

After some time, a tight-lipped, efficient woman with grayish hair in a bun and a starched uniform came to the door. "Yes?"

In English Father asked about the O'Neill family of eight and a Mrs. Donovan, but the servant shook her shoulders and frowned, like one interrupted in a task.

"I don't think she understood me," Father said. "My accent is not to her liking." He took out a bit of paper and wrote the names and a number eight. Again, she shook her head and was silent, but Father persisted. "Please, may we see the headmaster . . . head mas . . . ter?" he said with exaggerated pronunciation.

With a perturbed expression, she waddled off. When she reappeared, she ushered them into a receiving room where bookcases filled one wall, and on the other, heavy drapes covered tall windows. Liam gaped at the shiny furniture and polished woodwork. An ornate clock ticked loudly from the mantel of the large fireplace, and a framed certificate hung on the wall which told of the headmaster's commissioning in Her Majesty's army. Liam had just finished reading it when he entered.

Dressed in a black suit, the headmaster stood behind a massive desk and waved them to a pair of stuffed chairs, the softest Liam had ever seen. "I am the master of this workhouse. What is your business here?"

Father Mullen bowed. "Good afternoon, sir. Could you be so kind as to allow us to see the O'Neill family?"

"We do not allow visitors here, and the inmates are occupied," he replied with disdain.

"May I inquire as to their health and welfare?" Father asked.

"Mr. O'Neill was taken to the dying room, and the others are in their separate wards." Silence ensued.

Liam whispered to Father in Irish: "Ask about getting them out!"

"Is there any way to gain the release of the wife and children, sir?" Father asked.

"No, it is out of the question. They have no means to support themselves and are now in our custody and under the poor laws. If this is all you came for, your business is concluded."

"No, not yet," Liam said in Irish. In broken English, he begged, "We need . . . to see! Please! Colleen O'Neill?"

With the posture of a soldier, the master stood with head high. "I think this conversation is at an end, and I must be about my affairs here. Mrs. Peabody will show you to the door, sir." Father Mullen rose to leave. Dejected and powerless, Liam followed the servant down the dark hall. Colleen was here . . . somewhere . . . inside one of these cold and damp stone buildings.

Outside, he persuaded Father Mullen to circle the high wall

surrounding the complex and go to the rear. "Liam, I fear they are trapped in the workhouse. Look at these mounds of freshly turned earth where weeds and wild flowers are already taking root. Mass graves. See how uneven the ground is? That is because many graves are close together and shallow with dirt mounded up. This ground . . . all graves!"

They walked along the wall to the back far corner where Father Mullen pointed to a smaller building just inside the wall. "That is the fever ward where they put the sick and dying in an attempt to separate them. But with so many dying, it ends up being called the dead house. Patients who are sick with fever are mixed in with everyone else. To make the job of burying so many people easier, they have dug this large pit and built a slide of wooden planks that extends from a second-floor window in the dead house to the pit. But look away! Deep in the bottom is a child's body." Father pushed Liam away and crossed himself.

Father continued. "They used to carry the dead to the church grave yard in town, but the sight of so many bodies upset the local people, and new rules say the workhouse dead should be buried close by, preferably in the rear of the complex."

"Is this why they call the workhouse *Cosán na Marbh /* Pathway to the Dead?" Liam asked.

"Yes, I'm afraid so."

Liam erupted in fury and shouted, "Colleen is innocent and young, and it's not fair that she's confined in a death camp just because her family was evicted!"

As they walked around to the side of the workhouse, Liam found one heavy, oak door in the wall, but when he lifted the handle and leaned against it, it was locked and would not budge. This *was* a prison. In frustration, he began pounding his fist against the door and scanned the windows, high and inside the walls. The noise must have been heard by two haggard females who peered down for an instant, then disappeared.

Liam kept watching that same window, hoping someone might look out again. Then there appeared a single fair face. He squinted, trying to see more clearly. With the afternoon sun shining on her, he could tell it was a girl with hair, long and dark. His heart raced wildly. Could it be Colleen?

She raised one hand and laid her palm against the pane, and in return, he raised his open hand and held it up. Now she placed both palms on the window, and somehow, he felt it was a sign. Was she remembering their time at the wedding . . . their clasped hands . . . hers in his?

"Father, see that girl?"

"Where, Liam? I see no one."

"There! In the window near that chimney!"

"Colleen! Is that you?" Liam yelled. Suddenly she was gone. He kept searching that one window, but she did not return. Maybe someone had pulled her away. Was it against their rules to look out? "Colleen! Colleen!" he shouted, frantic with worry.

Father shoved him forward. "Hush! We could be arrested for trespassing." Liam knew he was right, but it was hard to let go, and he kept looking back at that window until it was out of sight.

"We best get home, Liam. They were not friendly to the likes of us and would just as soon send for the police."

It was mid-afternoon when they started south toward home, and the priest seemed to share Liam's depressed mood. Since they had no more food to give, they skirted around the starving clachan.

Father Mullen's shoulders slumped. "You know, Liam, the next time we pass through that village, no one will come out."

After an hour, he and the priest parted and took different roads. The sun gradually lowered on the western horizon. Having consumed only tea and bread since his breakfast of potatoes, Liam's energy ebbed and without realizing it, his pace slowed.

Her lovely face and pale eyes floated before him and took his mind elsewhere. He relived their kiss and remembered the warmth of her soft body when they embraced, the fresh scent of her hair, her smile when he looked back. How he yearned to hold her again. Imagining the horrors inside the death house, he clinched his fists. Would she die a little every day till the end came or would it be sudden? His outrage at this new injustice made him want to fight, but how?

The sun's glowing orb slipped behind the mountains, and the sky streaked purple and blue. No! It can't be sunset. He had promised Da he'd be home before this, and he started to jog.

Then he heard it: dogs barking and horses in canter just over the next hill. Soldiers! Quickly Liam jumped behind a stone fence at the roadside and wedged his body between it and the damp ground. Now they were close. Would the dogs pick up his scent? He could hear soldiers talking in muted English with an occasional laugh, and Liam could scarcely breathe. They were almost beside him on the other side of the wall, and he prayed the dogs would have no time to sniff him out! Still in a canter, the horses passed without slowing.

Then he heard growling. A dog had stopped on the other side of the wall and started to bark, at first hesitantly and then persistently! He knew the soldiers would turn around and investigate, and he could not wait to be found. In a low crouch, he ran along the wall, and the dog followed, barking incessantly. Another dog joined in rousing the alarm, but Liam kept running, staying low. Then he darted into a field of tall grass and hugged the ground.

The cantering hooves grew louder and told him the soldiers were returning. When they halted at the fence, the horses shook their bridles and snorted. As Liam peeped through the stand of grass, he saw the silhouettes of riders and steeds against the dusky

sky, looking over the field. When the dogs continued to yap and growl, the soldiers discussed the reasons for their arousal.

Liam's heart was beating so hard he could hear it in his ears. Then he heard a rifle cock and a bullet whistled past him. As he lay still and held his breath, a horse neighed. Lying on his stomach, Liam squinted through the green blades and saw the soldiers watching and listening. The shot was intended to spook out an animal or man, but nothing moved. The soldier cocked again, took aim, and shot a second time. The loud crack echoed through the quiet countryside.

Liam heard a rustling through the grass as a hare bolted into the small space next to the wall and froze there. The soldiers pointed to it and laughed, convinced that the animal had caused the alarm. Turning their mounts around, they commanded the dogs to follow. Liam heard them gallop away, and the sounds of barking and hooves grew distant.

The evening became quiet with only the night sounds of insects and frogs. Yet he still could not bring himself to leave his hiding place, and he continued to lay there, listening. Bird calls occasionally interrupted the stillness, and a dove's cooing in soft tones was reassuring. Finally, like a wary deer, he crept to the fence and peered over. The road was clear, so with new energy spawned by fear, he leaped over the wall and jogged toward home where his family would be waiting and worried.

He recalled Father's warning and realized that for violating curfew, the patrols could have shot him or banished him to a distant colony. With so many English soldiers swarming over the countryside and creating a state of terror, danger had come close and he knew it would again.

6
Spring's Passage: 1846

In the spring of 1846, the weather in County Mayo alternated between cold, drenching rain and sunshine, and Liam preferred the rain because it matched his mood. Sluggish, lacking energy or appetite, he caught Mother studying him.

"Liam, you act weary, but you're well, aren't you now?" She tried to touch his forehead, but he shrugged away from her hand. Mothers are like that . . . he mused . . . always sensitive to what their children are feeling no matter how old we are.

Liam forced a reassuring smile but was afraid his eyes told the truth. He rankled at the ruthless evictions of Ballinglass, but he grieved most for Colleen. Given time and not tragedy, their relationship would have grown, but now she would never leave the workhouse. He had lost the girl he could never forget and never be content without.

He watched romance kindle between Aine and Brian and was irritated by Sean's easy laughter as he celebrated each day with Maire, only two miles away. They exchanged tender looks and held hands even in Liam's present which intensified his melancholy, made him feel left out, lonely, and even jealous.

Father had always encouraged Sean's interest in Maire, which had been evident for over a year, and now he left him free from many chores. He made Liam take up the slack with tasks he normally shared with his brothers and accused him of being ungenerous when he complained.

Alone with Father in the potato bed, Liam decided to talk. "You know the Murphys are leaving, so why are you allowing Aine and Sean to spend so much time with them? You're setting them up for disappointment and heartache."

Standing in the trench, there was only the dull crunch of Father's hoe as he considered the question. Finally he answered: "Risking disappointment is part of life. If a person does not try to realize his hopes, he never finds out what's possible and he always wonders what might have been."

"Well, I'm sick and tired of doing Sean's work! You're favoring him over me and it's not fair!" Fuming, Liam hurled his hoe and strode to the house, but his outburst changed nothing.

His family continued to care for the Murphys who survived with potatoes from the Reillys, milk from the Murphy cow, and an occasional fish from the stream. Aine sometimes churned their cream into butter and luckily, no soldiers or agents detected their dugout. Brian hunted, but with hungry men everywhere searching for game, he usually returned empty handed.

A month had passed since the men left for England, and the trips between glen and cottage became a daily occurrence as the couples managed more time together. Liam had expected Mother to invite the Murphys often, but when the visits increased, he resented their happiness. In the heavy pot on the crane, *brotchán foltchep* – a delicious soup of leeks, oatmeal, and milk – simmered. Though it had always been his favorite, a sullen Liam now refused it.

If only he could be congenial again, but whenever he allowed himself to experience joy, he felt guilty because just twelve miles away, she was confined to the hellish workhouse. Pent up inside was a drive to reform what was brutal, cruel, and unjust, but being powerless, he had free-floating anger that he vented without direction. He knew he was taking his frustration and unhappiness out on his family, but he was either unable or unwilling to change.

After dinner in the pastel glow of the fire, bare feet warmed quickly, and the two families delighted each other with stories and music. Father played his violin, Sean and Brian, their tin whistles, and Patricia, Maire, and Aine sang trio. On these occasions, Liam acted preoccupied and stayed aloof, almost pouting. He wasn't proud of his behavior and wished he could put aside his feelings and join in, but his emotions were flat and he was unable to pretend otherwise.

One April evening as they sat at fireside, Father relayed a story that even intrigued Liam. Puffing on his curved pipe, he told about landlords who lived nearby on Lough Carra in a grand house called Moore Hall. "A hundred years ago, the Moore family left Ireland to escape English tyranny and settled in Spain where they became very rich in the wine and iodine business. But they still loved their homeland and dreamed of returning. In 1778 the English began to allow Irish Catholics to lease land, and by the 1790's the Moores came back to Mayo."

Grandda cleared his throat to add his own recollections. "I was just a child at the time, but my father always talked about how the Moores had to pledge an oath of loyalty to the English king in order to lease so much land. But they still saw themselves as Irish and even built a Catholic Church in 1835 in the village of Carnacon."

Da leaned forward, his elbows on his knees. "Since the blight last year, the present landlord of the estate, George Henry

Moore, has been greatly saddened by the suffering of his tenants and has come up with an idea. He's going to race his favorite horse for the English Chester Cup and use any winnings to help his people. Moore thinks his horse, Coranna, will run faster with the prayers of the poor, and all County Mayo is rooting for him!"

One morning in early May, Uncle Paddy burst into the door, shouting, "He won! Coranna won! He did it! People say Moore will have £17,000 with both the prize money and winnings from his bets, and he promises that none of his tenants will ever be evicted or go hungry. My Una has cousins who are his tenants, and they are dancing in the lanes!"

Grandda stood up and raised his arms in celebration. "The Moores have stayed true to their Irish Catholic roots, God bless 'em!" This news made even Liam smile, and that night, the Murphys and Reillys went to Uncle Paddy's for music and dancing themselves. They ran the short distance home after dark, two by two, staying quiet and watchful.

With the coming of June, it was again time for a vital and happy ritual of late spring — the annual mihul or turf cutting. Hearth and burning turf were the heart of every Irish cottage, and if the peat fire was permitted to go out, folklore said the soul of the family would leave. So replenishing the supply of peat was an important time when neighbors and relatives near the bog gathered for cooperative days of work, picnics, and music. They usually camped out in small shelters, but now because of curfew, they would have to return home each night. Despite this, they began the mihul in high spirits, except for Liam who went out of obligation.

Tiny white flowers called cean-a-bhans nodded and danced over the marshy earth, and the children begged permission to pick them. They raced here and there, squealing with delight, and despite himself, Liam enjoyed watching Caitlin's eyes sparkle with wonder at everything. In her frolic, she splashed into a hidden mud puddle but merely giggled at her misfortune. He wished he had her resilience.

Once the flowers were taken, the women set up the day's camp, and the men began to strip away the bog's past year of vegetation. Next, they would cut the sod into irregular, brick-like shapes and carry them to high ground to be dried by sun and wind. To get a year's supply of turf would take days.

Liam was assigned to cut in an area of the bog that was relatively dry and where cutting had halted the year before. The layers of exposed earth reminded him of a chocolate layer cake which he'd once seen in a tavern, and he wondered – how would chocolate taste?

The men were arranging an annual game to decide the strongest and most skilled cutter of turf. Although Uncle Paddy usually won, Brian Murphy aimed to give him competition. Liam heard men's laughter, but this year he felt apart from the festivities and as long as he stayed with his task, no one bothered him. His sandy hair fell over his face and conveniently hid his eyes.

He glanced up to see Aine and a flock of girls running toward him. "Liam, we're going to the hills to search for wild whortleberries and crab apples, and I need a basket."

Liam heaved a brick out of the ground. "I left it with Brighid. It's filled with potatoes in the skins and boiled eggs that you'll have to unload." With that, they ran to find her.

In a few hours, Liam noticed Aine and the girls returning, followed by a mounted cavalry officer. With Aine's flair for language, he knew she was enjoying this chance to practice her English. He guessed that the officer had been out for a ride when he came across the pretty lasses picking berries, and he probably saw them as a diversion from his boring duties. But did he think he could just join them for dancing and music? Liam predicted that most of the Irish families would welcome him because hospitality was their rule, but after his close encounter coming home from Castlebar, soldiers made him uneasy.

Yet because he felt protective of his younger sister, he put down his tool and approached the man. When Aine introduced the soldier as Captain Lawrence, the officer barely nodded, polite but cool, and focused his eyes on Aine. Liam understood his preference – Aine was pretty and spoke excellent English – but he still resented the soldier's cold arrogance.

Lawrence was tall and thin with an angular face, small dark eyes, very erect and proper in his bearing. At first, the captain inquired about turf cutting, camping, and the festivities, but then the questions became personal about Aine: her name, age, and where she lived. Liam winced when Aine explained the location of their cottage and pointed in its direction. Being less fluent in English and excluded, Liam felt awkward and returned to his turf cutting.

In late afternoon, the musicians began to play, and picnics were spread out on the ground. Father invited the captain to share their fare, but even though he declined, he made no move to leave. He seemed to enjoy the Irish music and when Aine and the other young girls began to step dance, his animated expression revealed his hopes. By this time, Brian was in the admiring audience, and when the captain complimented her dancing, Brian stood nearby, stern and almost hostile. Though the captain could only watch while the two of them danced the reel, he still returned the next afternoon and again hovered close to Aine. The situation became strained.

When he did not appear the following day, Liam was relieved and lost himself in the music of the tin whistle played by his talented cousin, Tomas. Wishing he had an instrument, he borrowed a neighbor's bodhran and soon drummed in time with the music. Then the delicate sounds of six harps playing together reminded him of *her*. She played the harp.

The next morning dawned bright, and on this the final day, everyone labored hard, including Liam. The cooperation made jobs easier and was good for the spirit. The men worked in pairs now and Liam partnered with Brian, with one driving in the slane and the other lifting the bricks out and tossing them aside. The young girls helped their mothers carry creels full of bricks to the high ground and stacked them tall with openings so air could pass through. These domes called "castles" grew numerous on the meadow and would continue drying for at least a week before each family would return and carry home its share.

Liam was inspecting the deep, three-foot cuts in the turf field when his eye was distracted by movement atop a hill. A group of men in the distance were waving their arms over their heads and yelling, though their calls were barely audible. Then he recognized them.

"Hey! Niall and the Murphys! They're back!" he shouted and started running. As the men on the hilltop scurried down the grassy knoll, Meg Murphy screamed with happiness and sprinted with amazing speed for her plumpness. They all met half way and embraced – with the Murphys, the Reillys, relatives, and neighbors taking turns to welcome them home.

Elated by Niall's return, Liam realized how much he had missed his brother. He thought Niall was too thin but was confident that Mother could fix that. After giving him a brotherly hug, he stepped away and let Mamai and his sisters have him. Caitlin jumped and begged to be lifted, while Brighid smiled, stayed close, but made no demands.

Denis Murphy patted his coat affectionately and announced: "It's right here – tickets and extra money for the journey! The

English paid us more than Irish diggers usually earn. In most years, twice as many men cross over for work, but this year with the blight, they wouldn't leave their families, hungry and alone. Niall sewed the money in my coat, and it's a good thing too! As I waited for the ferry, a rogue in Birmingham caught me asleep and tried to relieve me of our hard earned wages! He was a sly one and deft of hand, but he could not figure out where I had hidden it and finally awakened me with his search!"

"Whew! Denis!" Mom Murphy howled. "Someone should have been guarding over ya! How could you just sleep with our whole future there in your coat?" Liam found her dramatics amusing for just hearing about the close call left her breathless and about to faint.

Murphy put his hand on Niall's shoulder. "Me friend here is, indeed, a clever lad, and we would have been lost without him. His English improved fast over there, and he even read the newspapers we found lying about." During all this praise, Niall looked down. Liam appreciated Niall's humility for he never thought he was more intelligent than others, but he was.

When it was time for the relatives and friends to say goodbye, they held hands and recited the words that always ended the mihul: "In twelve months, may the roll call this day find us all present and none absent." After hand shakes and hugs, the families drifted home.

Mother walked with her arms around Niall, cheerful and smiling, but the couples – Aine and Brian, Maire and Sean – were reserved and somber. Liam attributed their sadness to the realization that their time together was short, and he wondered what remedies they would consider. Aine had no ticket to accompany Brian, but would Maire stay behind with Sean?

Then Liam recalled Da's words months ago in the potato

beds – *If a person does not try to realize his hopes, he always wonders what might have been.* Now Liam understood. Sean and Maire needed time to figure out what might still be and he hoped they could.

Once home, Mamai prepared Niall's favorite, colcannon, with just the right amounts of mashed potatoes, cream, butter, green onions, and herbs. When her three sons bragged that hers was the best in the land, she beamed broadly. For this homecoming meal, she added cabbage from her garden, warm milk, and stewed crab apples. While at the bog, Father had trapped a large rabbit, so each person took at least a few bites of roasted hare with Whortleberry sauce. After dinner, they gathered around the fire to hear tales of the journey.

Denis Murphy told about the day and a half ferry crossing to Liverpool on the open, top deck. "They shipped enough food out of Ireland on that one boat to feed all of Dublin for a month or more, and on the same ferry with all that food were starving people trying to get to Americay! The landlords paid less than five shillings for transporting sheep, and the animals had the shelter of a deck above them. Yet, we paid ten shillings for standing room only in wind and cold rain. The rough seas made us sick, but in the throng of passengers, it was a struggle to reach the rail, and we were miserable. I could barely walk on me legs after standing for thirty-one hours. The British shipping company packed so many people on the ferry that it floated low in the water, and waves washed onto the top deck, drenching us. They had only a few life boats, and I was afraid the ship might sink or some child would be swept out to sea."

Liam frowned. "Aren't there any laws against overloading a ferry like that?"

"Their only rule," Niall said, "was to make as much profit as possible off us Irish and our desperate need to leave."

"'Tis true," Peter chimed in. "Their prejudice against us runs deep." He pulled folded paper out of his jacket. "I've carried these cartoons back from England, and they'll make your blood boil! The British draw pictures of us in their newspapers as apes and criminals, worthless and lazy, plotting rebellion against England." They passed the cartoons hand to hand.

The one given to Liam pictured "the Irishman" as a hunched-over, furry ape with the expression of an idiot. The clothes were in tatters and even the children were drawn to look like demons. Underneath the picture, there was writing so he handed it to Niall for translation.

He read it easily. "It says, 'The Irish are a missing link.'"

Liam felt the blood rushing to his face. "That implies we're sub-human and part ape! Who writes these insults?"

"The government and its official newspaper, the London *Times,* and magazines like *Punch*, lots of them." Peter said. "The English people look down on us like we are inferior."

Gripping the paper tightly, Liam felt the sting of their contempt. "They must hate us!"

Peter retrieved the picture and carefully folded it. "Niall, tell about that black American, the runaway slave. What was his name? Frederick Douglass?"

Niall drank a ladle of water from the pail and wiped his mouth on his sleeve. "Yes, a British anti-slavery group brought him to England to protect him from slave hunters in America and to give speeches against slavery. He's really famous. When Daniel O'Connell invited him to visit Ireland last year, Douglass said we Irish were worse off than slaves in America. He claimed that both Southern whites in America and the English here use the same racist ideas to excuse their unfair and cruel treatment of slaves and of us.

The English claim to be superior to all people they rule."

Murphy jumped up and bellowed, "You're not going to believe this! But they talked about Ballinglass in the British Parliament – that fancy House of Lords – in London. 'Twas on March 23 that Niall saw the word Ballinglass in a newspaper he found and read it to us!"

"What did they say? Were they ashamed?" Liam asked.

"One of the Lords was. He said the hard working villagers had their rent ready but were evicted anyway, and he thought it was terrible. But then this Lord Brougham claimed the landlord had a sacred right to do whatever he wanted with his property, no matter what, and the villagers had no rights at all."

Peter stood up, excited. "On that same day in the House of Commons, Daniel O'Connell read the names of soldiers from Ballinglass who had died in battles for England in India."

"Yes, indeed!" Grandfather slapped his knee. "O'Connell's a voice for Ireland. And did that make them feel guilty . . . those boys giving their lives?"

Peter continued. "Only a few English have sympathy with us. But one man, Lord Earl Grey, said that conditions in Ireland were awful and that only the presence of an overwhelming army in Ireland kept us down. He said it would be no wonder if the Irish rebelled! The other Lords booed and heckled him, but he stood his ground." The group around the hearth chuckled at the thought that Ballinglass and Ireland had even a few defenders in London.

"But don't get too hopeful," Niall warned. "From what I've read while there, the government will not help us if blight returns. They call Irish farmers 'excess people,' and if this year's potatoes fail, Government officials expect two million to die, and they seem indifferent to that prospect. They would welcome the chance to get rid of us any way they can in order to clear the land for grazing livestock. The government wants cheap meat for British factory workers because they are paid low wages."

"You must be wrong there, Niall," Father said as he lit his pipe. "Everyone here says that finally England is going to help Ireland, and even our newspapers believe that."

"That's Irish optimism," Niall said. "This Charles Trevelyan, the man in charge of Irish relief? He talks like he *hates* Irish! Last year he tried to prevent Prime Minister Peel from importing Indian maize, but Peel did it anyway. Now, with the new Prime Minister, Lord John Russell, Trevelyan has gained control of what the government does. That worries me."

Gloom settled over the hearth. Liam disliked these predictions of doom, and besides, blight might not even return.

Mom Murphy leaned over and confided to her daughter Patricia in a loud whisper: "Maybe if the blight comes again, we'll be *glad* we're in Americay."

Niall overheard. "That's true, Meg, hard as it is to uproot. In fact, I've made a decision." He turned toward Father. "With the money I earned in England, I'm sailing to Americay with the Murphys. On our way home, we bought tickets on a ship that leaves Westport in ten days."

Mother gasped, her hand over her mouth. Liam could not believe it. Niall leave? His face felt hot, and he had a sinking feeling. No! How could he?

Caitlin's eyes were bright with excitement. "Niall, are you really going on a big boat across the ocean to Americay?"

"Yes, Cait."

"But you'll be back for my birthday, won't ya?"

Niall turned pale, and his eyes saddened. "I'm afraid I won't, but I'll find a special present and mail it to you."

"That would be nice. But . . . when *will* you be back?" She looked at him squarely.

Niall struggled. "Well . . . little sister . . . probably . . . not ever." He swallowed hard.

Caitlin sat motionless and stared at him in disbelief. Then hope ebbed. "Not ever?" With tears brimming in her eyes, she bolted up the ladder to the loft, and Aine scurried after her, followed by Brighid. In the still room below, everyone could hear their stifled sobs and sat stunned and somber. Mother backed away from the hearth and ran into the side room, her hands covering her face. Sean opened his mouth to speak, but had no words.

Always reasonable and calm, Father spoke in even tones. "Niall, you have thought this through, have you now? Are you sure this is what you're wanting, lad? You know, few who go across the great ocean can ever return to Ireland. We can write letters, but you'll never see your Mamai or any of us again."

"It's the hardest thing I'll ever do," Niall admitted. He paused and sighed deeply. "But rents and taxes are rising here, and we Irish are getting poorer. Our rents here in Ireland are almost twice as high as they are in England, and when English tenants are evicted, they have some legal rights, but not so here. All their laws oppress us."

With blood pounding in his temples, Liam yelled at Niall. "But what is more important than family! Can you really be happy never seeing any of us again? You're forsaking Ireland!"

"Liam, I don't *want* to leave. My family is dear to my heart, and I love Ireland and would fight to free her, but the British have placed an overwhelming army here. I know America does not welcome the Irish Catholic, but there I have a chance, and if I'm ever to go, now is the time."

Father intervened. "What you say is true, but . . . Niall . . .

even on the last day of my life, my heart will still ache for you. Yet, if it's what you really want . . . you have my blessing and prayers."

Grandfather slumped over and looked into the fire's depths as though answers were there. "Just don't go to British Canada or you'll still be under English rule."

Murphy tried to put in a cheerful word. "We'll look after him like one of our own, I can promise ya that."

Grim and resigned, Father bit down on the pipe held tightly between his jaws. "We appreciate that, Denis, but we've got a lot to get used to at the moment."

Liam could no longer remain in the cottage and retreated to the yard. Out in the night, he gazed up at the moon, surrounded by a halo of haze, and though it looked like nothing had changed, everything had. His world was coming apart and the family cracking open, shattering into pieces. How could anything ever be right again . . . with Niall gone. As the cool air hit his hot face, he felt chills and shivered in dread of unknowns still hidden.

Besieged by a storm of emotions, he paced back and forth. He felt abandoned and betrayed by his brother, disgusted with his father for giving Niall his blessing and not trying to stop him, and grief for his heart-broken mother and sisters. He loathed the British and their tyranny for driving Niall away and pitied little Caitlin . . . dear Caitlin who was still crying when he left the room. In the hours of darkness that remained, Liam watched the moon inch across the sky. He had long feared that Niall would leave . . . now it was coming true.

7

The Feast of Departure

The next day there was a forced cheerfulness as everyone in the family tried to be strong for each other and for Niall. Grandmamai and Aine hovered over Mother who was a special concern, and Liam, too, kept his eye on her for it couldn't be easy to give up a son. Uncle Paddy had always described her as "a typical Irish mother, only more so," and living up to that tribute, she focused on Niall when he needed it the most. Though heavy-hearted, she immersed herself in the preparations for his feast of departure, as it was called in County Mayo.

"We must have a proper farewell and send him off with good memories," she reminded.

Most Irish called this gathering an "American wake" because those who were leaving were generally headed for America, but in Kilkenny and in Tipperary they called it "a live wake." Liam pondered the similarities these gatherings had to a real wake for a dead person. Both began with a jolly reminiscing of past times enjoyed together and ended with mourning the loss of a loved one whom they would never see again on this earth. Regardless of whether the separation came through death or departure, the person was gone, and both wakes ended with saying goodbye forever. In the past, Liam had enjoyed the American wake as a social occasion with music, dance, food, and toasting, but now that he was losing his own brother, he was depressed and dreaded it.

The time and attention necessary to make all the arrangements were a welcome distraction from the reality facing them. Mother sent Niall and Sean to cottages all around to tell relatives and neighbors of his decision to leave Ireland and to invite them to his feast of departure. They had lived in the same place with these families for generations and had strong bonds of friendship and mutual help. Niall reported that each cottage welcomed him with great affection and invited him in for a lengthy visit. Liam and Da went to a hillside hiding place and retrieved some poteen distilled from either potatoes or barley. The strong homebrew was illegal to make, but would be used for late-night toasting.

Father decided to roast a pig now, instead of saving it for Christmas. "It's a rare day that my first born son leaves for Americay. Besides, I can dry some pork for him to take along." Mother finished knitting Niall a heavy wool sweater from yarn she had spun earlier, and Grandmother prepared oat cakes and boiled eggs for the journey. Aine used the Bible to press a shamrock on a husk and collected shamrock seed from the glen to be planted in an American pot. Sean chipped some stucco off the cottage as a memory of home, but Liam had no gift and no plans to find one. Niall would stay here, if he loved us.

One afternoon when Liam had finished milking the cow, he found Maire and Sean sitting on the stone fence with their backs to him and heard Sean pleading with her to stay in Ireland and be his wife. Her tearful replies and their tortured arguments were too painful and private so Liam hurried past, but their despondent mood when they returned to the cottage told him that the choice to marry and separate from her family at this time was too difficult for Maire.

When she ran back to the glen alone, Sean acted hurt and angry but confided in no one. Liam felt sympathetic and assured him, "I'm here if you need to talk," but he stayed to himself. Maire's red and swollen eyes bore evidence of frequent weeping, and it was clear that her decision not to marry was constantly being reconsidered.

As time grew short, all concerns other than the departure were buried under the preparations. The Murphys kept adding things to the Reilly's cart: a cooking pot, blankets, clothing, and sleeping mats till it was piled high. One morning Denis Murphy milked Daisy, his much-loved cow, for the last time and tearfully sent her away with Brian and Mick to sell in Ballinrobe. Grandda gave Niall a special gift which Liam coveted: a small wooden trunk built by their great-grandfather, Tomas Cian Reilly. But seeing the pride with which Niall packed it dissuaded Liam from complaining. According to the plan, Father, Sean, and Liam would escort the group to Westport where they would board the ship to New York City, but in route, they would make a pilgrimage to Croagh Patrick, the holy mountain of the great saint.

That final evening, the Feast of Departure – or Farewell Supper as the Murphys and people in County Galway called it – came "in the wink of an eye," as Grandmother said. Women with black shawls draped over their heads ambled up the lane, carrying dishes of food, while men in patched pants and frieze coats walked in a separate procession, bringing their musical instruments or small gifts. Children circled around them in games of tag, chased by devoted dogs that refused to stay home. They all came to honor Niall in his last hours at home, and soon the cottage was full of friends and relatives, with other neighbors spilling over into the yard.

Tomas, with a soft hat cocked at an angle, peered over the half-door and called to Liam. "Hey Cousin, here's some frog bread. I caught the frog, Da roasted and pulverized it, and Mamai baked it into the dough. It's supposed to prevent a case of fever, but at least it's nourishing."

The oak table, pushed to one side to leave more room for dancing, was now the place for gifts, and Liam added his cousin's bread to the crocks of butter, rye cakes, and a knit cap which were already there. When Mittens the cat leaped onto the table to sniff the foods, he shooed her away with a loud clap and carefully monitored her whereabouts afterward.

"Where is our Nialleen?" crooned the high pitched, unsteady voice of elderly Aunt Ber. Liam had almost forgotten the custom of adding "een" to a name as a sign of affection. As he opened the half door and helped the old woman over the threshold, her words flowed in an unbroken stream. "When I heard that our Nialleen was going away, I was never so surprised since the day I was born! But you know what they say: 'The only part of Ireland where a man can get ahead is in Americay!'"

"I know all about it," said Cousin Taidhgh. "Here's a letter from my three sons in Boston. That's just the next village over from County Mayo, don't ya know." He tilted his head toward the Atlantic and unfolded a letter for the fiftieth time, all frayed, limp, and precious. "My son says everyone can vote in Americay, and you can own your own land. No taxes paid to a foreign church either! But watch out, Niall! They'll change your last name, if you're not careful. When you enter the country, an official will ask for your name. They don't know how to spell the Irish names, and they put down their best guess, and you'll be stuck with that. Since they entered at different times, me sons all have a different spelling of O'Neill!"

Liam remembered Cousin Taidhgh's bragging that his

children made an even dozen, all healthy and raised on potatoes, buttermilk, and an occasional egg. Good thing that he had numerous children still in Ireland, Liam reasoned, to comfort him for the three sons he had lost to emigration. Yet when Cousin Taidhgh begged Niall to "take this letter to my sons," he looked so desperate for a messenger that Liam realized those three had left a hole in his heart.

"Laugh at your problems like the breakdown of a cart," old Granny Walsh squeaked. Then came a warning from a close neighbor, Barra Fleming: "But the Yankee hates us. For some jobs there are signs in English that say 'Irish need not apply.' Many Irish just go there to die young in dangerous work that breaks a man, like building bridges and digging deep tunnels."

"But unlike here," Cousin Eamon interrupted, "They'll pay you money for the work you do!"

Aunt Una, full of importance, rushed to the guest of honor. "Mind you now, Niall, take straw mats, not feather ones, because water from the sea splashes down into steerage and ruins the feathers. My cousin's youngest brother wrote us that." Aunt Una was a bit bossy, Liam thought, but tonight her advice made good sense.

Father Mullen, who first had to visit a village of dying parishioners, arrived late, but he lost no time in counseling the emigrants. "With bad weather, it can take months to cross the Atlantic, but the ship will only put in enough water and food for a voyage of six weeks, so take extra."

"Yes, Father . . . but it's not easy to make up such a shortfall!" Murphy fretted.

"Might you be taking an American ship?" Father Mullen asked. "The British ships have fewer regulations to protect the passengers, and even those are not enforced! They say even the Canada people are complaining to Her Majesty's government about the horrid conditions aboard British ships landing there. It's a cheaper fare, but then our people, if they survive, walk long distances to the northern states of Maine and the like, all to avoid English rule."

Murphy raised his bushy eyebrows. "We've bought the tickets already, and I never knew to ask if it was an American ship!"

Father continued with his warnings. "And beware of swarms of runners who meet the boats and want to take you to high-priced lodging. They'll grab your luggage and force you to chase them. The Irish Emigrant Society in New York has agents that meet the ships and will give you honest advice, so ask for them."

"Yes, Father . . . Remember that name, Irish Emigrant Society," he said, turning to his sons.

Since he got a late start in giving advice, Father Mullen hardly paused for a breath. "I will be praying for you, and always remember: we carry our faith wherever we go, and in Ireland, religion matters more than anywhere else."

"That's the truth, Father," agreed Uncle Padraig. "An Irish atheist is one who wishes to God he could believe in God!" Giggles rippled through the room as people caught on to the joke, and even the priest grinned before resuming.

"They have a St. Patrick's Church in New York . . . on Mott Street, I believe. Go to Mass the first Sunday, and God willin,' Niall, you'll find a good Irish girl to be your wife and maybe even from County Mayo!"

"Or a good girl from Galway," put in Murphy, his eyes twinkling.

Liam glanced at Aine and Brian. The light in their eyes that came with first love was clouded by the impending separation, and she seemed bothered by this talk of "finding an Irish girl in Americay." Brian gave her a hug, whispered to her, and whatever he said made her smile.

The advice gave way to stories about Niall, all funny and most true. Those guests who were too poor to give him a gift of butter or berries read poems they had written or told stories about the huge fish they caught together or the close call they barely escaped.

"Niall was the most sharp-witted of lads!" declared Uncle Padraig. Liam noticed that he, like many of the others, used the past tense as if Niall were already gone or dead.

Because Niall was leaving forever, some people decided to ignore the curfew and gambled that this lane, not on a main road, would escape the eyes of patrols. "We can stay 'till the morn and sleep the children in the loft," said Mrs. Carroll.

Next there was music and dancing for the last time with the local musicians who allowed Niall, Sean, and Cousin Tomas to take the lead and solo parts. The fast music provided an escape from the reality they faced in the coming dawn. With other young girls, Aine, Patricia, Maire and the Riley cousins danced well for Niall and gave him a memory of fine step dancing that he would never forget. Sean entertained the guests with the superb solo dancing for which he was known, and they roared in appreciation and clapped along. The crowd whirled with partners to the Kerry Set and the fast motion was a release for the tension that was building as the hours passed. Liam sensed an undercurrent of sorrow in the festivities and wished the music would never end . . . or the night.

Since the toasting came last, Liam realized the hour was late when Father got out the poteen. Lucas Quinn was the first to raise his cup and salute Niall: "God be on your road every way you go and bring you back to Ireland."

Everyone shouted "*Sláinte.*" Though he could never return, it was their heart-felt wish.

"May there be land without rent for you," said Nic Flannery.

"*Sláinte*," voices repeated like a chorus. To own his farm land was the dream of every Irish Catholic . . . a dream denied by the British government in Ireland, but not in America.

Uncle Padraig cleared his throat and put his arm around Niall, a boy he had helped his brother raise. He began to recite Liam's favorite, the "Blessing of Light."

"May the blessing of light be with you – light outside and light within.

> May sunlight shine upon you and warm your heart till it glows like a great peat fire so that the stranger may come and warm himself by it . . . ."

Liam knew the verse well and under his breath, he mouthed the words. The lyrics flowed on, wishing in turn generosity, kindness, and love of the good earth. Uncle's voice faltered and grew hoarse as he recited the last lines.

Then at the end of life, when death comes . . . "may your spirit quickly be up, and off, and on its way to God." After a long embrace, Uncle Paddy turned away and dabbing his eyes, he blew his nose and moved to the back of the room.

Now the last toast. It was Father's turn, and as he raised his glass, he spoke in a voice heavy with emotion:

> "May the road rise up to meet you,
> May the wind be always at your back,
> May the sun shine warm upon your face,
> May the rains fall soft upon your fields and,
> Until we meet again, may God hold you in the
> palm of his hand."

Then Da added, "And I'll be waiting in heaven, never again to part." Everyone felt his pain, and a hushed murmur went through the room.

It was time for the traditional last jig for father and son, and they stood with hands on hips, elbows pointed outward, and feet in place. The musicians struck a lively tune, and the men leaped to the prescribed step in unison with an energy that spoke of hope. The concentration required was so great that they stared straight ahead, expressionless, with no hint of grief. At song's end, father and son came down together on the same exact note with perfect teamwork, and it was finished.

When Father placed his hand on Niall's shoulder and smiled with pride, Liam heard sniffling and coughing around the room and saw tears standing in many eyes. He felt his own emotions coming to the surface. Why did Niall have to leave? WHY! He wanted time to stop.

The crowd moved in to embrace Niall.

"God bless, Niall, take care o' yourself."

"All the best . . . God bless."

"*Dia's Muire dhuit agus Pádraig* / God and Mary and Patrick be with you."

"*Go raiabh maith agat* / May it go well with you."

"*Slán* / Goodbye."

Niall gripped the outstretched hands and hugged those with open arms. "Aye" he mumbled to each.

Father Mullen gave the exiles small Irish crosses and gathered them for a blessing. As they knelt, he held his hands over their heads and asked God's protection against storms, accidents, illness, hunger, and all calamity. He radiated paternal love as he went to each person for a special word, even squatting down to talk to little Donal Murphy.

At last, it was time for the Reilly family to come and huddle around Niall. "Forget not the land of your birth," Grandda said gruffly and gave him a bit of Irish sod tied in a cloth. He stood stiffly and the gruffness of his voice was his defense to rein in the powerful emotions that were almost loose. Niall took Grandfather's frail hands and studied them for a long moment before he unclasped them.

Then Niall turned to Aine who stoically held her gifts of shamrocks. Trying not to cry, Aine swallowed hard and laid a little bag of seeds in his hand. "Plant these." She slipped the pressed shamrock into his pocket and could only say, "For luck." Liam could hear the quiver in her voice and knew that Niall could too.

Sean put the stucco from the cottage in Niall's other pocket. "A piece of home," he croaked. His face could not have been more despondent if this had been a real wake. Niall was bending under the strain, so Liam decided to postpone his goodbye and stepped behind Sean. Besides, he had no gift.

Stooped little Grandmother inched up and gave final instructions for the prepared foods she had in a cloth bag. Standing on tip-toes, she reached up to her tall grandson and hugged him tightly, whimpering like a kitten until Grandfather came and drew her away.

Caitlin and Brighid impatiently patted Niall's leg until he attended to them. Brighid was the first to speak: "We are giving this gift together because I did not have anything good and Caitlin did!"

Niall smiled down at her. "Your love is enough."

Caitlin, holding something behind her back, cleared her throat, and announced: "Niall, this is yours now!" Then she thrust forward her cherished holy card of St. Patrick and waited for him to take it.

Niall's eyes grew misty and he shook his head. "Oh, no, Cait! Not your picture. I know how you love it."

"Go ahead . . . Take it," Aine urged. "She's sending part of herself with you to Americay, aren't you, Cait!" With Aine's persistent prompting, Caitlin slowly gave it over with a touch of reluctance. He accepted it but slumped with the burden of this sorrow – his and theirs.

Now it was time for Niall to say goodbye to the last member of his family, and he postponed that farewell as long as he could. He could hardly bear to look at her, and instead, he slowly put his gifts into great-grandfather's trunk. "Is the cart ready, Da? Is it time to go?" Light was peeping over the hills in pink, gold, and orange rays.

"Yes, son. We're all waiting." Father and the brothers could be brave, knowing that their last goodbye was two days away, but Mother was staying behind. Liam knew she was trying to remain calm, and his heart went out to her. She did not want to embarrass her son with an outburst, but she was drained and exhausted. With the new sweater she had knitted neatly folded in her upturned hands, she waited, and finally, he turned to her.

"Mamai." He opened his arms. Her embrace was long and tender, but when he began to pull away, she moaned and her composure crumbled. She clung to him and began to weep, knowing she would never again hear his voice, or hold him, or see his smile . . . never again. She gasped and groaned . . . "Niall! No! . . . Don't go! Please! . . . NO!" With each plea, her voice grew stronger and shriller. Her grief made him hesitate, and Liam could see Niall's doubts. As Mother's pent-up emotions broke like a dam and the torment flowed out, she gripped his arms and buried her head in his chest, desperately holding on and crying. "Oh! . . . don't leave! Niall, *a ghrá mo chroí* / Niall, beloved of my heart!"

Grandfather tried to pry her hands away, but she clutched Niall all the more tightly. "Oh, help me, dear Jesus . . . Niall . . . DON'T go!" Her voice got louder and more frantic, her eyes begging with tears flowing. "Please! . . . Oh, God . . . Niall . . . STAY!" Father yanked hard on her hands and broke Mother's grip, while Grandfather and Uncle Padraig restrained her in a tight hold. As she sobbed and wailed in despair with her arms outstretched, Niall looked back at her, his eyes glistening with tears.

The women began the shrill, high wail called keening. Following the cart, Liam looked down to hide his own heavy heart and misery. How could Niall do this to their mother? The sounds of sorrow were soon muted by distance, and the cottage gradually became smaller until it was lost behind the hills. All was quiet with that deep sadness of separation that comes after a death.

Liam knew that his mother's anguish was burned into Niall's memory and he wondered – how can he bear it . . . remembering this the rest of his life? Liam, too, could still hear her cries and ached to go back and comfort her, but all he could do was keep walking, walking. They all plodded on for an hour without a single word as they turned their thoughts inward.

Then, Liam intuitively sensed her. He looked back and there she was . . . down the road behind them. She must have broken free! They stopped and waited. In trying to overtake them, she had sprinted some distance and was now breathless and pale.

Niall jogged back and held her tenderly for a long private goodbye. Then hand in hand, they walked together with the group and this seemed to comfort her. Liam did not want to intrude into this moment, but now and then he glanced sideways at his mother and her first born son, and he could tell that each wanted to mend the other's broken places.

"Niall, I didn't want you to remember me like that," she managed to say. After a few miles, they topped a hill, and when she stopped, Liam knew that she would now try again to let him go. She managed a half-smile but dared not speak, and with a gesture, she motioned him ahead. They walked on without her, but every time they looked back, she was still standing on that hill, unable to leave. Then finally, with head low and shoulders bowed, she turned and passed from sight.

8

The Final Farewell

Despite the sorrow and wrenching farewells of the feast of departure, dawn turned into a fair day with honeysuckle filling the air with its strong, sweet scent. As the road curved through the Partry hills, a large lough came into view with magenta foxgloves crowding its bank and still water reflecting blue sky and passing clouds. A wild swan, with wings lifted to catch any breeze, skimmed its surface, while another bobbed nearby. Liam had heard that years after leaving their homeland, exiles still dreamed of the green of Ireland in all its forty shades. He sensed a bitter-sweet mix of regret and anticipation as Niall and the Murphys departed from this corner of the world.

Heaving a long sigh, Murphy told his family, "Remember the peace and beauty of this country road, and then you can always come back . . . in your memory." Liam was glad he was staying.

Winding through the sleepy hamlets of Kiltharshachaun and Dereendaffderg, the donkey's hooves caused an occasional plume of dust to rise from the road. The cart was so loaded that Niall's trunk occupied the seat, and Da had to walk beside the donkey, pulling the reins.

As they approached the Ballintubber Abbey, Murphy raised his hand. "Ah . . . before I leave Ireland, I must say one last word over the grave of *Sean Na Sagart* / Sean the priest hunter." The group followed him as he marched past the stone markers of six centuries and stopped at a grave which lay in a different direction to those surrounding it. Murphy pointed to an old ash tree that grew next to it. "See the upper branches? They turn down as though to point him out."

Liam looked up, intrigued. "Tell us about him."

"He was a drunk and a thief, and the magistrate at Castlebar condemned him to die, but the English made a deal to commute his sentence if he would become a bounty hunter for priests. In those days, they paid one hundred pounds for the head of a bishop, twenty for a priest, and ten for a monk, and for sixteen years, he earned his money with this bloody work. He even pretended once that he was dying and begged his own sister to send for a priest. As the priest bent over his groaning body to pray, Sean thrust a dagger into his side!"

Hunched over, Murphy spat on the grave and cursed him in haunting tones. "May you fall into the abyss of darkness . . . and never see the Light." Then he roared, "Never!" The hills resounded with the echo . . . *never* . . . *never* . . . . Liam shivered. Never was a long time.

"So did someone finally kill him?" he asked.

"Yes." Father pointed south. "There's a stone marker near Partry on the spot where he was slain around 1726. While chasing a priest, he was surprised by a man who was chasing after *him*."

Feeling gratified by the victory over the murderer, the group trudged past the abbey's ruins which were partially destroyed long ago by Cromwell. As they merged with the gravel post road to Westport, Liam was surprised by the large number of people heading the same way, and he wondered if an exodus was building.

Strong ties to place and family had kept most Irish from leaving before, but now, hunger and mass evictions were overcoming love of home – *if* they could come up with the passage money.

Liam cherished the warm camaraderie which bound Irish together and how travelers freely exchanged handshakes and greetings. Soon the gregarious Murphy knew the names of most people they met on the road, and he reminded Liam of the old saying, "There are no strangers in Ireland, only friends you've yet to meet." Encouraged by his friendly manner, the rural folk shared their troubles, hopes, and plans in a trusting openness.

Briana, the fiancée of Conor O'Hare, hooked her elbow through his arm affectionately and explained their situation. "My family won't allow us to marry till I'm older so we're eloping to Americay."

Looking across the fields and frowning, Conor took off his hat and scratched his head as though it made him think better. "How far ya reckon it is before ya hit land?"

"Probably six weeks sail . . . or more," Murphy answered.

Conor became glum. "How deep is that ocean?"

"Mighty deep." Murphy kept looking ahead.

After a period of quiet thought, Conor cleared his throat. "After Liverpool, our tickets are for New Orleans. How big's that?"

"Mighty big."

Conor's frown deepened to a pout, and he slouched inside his jacket.

Murphy observed him out of the corner of his eye. "You're not thinking of staying in Ireland, are ya now?" Conor squinted into the sun and said nothing, but doubts were hanging all over him. Briana kissed his cheek and snuggled up to him, but Liam questioned how far that would take him. When their pace slowed and they fell behind, Murphy proposed a wager to Peter: "Two of my potatoes that we don't see them in Westport," but with a chuckle, Peter declined the bet.

Nicolas Malloy, a young father who was slight of build, pulled a loaded cart by himself since his wife carried a babe in arms and herded two other children. With a reddened face and great determination, he staggered up hills, straining against the weight until Liam feared that the cart might roll backwards. Going downhill, he braced himself and planted his feet sideways, but clearly, he could not sustain this struggle for long. So looking at Brian, Liam indicated that he wanted to help the little guy.

When Brian nodded agreement, Liam turned to Malloy. "Can we give you a hand? Less grueling for the two of us."

With a flood of blessings, Malloy dropped the shafts of the cart. "Ah . . . thank you! 'Twas wonderin' how I was gonna make it and then . . . *D'ordaigh Dia cúnamh* / God ordered help. He must have put the idea into your head." Once freed of the burden, Malloy talked non-stop.

"We're trying to get to Americay. The Earl of Lucan took our rent, but evicted us anyway!" His voice turned hoarse with hate. "He evicted 10,000 people from Ballinrobe alone and put Scotsmen in charge of a 15,000 acre ranch. Threw out another 23 families from Swinford . . . all to clear land for pasture. Now people are begging door to door and calling him the *exterminator*."

Murphy's eyes narrowed. "And that's what he is, the greedy blood sucker! Just think, most of his people will die from hunger, exposure, and the fevers!"

A grim Liam recognized the name – Lord Lucan – the wealthy nobleman who was slowly starving the Castlebar workhouse. They should add those inmates to his tally of victims.

Murphy waved his hand over the fields of grain growing around them. "After Lucan and the other landlords turn it all to pasture, they'll probably overgraze and destroy what fertility we worked generations to cultivate. Malloy, tell me now! Since that scoundrel Lucan didn't even give your rent back, how will you get the price of a ticket?"

Malloy tossed his hat into the cart. "Over the years I set back money for my parents' funeral, but since they're still alive, they insisted that I use it now, and they have gone to live with my sister. I plan to pawn this cart and some of the stuff in it to make up the difference."

After Peter and Mick took their turn with Malloy's cart, Liam found a downcast Niall in the rear and fell into step with him. If only he had never gone to England because, unlike the Murphys, his brother did not *have* to leave. Although still determined to emigrate, Niall was finding it painful and only gave Liam a weak smile and a nod. He kept looking down at his feet and continued the same brisk pace. Emotions were too strong for either of them to talk, but there was still time. Just ahead, Liam observed Sean and Maire walking with arms entwined. Sean must have accepted her decision to leave and wanted to make the most of the time they had left.

The Malloy and Murphy children became tired and thirsty and started to whine. When Father suggested the group stop at a small hamlet up ahead that had a well, Mom Murphy herded the children forward and gave the Malloy baby to her daughter Patricia to carry. But when they got to the top of the hill, the women stopped and gasped. Patricia let out a high pitched cry. "Oh! Oh, my God!"

Liam dashed to the front. Before him lay the village, black and smoldering, as if it had been attacked by a conquering army. Indeed, it had. With the scent of smoke still strong, he guessed the soldiers had torched the thatched roofs yesterday. Judging from the way the thick walls had been forced to crumble inward, he surmised that the wreckers had been provided with a battering ram.

Liam loped down into the village. Stepping over a threshold, he saw four charred stools, a baby cradle covered with soot, broken pottery, and burned clothing scattered about. Hanging from the crane inside the stone fireplace was a pot of potatoes for the next meal which never came. How frightened they must have been, with fires raging . . . to flee and not even take food. These people had lived here for generations and to have potatoes, they must not have suffered from blight. Where were they now? He felt sick, and like the other travelers, he drifted about reverently as if visiting a graveyard. This village had died and soon its people would also.

Liam spoke through clinched teeth. "Why do the powerful think they have a right to do this! Why?"

"It's arrogance," Niall answered.

"And greed without mercy," Liam replied.

Sean held up a weeping Maire, who was reliving the pain of Ballinglass, and Liam, too, became emotional as he remembered Colleen's ice-blue eyes, filled with tears . . . something impossible to forget.

Father became the caretaker and urged them to sit and rest while he collected soggy potatoes from the pots and passed them around. Liam located the well and drew water. After the children drank from the pail, they were the first to recover. When a small black and white rooster peeped around a wall and surprised them with a cluck, they squealed and gave chase.

Liam jumped up, cornered it, and held it by its neck. "Tonight's dinner."

Malloy caught a scrawny hen, building a nest out of loose thatch. "I hate to take this, but they'll never return." After watering the donkey, the group lifted their bundles and resumed the journey. Liam and Brian again shouldered Malloy's cart shafts and pulled it forward.

Suddenly, Denis Murphy stopped in the road and cleared his throat. "Seamus Reilly, without your help . . . well . . . Instead of heading to New York, we Murphys would be going to early graves like those people back there!" He put his hand on Father's shoulder and the two embraced.

"You'd do the same for us, Denis."

Taking a cue from Murphy, Malloy shook the free hands of Mick and Peter. "And thanks to ye lads, I'm gonna make it! Maybe we Mayo people can get on the same boat and live nearby in New York."

"Aye, t'would be a comfort to hear a familiar accent," Peter said.

Against the road-side wall, a man, too weak to go farther had collapsed, and crowded around his feet were three small sons who pulled their shriveled limbs in close. The boys looked passively at the travelers from deep, sunken eyes, and Da was so moved by the children that he laid the remaining soggy potatoes in the lap of the oldest. The boy stared at them and then touched his father who opened his eyes and raised his head. Liam pitied them and wondered if they were trying to reach Westport to beg from the prosperous English living there.

Niall, who had walked ahead, called back to Da, "Is that Croagh Patrick on the horizon?"

Father shaded his eyes and peered into the distance. "Yes. On that mountain, in the year 441, St. Patrick spent the forty days of Lent in prayer and fasting for the conversion of Ireland. When we get there, we'll climb about three miles to the top and pray for a safe journey."

Murphy laughed easily, like a man who had never lost the boy in himself. "That's a *long* way to go to pray."

Liam searched the hills and saw a mountain of perfect conical shape which stood out from the rest. He could see a pale line encircling it to its peak and knew it must be the path of pilgrims, carved by generations of feet for the past fourteen hundred years. This was Liam's first time to visit the holy mountain, and it was a daunting sight. "Is there a church at the top?" he asked.

"Yes," Father said. "A small, stone church has stood there for more than eight hundred years. We'll start the climb upward from the village of Murrisk."

When the road to Croagh Patrick turned southwest, the Malloys said goodbye. With Westport now only a few hours away, they needed to move on and could not manage a detour that would lengthen their journey. They all hugged each other with a sincere affection that had grown from sharing common adversity and camaraderie.

Liam shook his hand, "We'll see you at the dock, Malloy."

"Yes, God willing."

A straggling column of old men, wives with babes, teenagers, fathers, and grandmothers merged from side roads and traveled with them. After passing through the old town, they stood at the foot of the mountain. Those who were descending gave them walking sticks and only asked that they pass the sticks on when they were finished. Meg Murphy spread blankets on the ground for her weary children and stayed behind with the cart while the others made the assent.

They began the climb at *Tobair Pádraig* / Patrick's Well where the saint baptized his first converts in a natural spring. As Liam traced the path which was worn into the white, quartzite rock, he felt united to souls, past and present. Whenever fellow pilgrims sensed that fatigue was causing a neighbor's feet to falter, they would call out words of encouragement like "You can make it, just a little farther." People paused at stations along the way to rest, pray, and contemplate Christ's suffering on the way to the cross.

About half way up, the weather turned foul with mist falling and wind whipping the stony path. As Liam's pace slowed, the distance between him and his group increased. The carts and people below were now only dots on the fields, and a tired Liam considered stopping here or even turning back.

Then a stooped but nimble granny with a staff guessed his thoughts and shuffled up next to him. Her skin was wrinkled and creased by decades of trouble, but she still smiled and her eyes had a twinkle as she looked squarely into Liam's face.

"Now, sonny, you can do it!" she said in a scratchy voice. "This path is like the road to heaven." She pointed her gnarled walking stick toward the summit. "Life's a struggle and a journey, don't ya know. These sharp rocks are like hardships that we can overcome with God's help, so come on now and follow me!" With that, the old lady stepped forward, as sure-footed as a mountain goat and amazed Liam with her vigor.

With new determination, he set off behind her, and when he caught up, she giggled. "That's the way, sonny! You're almost there, but don't show me up, now!" Liam grinned at her and guessed she lived nearby and had made this climb many times. Yet youth easily won, and reaching the top first, he was rewarded with a view that took his breath away.

From the bare, windswept summit, he could see the magnificent bay and its hundreds of islands, shimmering in a blue sea. The mountains of Achill lay to the north and the Atlantic Ocean stretched to the west in an unending expanse to the horizon. In this mystical, high place of peace and beauty, Liam felt St. Patrick's unselfish spirit. He remembered hearing how the saint had risked his life to bring the faith to Ireland and had used a shamrock with its three leaves on one stem to teach about the Trinity. Liam followed the others into the little stone church, and in the cool stillness he reflected on the symbols of the pilgrimage and prayed for their safe journey.

When they emerged and stood gazing at the breath-taking view of mountains, ocean, and islands, Liam sensed the melancholy of the exiles as they said farewell to their homeland for the last time. The mist had moved out to sea and left a rainbow arcing over the water.

"It's a good sign, that rainbow," Murphy said. As they followed the steep, rocky path back down to the base, the sun slipped behind the horizon, and the sky blazed a radiant orange over Clew Bay.

When they rejoined Meg Murphy, she had plucked the chicken clean and cooked it in the turf fire of pilgrims from nearby Louisburgh. Since the travelers lacked musical instruments, some entertained with lilting music that they made with their mouths. The singers sang wordlessly, yet they skillfully emulated the fiddle and drum with just their voices. The rhythm matched the beat of the reel so those hearing could step dance on the soft earth by the light of the fires. "Deddle-de-dum-de do-da-dum de-de . . . ." The beat and momentum drew Liam and Sean into the group. They moved to the beat and danced the steps of generations, feeling a common bond as their shadows bobbed and circled. Finally, after all grew quiet, they wrapped themselves in blankets under the starry sky.

Skylarks, celebrating dawn, woke them at the first hint of morning, and before noon, they covered the six miles to Westport. On the outskirts was an Irish town of cottages. When Liam asked why it was separated from the main community, Father explained that it started with the Penal Laws passed after Cromwell that allowed only English to live inside the city limits of corporate townships.

Soon they reached Westport, the largest town Liam had ever seen, with its crowded, noisy, and bustling streets. Dust irritated his eyes as it rose from the wheels of coaches, wagons, and carts, each jostling for the right to pass. He gawked at buildings four stories high which housed a flour mill, a bank, and a brewery. Fine townhouses lined the streets where English residents lived and small shops and taverns competed for the attention of customers with colorful, handmade signs.

"Our own landlord, the Marquis of Sligo, has a great mansion here called Westport House," Father said. "He resides there, when he's not at his London house or his hunting lodge at Delphi."

Everywhere Liam looked, he saw British soldiers in coats with gold buttons and beggars in rags. Like breathing skeletons, the beggars' skin stretched over their bones so that he could see every rib and curve. Since their shins had no muscle, their knees looked large and prominent.

A woman, eyes half-closed, approached Liam with a boney hand extended. In a monotonous tone, she murmured, "Please, have mercy . . . a crust of bread . . . a coin . . . for my babies." Her children stood near, their shoulder joints protruding, with necks that seemed too thin to bear the weight of their skulls. Liam could hardly bear to look at them, for hunger had not only taken their strength, but their dignity and pride. When he laid his crust of morning oat cake in her hand, she gave this small morsel to her closest child. As she overwhelmed Liam with words of gratitude, he felt guilty for giving so little.

Turning to move on, she suddenly halted as if startled. "Denis . . . it's me."

Murphy stared at her, and from his puzzled expression, Liam could tell he did not recognize her, yet something was familiar . . . perhaps her voice. Then his eyes widened in disbelief and horror: "Maureen . . . McGuinness? . . . Oh my God! . . . Is that you?" Tears rose to his eyes as he embraced her frail body, but when her protruding skeleton poked his arms, he pulled back. "Meg . . . It's

Maureen . . . from Ballinglass!"

Meg ran up and gaped, incredulous. Then she comprehended: her life-long friend was in the last stages of starvation, and with great tenderness, she hugged her delicate torso. Ever since the destruction of Ballinglass, she must have been wandering and begging, living in ditches and odd places. When asked about her other two children and her husband, all she could do was shudder and shake. She could not speak the awful truth, but they sensed they were already dead. She had these three left, and not for much longer.

"Oh, Denis, give her some of our food!" Meg pleaded. Without hesitation, Murphy clambered back to the cart and rummaged in the food bags. When he returned with oat cakes and potatoes, Maureen bowed with an outpouring of blessings that embarrassed him.

He waved his hands. "No, no! Take these and don't thank us. My deepest regret is that I cannot take you away with us." Murphy slumped with a sadness that went to his core.

Unable to let go, Meg cried and clung to her friend. Irish on the street witnessed the scene with long faces, and Liam swallowed hard.

Brian and Patricia stood on either side of their mother. "Mamai, you have to let her go," Brian whispered, and at last, he convinced Meg to release her.

Maureen's expression remained unchanged and her eyelids drooped with the look of a trance. "Go . . . my friends," she murmured hoarsely. "Flee, if you can, and pray for me!" With that, she turned to leave with her small ones following.

A kind English vicar in his collar must have been watching and grabbed her arm. "Eat slowly . . . only a little at a time . . . or you and your children will be sickened." With that advice, Maureen disappeared into the crowd.

Murphy was morose. "The sight of them will haunt me

forever! The hunger is a slow torture but murderous, just the same, and it t'would be quicker and kinder if Mrs. Gerrard had executed them with a gun." Liam now understood more than ever why the same word in Irish – *fabhair* – meant both eviction and extermination.

Dusty travelers poured into the road leading to the quay, and if they had no cart, they carried bags, chests, bundles, and iron pots on their backs. Most people had never been more than twenty miles from home, and Liam could see fear on their faces. Saloon keepers urged the nervous exiles to come in for one last drink of stout to calm themselves, and some even promised that it would prevent fever and seasickness. Wives clung to their husbands' arms and fretted when they listened too intently. Agents selling tickets pictured a cornucopia beyond the sea where land, food, and jobs were pouring out in abundance. Some dishonest agents charged as much for steerage as second class and pledged that the ships would have plenty of water and food.

Yet, peddlers warned the exiles that rations would be meager on board and urged them to buy their cow organs, oats, dried fish, and moldy bread. One man selling fishing tackle attracted Niall's interest. He and Liam discussed whether a person could fish off such a large boat or if it might be just another scheme to get his precious money, but at last, Niall decided to buy it, on the chance.

One peddler captured Meg Murphy's attention: "All you Irish women, hear this! The ships have made little provision for you, and it's yourselves you'll be cursing if you leave without this chamber pot."

She tugged on Murphy's coat sleeve. "Denis, did you hear that? With our daughters, you should buy one."

He dug into his pockets. "It's a good thing we bought the

tickets when we came through from England, or you and the peddlers would take it all beforehand." He counted out the required amount with painstaking care, and she hurried off to make the purchase, lest the peddler sell out.

Murphy pulled his tickets out of his pocket and counted them again. "Liam, we worked on a number of farms to earn enough money for these. The wage, usually just two pounds, was higher this year because fewer men went to England. With the blight, they couldn't leave their families, don't ya know. Our adult tickets to America cost around six pounds sterling each! If a family can scrape together enough money for only one ticket, the father sometimes goes alone and leaves the family behind, provided they can survive without him. Once in America, he tries to earn enough money to bring them over."

Liam recalled Maureen's last words: "Go! Flee if you can!" But with such a high price for tickets, most people clearly could not.

Murphy tucked his tickets away. "If you Reillys had not protected Meg and the children, my boys and I could never have gone to England, and then where would we be?"

"Hey! There's Malloy!" Brian called out. "He's irate and quarreling with that ticket agent." Brian went to inquire about his difficulties, and when he returned, he reported that Malloy had been tricked and sold tickets to Liverpool on the ferry, instead of passage to America. "From there, he will have to buy another ticket, and he's afraid he won't have enough money," Brian explained.

"Poor lad." Murphy said. "I'm sorry for his troubles. In Liverpool they'll charge him large sums for each night's lodging until the second ship leaves. He'll be on a vermin-infested floor with twenty others and many get sick, run out of money, and never make it."

As they walked toward the ship, Murphy pointed toward a nearby dock excitedly. "Liam, you were right when you said this isn't a *real* famine! Look at all that food piled there, waiting to be put on a boat to cross the channel. If only the landlords would let us eat even part of what we've produced, starvation could be avoided."

The sight of huge stores of food of all kinds and livestock in pens infuriated Liam. Dock hands steadily unloaded more produce as the starving gawked with longing at the food stacked up in front of them. Soldiers with bayonets stood on guard against the swarming beggars, lest they try to take anything. Everywhere Liam looked, he saw armed soldiers on foot and on horseback and realized that to send so many troops to Ireland, the British government must be worried about keeping people under control.

Wandering the waterfront, Liam discovered Niall's ship floating in the river inlet. Since the water level was below the docks, he could see onto its decks where sailors loaded crates and barrels. It looked top-heavy with a narrow hull and slender masts. A loose fold of sail flapped in the wind like on a giant clothes line. Though one slip could mean death, sailors balanced on beams high above, checking the rigging and making adjustments with nonchalance. The ship, rising and falling like a toy in the tide, needed paint and looked old and weathered. Even in this harbor, it creaked with the shifting tide. Liam worried about how it would fare in a violent gale, but decided he would keep his fears to himself.

Where *was* Niall? Since leaving home, he had been withdrawn and difficult to approach. Liam found him with Father, leaning on the pier, lost in thought and the hypnotic motion of the waves. Liam did not want to intrude on their last moments together so he stood quietly nearby, watching the foam curl around the quay. Clacking sea gulls glided in, perched on posts, and hopped just out of reach.

Not far away, he observed Sean and Maire locked in an embrace, their hair whipped by the salty wind. Even with an ocean between, Liam believed their love could not be denied and would endure as both a cross and a craving. Even if it took years, Sean would find a way to join her in Americay where she would be waiting. Liam knew this was their dream, if the fates allow.

In the cobblestone area close to the ship, relatives gathered near the gang plank and milled about where a mound of luggage, food, sleeping mats, two live geese, and a pig waited to board. Da had brought the cart to this area and unloaded it. Liam noticed a family hiding behind their sleeping mats while they struggled with a trunk. Walking behind, he saw they were putting a small boy inside and guessed they planned to get him aboard as a stow-a-way.

In passing the time before sailing, family and friends gave words of devotion and farewell. Even little Donal tugged at Liam's pant's leg to say goodbye, and Liam tousled his red hair affectionately. Then he turned to his father. "Murphy, keep your humor on the ready. You're always like a sunny day." Peter, Patricia and Mick lined up to shake Liam's hand and express their gratitude.

Then Mom Murphy ambled over, squeezed Liam, and planted a kiss on his cheek. "Take care of your sister Aine for my Brian! He loves her so."

Brian, himself, exchanged a hearty arm grip. "Tell Aine my letter will come as soon as I'm able. No one can ever take her place with me." He quickly moved away, not trusting his emotions. Brian was steady and strong, and Liam wished that their relationship could have had a chance.

Passengers were startled when, without fanfare, the officer removed the barricade. "Boarding can begin!" he yelled. Pandemonium broke out. Realizing their worlds were diverging forever, the relatives who were staying behind wailed, cried, and resisted. Letting go was painful. In the chaos, Liam rushed to find his brother and embrace him.

"Niall, goodbye!"

"I'll write," Niall promised. Liam choked up. He had so much he wanted to say, but it was too late and Niall turned away.

In the excitement, Niall struggled to drag great-grandfather's trunk, while also juggling his mandolin and fishing tackle. Brian Murphy, seeing his problem, grabbed one end of the trunk and together they jostled through the crowd and down the gang plank. As Niall neared the deck, he turned and gave a brief wave before he and the Murphys were lost in the crowd.

Numb, Liam realized it was over and he would never see Niall again. The brother who was always on his side in every squabble . . . his best friend . . . his leader and example was cut off forever. His face grew hot and his chest felt weighted with a sense of irretrievable loss.

Sean, too, was grappling with grief. Losing Maire was heartbreaking, and Liam could sense his anguish. His eyes were red-rimmed, and his hands quivered as they rested on the rail. Normally stoic, he kept biting his lip, struggling to contain a tide of feelings.

Because the ship was not *really* gone until they could no longer see it, Father, Liam, and Sean pressed against the railing with the other families, refusing to leave. The Reillys craned their necks and tried to hear what was happening on the ship's deck. An Irish clerk called the roll, and with great trepidation, the travelers awaited the inspection. Each passenger passed by the captain and stuck out his tongue. The captain looked long and hard at a few who appeared too sick, but none were denied.

Several crewmen went below to look for stowaways, while others moved among the luggage and turned each trunk on its end. Watching from the dock, Liam worried about the young boy who was hidden and now upside down. When the child began to whimper, the sailor opened the trunk and grabbed him by the hair. "Out! You rotten pig!"

The father rushed forward. "Please, have mercy! We are evicted and I have a large family! I cannot pay another fare but let me work for the half fare of the child!" Without waiting for the translation of this plea, the Captain glowered and motioned for a crewman to put the child ashore. But when the sailor tried to grab the little boy, he kicked and broke free, crying for his Mamai.

The mother threw her body over him and screamed. "No! My baby! We cannot leave him! Take me off instead!" The other children in the family began to wail and cry. Their tragic dilemma was one the passengers knew well, and despite their own poverty, a young girl started passing a hat for a collection. People dug into their pockets and calculated how generous they could afford to be, but most gave something.

At last, the hat was handed to the captain and tension filled the air. His officer counted out the coins one at a time while the passengers waited. At last, he nodded that the half fare was there, and a cheer rose from the steerage. The mother hugged her child and wept with gratitude, as did many watching from the shore.

On the dock, a bailiff and seven soldiers strutted through the crowd. "Stand aside!" the leader commanded as he pushed open a path. The knock of their boot heels on the wooden dock sounded loud and intimidating, and Liam bristled as they forced their way through. The passengers scowled and grumbled as this strong arm of the British government came on board in the final minutes.

The soldiers approached the captain with an official arrogance, and after a brief conference, the officer announced a name: "Cian Kennedy. Come forward." A lanky, timid fellow carrying his hat stepped up, his face full of questions.

"'Tis me you're calling, sir?"

The Irish clerk again served as interpreter: "Your landlord says you sold three pigs for your tickets on this ship, pigs which are owed him for rent next Gale Day. You are under arrest."

The young man stood bewildered. "But I raised those pigs myself. I paid the last rent in November when it was due with oats, and I'm leaving Ireland so no more is due!"

The soldiers seized him by the arm and began pulling him off the ship. The crowd of steerage passengers became rowdy and cursed at the soldiers with reckless abandon, knowing they would soon be beyond their reach. "Devils you are! Let him go in peace!" The frightened lad was taken away. Liam asked Father what they would do to him.

"I'm not sure, but the authorities will only listen to the landlord."

The roll-call clerk tried to calm the surly passengers. "Lucky for you those soldiers don't understand Irish! You may now take your luggage below." Confusion erupted as they scrambled to gather belongings and descend into the ship's depths. Liam knew that filthy conditions there caused disease that buried many at sea.

"Hope they make it," he mumbled, "and there are no great storms."

No families on shore stirred from the dock, and with emotions on edge, they watched the sailors loosen the moorings. They heard the luffing sounds of the sails being unfurled and filled with wind as they were drawn taut.

The passengers must have heard it too because they rushed to the top deck for their last look at relatives and beloved Ireland. Liam searched for Niall, but he was lost in a wall of faces. As the full sails pushed the ship out, it creaked and groaned, but then it silently started its slide down the river inlet to the Atlantic Ocean. At first the passengers stood transfixed at the rail; then suddenly, there was frantic waving and cries of goodbye on both ship and shore. Liam strained to see the ship until it was only a speck on the horizon because to leave made the separation final and complete.

Families drifted away, until only the Reillys alone stood watching the sea. Then, from down the dock where soldiers were guarding livestock and food, they heard a noisy commotion as women shrieked and men moaned. The Reillys loped down to where a crowd had gathered and saw someone lying on the dock, surrounded. Being tall, Liam peered over heads and looked down at a gaunt man, only bones and sinew. As he lay moaning, blood gushed from his side and pooled on the planks in an ever widening, maroon circle. A soldier, with his bayonet dripping, explained to an officer that the man had tried to steal a bag of oats. He seemed to take great satisfaction in preventing the theft, and the approving officer commended him with a nod and a pat on his back.

The dying man's cheeks were sunken and his lips dry, but he was trying to say something. A woman crouched beside him and put her ear to his mouth to catch his last words. Then she raised her head. "He says . . . 'my children . . . by the ship.' He must have left them there!"

Liam, Father, and Sean followed her back to the dock where the ship had been, and there waiting in the shadows were three little boys, looking too weak to stand, yet somehow they did. The man must have hoped the ship's departure would distract the soldiers long enough for him to get away with a bag of grain. Sadly, Liam recognized them as the boys they had seen yesterday at the side of the road and to whom Father had given soggy potatoes.

The children said over and over *"Tá sinn ocrach /* We are hungry." It was a touching lament and sympathetic people gathered around them. As several women took them by the hand and led them away, Liam was deeply moved. These people, forgetting their own distress, rendered all the aid in their power to these helpless waifs.

Liam gritted his teeth. "How could that soldier feel justified in spearing a starving man, stealing food? That is inhuman." Desiring revenge, he imagined thrusting a bayonet into the soldier's side and twisting it.

Father nodded. "I know how you feel, but not all soldiers are willing to do that. This spring in Mitchelstown, a mob of a hundred starving women and children held up carts carrying maize to a depot and took some. That time the soldiers didn't fire on them, although afterwards their superior officers reprimanded them."

Sean was thoughtful. "Well, even if you are in the army and they order you to shoot the starving, it is wrong. Have they no compassion? God help us if the next potato harvest is blighted."

Father put his arms around his two remaining sons. "Remember. Good fortune always follows bad. Things will get better." Liam heard his words, but Father's eyes did not quite agree. Liam could only think of those children, now orphaned. With heavy hearts, the Reillys started for home . . . a home without Niall.

9

Summer of Shadows

In the summer of 1846, the Reilly family was haunted by memories. At times, they forgot Niall was gone and listened for his laugh in the morning and for his mandolin when the fire burned low. He was like a shadow lurking nearby that always escaped detection. If a neighbor stepped across the threshold, Liam for an instant would think it might be Niall.

He could only imagine what Mother must feel. Out of habit, she sometimes set out Niall's bowl, and then with a forlorn look, she removed it. The joy she might have had in old age with her children and children's children around her would now be incomplete.

Since she could not bear to send gaunt beggars away with nothing, she kept sharing their dwindling stock of potatoes with those who came to the door. Liam realized that Irish tradition expected people to share with the needy, but with the rescue of the Murphys and the large number of beggars since the blight, the supply of potatoes had sunk lower than ever before.

He was alarmed and told Mother so, but he had no way to counter her replies: "But, for the grace of God, go we." She quoted scripture. "It might be Christ himself, and on judgment day, the Bible says God will ask us: 'Did you feed me when I was hungry?'" One cool evening after passing out potatoes, she must have noticed Liam's worried expression, and leaning over, she whispered, "Someone on the ship is sharing with Niall."

Father supported her generosity with optimistic forecasts. "The next harvest will make it up and promises to be the best in years. The weather this May and June has been warm, and the potato plants at this stage are more vigorous than usual." His parents made him feel selfish and stingy, and he hoped they were right.

Sean and Aine went through the motions of their tasks, but were listless, and Liam could see that loneliness for Maire and Brian had sapped their normal buoyancy and vigor. They were not only missing a brother, but mourning lost loves as well.

One afternoon, Sean asked Liam to go fishing in the glen and, looking forward to an afternoon in its deep shade, he agreed. But once there, Sean was gripped by nostalgia and wandered the bank, searching for anything that was hers: a forgotten ribbon, a button left behind, a footprint. He peered into the now deserted scalp and seemed to be listening for her voice, but the only sounds were occasional bird calls and gurgling water. Wistful, he slumped on a boulder near the stream. "We used to sit here and talk for hours." Liam felt powerless to ease his sadness, and it was a long walk home.

Several days later, Sean again suggested fishing in the glen, but Liam declined and explained that he needed to help Da shear the two lambs. Sean went on alone, but returned within the hour.

"Liam! I saw smoke and heard voices. An evicted family has moved into the Murphy's scalp."

Liam approved. "Good! 'Tis better than a ditch."

"But now I feel really cut off from her."

"I know," Liam murmured. He wished he could console him, but Sean and Maire had been in love for more than a year, and only yesterday, Grandmother had said, "It's clear that Sean's heart is in a hundred pieces." When Liam remembered Colleen, he was seized by a persistent longing, so how must Sean feel?

Mother tried to fill the voids in the family by keeping everyone busy, and since the men were now occupied with harvest, it was the girls who needed a task. When Liam came in from the fields for a cup of milk, he found a yarn workshop underway. A mound of fleece lay between two stools, and Caitlin's job was to pick it clean of heather and debris.

Grandmother was showing Brighid how to pull a bit of wool between a pair of special wire brushes called cards. "Once you get a flat piece stretched out, put it at Aine's feet." After much effort, Brighid laid her first clump on the floor.

When the playful Mittens batted it away with her paw, everyone laughed, and Caitlin chased after her. "Mittens, no!" Once retrieved, Aine attached the wool to the spindle and, under Mamai's watchful eye, she spun it into a long yarn.

When the cards stuck together in a tangle of fleece, Brighid threw them down. "I can't do this!"

"Ah, now." Grandmother said. "You're catching on well, but don't press quite so hard." She chuckled and murmured into Mother's ear, "*Mol an óige agus tiocfaidh sí* / Praise the young and they will blossom." Liam was heartened to see a smile flicker over Mother's countenance, which had been too solemn of late.

Grandda, sitting in his habitual niche next to the hearth, stoked the fire even when it did not need it. "How's the cutting?" he asked.

Liam set his empty cup on the table. "The harvest is good, thick with heavy heads. We should be able to hide back a little barley for ourselves, and in a few days, we'll be ready to start on the oats."

As he was leaving, Grandda called after him. "Cousin Eamon is in need of thatch, so lay out some straw to dry."

Back in the fields, Liam picked up the waiting scythe and took his place beside his brother who was cutting in a smooth motion, but suddenly Sean stopped. "Niall is thinking of us . . . somewhere on the ocean. Don't you feel it?"

Liam looked off toward the horizon and then frowned. "Maybe, but I just hope it's not because he's sick or there's a storm at sea." The brothers faced west as if they could reach him with their minds, and then with pensive looks, they resumed their mowing. Liam regretted having voiced such a negative worry . . . lest it be prophetic.

That evening Uncle Padraig, along with cousins Tomas and Eamon came after dinner to play a game of "five cards." Sitting around the table, each began with jovial predictions of winning, but after Grandda lost hand after hand, he tossed down his cards with disgust. "Not sitting under a rafter, am I?" Referring to a superstition, he checked the ceiling. "My luck is missing me entirely, and I'm gonna change it," and with that, he turned his hat around backwards. They chuckled at him, but stopped when he won the very next hand and the next. Beneath his hatband, his eyes had a merry twinkle at getting the best of them.

Then the bad luck shifted to Father, and he, too, called upon a superstition. "Erin, come stick your needle in my shirt!" he said. The teasing and jokes were passed around the table as freely as the cards.

For their entertainment, Caitlin and Brighid begged for fairy tales, told next to the fire where shadows danced and the mysterious seemed possible. Grandmother repeated the old story about a wicked land agent who ordered a hunchback farmer to level the ruins of a fort. But knowing that leprechauns lived there, the farmer refused, not wanting to harm the little people. To reward him, the leprechauns moved the hump to the land agent's back! Caitlin and Brighid clapped with glee.

"Tell us another," they urged. Aine repeated the tale of the Children of Lir in which a jealous stepmother cast a spell on four children and transformed them into beautiful swans with human voices. After struggling for hundreds of years, they were set free. Half-listening, Liam was distracted by Aine's dramatic flair and missed a chance to win the game.

When cards had run their course, the table was pushed aside, and the relatives retrieved their instruments from the front door. Uncle Paddy picked on his mandolin, Da took the fiddle from the wall, and Eamon placed his drum on his knee. Sean and Tomas played tin whistles, and the lively tunes brought Aine, Brighid, and Mamai to their feet, dancing the three-person reel with quick steps and leaps. Caitlin copied their moves as best she could, while the grandparents clapped the beat.

The music and motion filled the room and blotted out all sadness. As the beat got faster, it drew Liam in and he danced the reel till he was breathless and invigorated. Hearts and feet stepped to the same rhythm, united by the joyous celebration of the moment. The lively melodies lifted Liam up and out of the gloom which had lingered since Colleen and Niall had been taken from him. As often happened, the music, dance, and storytelling worked a kind of magic that served as a temporary release from poverty and worry. Living nearby, the relatives sneaked home after dark, one at a time.

The next day, the barley harvest continued, and the father and sons whipped the straw and heads, leaving grain and debris behind. When a pound of barley seed was separated out, Liam took it to his mother for grinding in the quern, hoping she would bake bread later in the day.

Cousin Tomas wandered over, and with his hat cocked to one side, he projected a carefree attitude. "I have good news! George Henry Moore, the best landlord in all Ireland, chartered an American ship, the *Martha Washington,* and now it has docked in Westport with 4,000 tons of maize. They're loading carts now to bring it to his tenants near Lough Carra!" Cheers for Moore erupted.

Father handed Tomas the winnowing tray. "Here . . . help us shake out Sligo's barley." But instead of working, Tomas began amusing them with convincing mimes. He pretended that a leprechaun had stolen some barley and jumped into his shirt. He squirmed and yelled and made them laugh.

Finally the clouds glowed violet and pink with the setting sun, and Tomas said goodbye. After washing up at the well, Liam and Sean entered the cottage and smelled fresh barley bread, cooking on the open hearth.

"Hmn! Smells delicious!" Liam said as he peered into the pots. "I wish we could share some barley bread with Niall, but not *much* of it, mind you!" A clay urn filled with red hollyhocks from the yard brightened the table. Outside the little sisters were playing with Curley, the lamb, when Brighid's excited face appeared over the half-door.

"Someone's coming! On a big horse! A soldier!"

Liam peered out. Captain Lawrence from the turf cutting had followed Aine's directions and was dismounting in the yard. Caitlin and Brighid stood back with more than a little fear as the muscular, black horse with shiny coat snorted, shook its mane, and pawed the ground.

"He's sure bigger than our donkey," Caitlin said as she continued to back away.

As Lawrence strolled up to the door, he looked dapper in

black boots, riding pants, and uniform coat, and his hair was combed and groomed with oil. Liam had been secretly expecting this visit, but his parents seemed surprised and wary.

However, true to the Irish rule of hospitality, they welcomed him. The spinning wheel in the corner was humming as Aine practiced her new skill, but when she stopped and proudly showed him her ball of yarn, he seemed disinterested.

Assuming the role of interpreter, she introduced him in turns to everyone. Uncomfortable with a British officer as a guest, Grandda's manner was gruff. Although Sean and Liam understood some English, they appreciated Aine's translations.

"Will he be joining us for dinner?" Mother asked. Aine echoed her question in English.

"Yes, if it's not an imposition," he replied. He gave Aine admiring glances, but she acted oblivious and treated him with the respect due a teacher. After all, he was probably nine or ten years older, Liam guessed, and Brian still had her heart. As they recited grace, Captain Lawrence bowed his head but looked at Aine. At first he took small portions of the colcannon, but its delicious flavor evidently surprised him and he eagerly accepted more. Since guests were expected to entertain their hosts with stories, poems, music, or news, Father lost no time in asking.

"What do you think we can expect from the government? Is it going to help us?" Aine repeated Da's question in English. The table was quiet while Lawrence cleared his throat and dabbed his mouth with his white linen handkerchief, as if considering how candid he should be. He glanced over at Aine, whose large sea-green eyes looked back with curiosity. He took a quick breath, as though she had stolen it, and turned to her father.

"Unfortunately, I rather doubt any help will be forthcoming. This April, one of our revenue cutters, *Eliza*, was inspecting in the

Killeries . . . you know . . . that wild district of deep ocean inlets in northwest Mayo? A boatload of men, so weak they couldn't stand, floated out to the ship to beg for food. The sympathetic captain ordered Indian maize to be sent to the area from the Westport depot. While it seemed a reasonable thing to do, Charles Trevelyan denounced it as unnecessary."

"This man Trevelyan . . . I've heard of him," Father admitted.

"He's the Assistant Secretary of the British Treasury and controls Irish relief," Lawrence explained. "He and Sir Charles Wood, an important cabinet official, both seem inclined to do as little as possible for Ireland."

After Aine's translations, Father looked solemn. "Peel, the former Prime Minister, imported maize from America last spring, but hardly any has been sold! Is there any chance that the new Prime Minister, Lord Russell, will bring in more maize at least?"

"Months ago, Sir Randolph Routh, who heads the Relief Commission in Dublin, urged Trevelyan to import more maize, but he refused. Despite the fact that blight is returning in some places, Trevelyan has ordered all food depots selling maize to close by July 17th."

Father's eyes widened. "What is his idea? First, no imports and then to halt the sale of stored maize?"

The captain shrugged as if a bit baffled himself. "I'm sure he must have his reasons, but another rather surprising thing happened this month. A ship called *Sorciere* was bringing the last of the maize Peel had purchased from America, yet Trevelyan wouldn't let it unload. He told them that Ireland had no need of it and to dispose of it elsewhere."

Father's eyes flashed alarm. "He said Ireland did not *need* it! He actually sent them away, not letting them unload?" Exasperated, his voice grew louder with each word.

Lawrence shook his head apologetically. "Yes, and I confess, I am also perplexed. Anyone here can see there's a food shortage."

Liam felt anxious. He remembered Niall describing this Trevelyan as a man who hated the Irish, but what could possibly be his motives for sending away food? Food the government had already purchased! Father looked pale, but Liam guessed he would say nothing too critical of the government in the hearing of this officer.

Da sighed. "Well, if potato blight returns to Ireland, surely it will be limited and not as bad as last year." Since the captain was the only representative of the British government in the room, Grandda glared at him from beneath his bushy brows.

Caitlin had grown tired of grown-up talk and wiggled on the bench. "Do you know who is having a birthday, Mr. Soldier?" Aine translated.

"You, perhaps?"

"I have one soon, but tomorrow it's Aine, my sister!"

"Indeed." He turned to Aine. "And what birthday is this?"

"I will be fifteen. The years between me and my sister Brighid are seven because two sisters died between us."

When the other family members gathered at the hearth, Aine spoke English at the table without translation. Liam only pretended to stare into the fire and strained to overhear.

Lawrence faced Aine. "My cavalry rides a circuit between Ballinrobe and Westport."

She looked surprised. "That far? Back and forth all the way to the coast?"

"Yes. We help patrol Westport for several days before we start riding back this way. I find this rural post a bore, and Westport is an improvement. But when I'm nearby in Ballintrobe, I would enjoy the company of one like you who speaks English, even though you're of the peasant class." A slight frown creased Aine's forehead at his remark about class, but he either failed to notice or ignored it. His eyes moved over her admiringly. "I suppose you're as intelligent as you are beautiful. Do you also read?"

She sat up straight and proud. "Yes. Our teacher, who comes every summer, is studying for the priesthood and speaks Irish, English, Latin, and reads Greek. It was he who taught me the Sasanach – that's the Irish word for your language."

"You must learn with ease. And when can I see you dance again?"

"After our cousin's roof thatching the last day of July, there will be festivities with music and dance." When Lawrence asked for the details of time and place, she gave them, and Liam squirmed in his seat, wishing Aine was less open and trusting.

The next day the harvest continued. After mowing all day until hands were blistered, Liam strolled back to the cottage with Sean and admired the tumbling clouds, tinted pastel. Then on the hill not far away, he saw the silhouette of a fine steed and rider.

"Looks like we're having the soldier's company again," Liam said.

Sean grimaced. "I've heard enough of attitudes in London, but Lawrence surprised me by being open, frank, and almost sympathetic."

Liam lowered his voice. "It's Aine. He wants time with her and shares news just to win favor with Da."

Perturbed, Sean nodded. "Our parents will invite him for dinner – you know it – and we have no potatoes to spare."

When they reached the cottage, the captain was seated next to Aine, and in his lap was a gift wrapped in white paper and red ribbon.

Caitlin spied it. "Is that for me or for Aine? My birthday's coming soon, and my brother is sending me something good from

Americay!"

"Caitlin, Niall's not even there yet," Aine tried to explain. "He's still on the ship." After translating for Lawrence, she added, "I'm afraid she's going to be disappointed."

"Maybe not." He reached in his coat and pulled out some English taffy tied with a ribbon. "I remembered her, too."

Caitlin had seen candy in the shops but never tasted it. "Oh! Thank you, Mr. Soldier!" She could not take her eyes off the sweet, and he teased her by dangling it too long before he finally dropped it in her hands. "There!"

"Save the paper." Aine instructed. Caitlin and Brighid each pulled off a bite of sticky taffy and skipped around the room with wads bulging in their cheeks.

Aine enjoyed their delight and smiled. "That was generous of you."

"Now for the one who really counts!" He laid the gift in her lap. "I think this will further your English studies. I brought it from London for myself, and it's in good condition, though I regret it's not new." She unwrapped a book of English poetry by Lord Byron.

"Thank you!" she murmured, eyes sparkling, as she began to thumb through the pages.

He moved closer, ostensibly to see the book, and pointing to the page, he touched her hand. "This poem here is so like you: "She Walks in Beauty." Lawrence's eyes gleamed as he watched for her reaction, but Aine continued to leaf through the book and ignored the compliment. Liam still had suspicions about the captain's motives and listened with mixed feelings. He appreciated the gifts to his sisters, and perhaps the soldier was sincerely kind, but it was hard to know.

After dinner, they gathered around the hearth for music. Accompanied by Father's violin and Sean's whistle, mother sang in a clear soprano voice with artful control, and Aine joined her for a duet. After an hour, Father signaled evening's end by hanging his fiddle back on the wall.

Aine saw the cue and walked Lawrence to the door, but before leaving, he took her hand and lifted it to his lips for a long kiss, and all the while, he looked into her eyes intently without blinking. His boldness made her uncomfortable, and her face flushed as she looked away. Liam guessed she was loath to offend him by withdrawing her hand, but he knew Father saw the move and would be protective of Aine for he guarded his flock like an archangel.

By the first of July, it was clear that the traveling teacher was late, and since the little sisters were impatient to start school, Aine dug the books out of the trunk and started teaching them herself. Five years before, Mother had made cheese to sell at the fair in Ballinrobe and purchased a manual to teach reading from a peddler for three shillings. Aunt Una sold her crochet to buy *Gough's Arithmetic*, and to protect the precious books, the mothers covered them with lamb skin, woolly side out.

When Liam was ten, Da and Uncle Paddy had rubbed sea-stone on pieces of slate until they were smooth and then asked a skilled cousin to put wooden frames around them. Liam recalled using shaped limestone on the slates to do his figuring, and these, too, were lifted from the trunk.

Aine began reading lessons with Caitlin, while Grandda taught Brighid how to add and subtract. One afternoon Caitlin ran to meet Liam with reddish ringlets flying and the Bible in her arms. As they walked, she read a passage so well that Liam could not decide if Aine was an exceptional teacher or if Caitlin was very bright, but Grandmother said it was both.

A week later, Tomas stuck his head over the door and shouted, "Come to our cottage, cousins! Mr. Barrett came last night, and classes begin this morning!"

Caitlin jumped for joy, her braids bobbing. "I'm going to show the teacher how smart I am!" The family laughed at her lack of modesty, but knew she spoke the truth.

The lessons went on for three weeks in various locations for the twenty-three students of neighbors. The families pooled their resources to feed Mr. Barrett. Adding to this, Mother made two sturdy wicker baskets to hang on the sides of his donkey, and Aunt Una knitted a sweater.

But due to the reduced supply of potatoes, school ended early, much to the students' disappointment. Da suggested Aine continue the school herself, and it proved an answer. Even Liam and Sean, while working on English with Aine, taught others by reading the English poetry book. Aine recruited Grandda as history instructor, and when appreciative parents praised her organization and talent, she vowed to become a real teacher someday.

On the last day of July, it was time to give Eamon a new roof. "It's a perfect day for thatching," Da said. "Calm, with only a breeze, and lots of "*comhar na gComharsan* / neighbors helping neighbors." After Sunday Mass in Partry, carts congregated around Eamon's cottage, heaped with straw that would be sewn onto the sod which rested above the roof timbers.

Uncle Paddy, the expert on thatching, organized the work and assigned Liam, Sean, and Tomas the job of removing old and broken thatch. When Liam disturbed a nest and angered a mother bird, she circled his head, squawking. They laughed as he ducked her sharp beak and batted her away, but then his ladder shifted backwards and was precariously off balance. They held their breath as he leaned forward in time to avoid a disastrous fall.

"Careful, you lads!" Uncle Paddy yelled. "No time for clowning."

By mid-afternoon, Uncle Paddy trimmed the surface with the Dutch mallet to a neat exterior, and the roof was complete. After Eamon offered both poteen or milk for the toasting, Uncle Paddy held up his cup: "May your thatch never fall in and may we, as friends, never fall out!"

The men answered in unison, "*Sláinte* / health."

Family groups of grandparents, children, and wives strolled over to Eamon's cottage with baskets of food, and musicians lent a gaiety to the occasion. They placed the food table in the yard to leave the cottage free for dancing and set up a game of road bowling in the lane. Liam was about to take his turn when he saw the black steed and rider.

A low murmur went through the crowd at the sight of a British officer, but no one changed their activities. Liam observed Lawrence out of the corner of his eye as he and Da nodded politely. The captain went at once to Aine's side, monopolizing her attention and cutting her off from friends and cousins.

When Aine and the other young girls lined up to dance, Liam noticed how Lawrence brightened, and though the attraction was understandable, Liam was irritated. Aine was light on her feet with a shapely figure, a small waist, and flowing, blond hair that bobbed as she hopped to the beat. Her lovely face glowed with the joy of the dance, youth, and life.

After Liam and the lads danced, the crowd called for Sean, and they turned a table upside down to give him a hard, wooden surface. His fast rhythms and clicking steps resounded in the room, and Aine beamed with pride.

"My brother," she reminded the captain.

Lawrence nodded. "He's remarkable . . . I must say." Next, people of all ages swirled to the reel, and Liam danced with Aine to get her away from the captain, back to her friends and the dancing she loved.

At dusk, the group began to disburse, and Da seemed to take satisfaction in telling Lawrence that this gathering was ending now because of the curfew and Coercion law passed by the British Parliament. Faced with having to leave Aine, the captain turned to her. "Ask your father if you can ride home with me on my horse." She repeated his question to Father in Irish.

"You and he by yourselves?" he asked her directly.

"That's what he has in mind." Her eyes said – say no – and Liam guessed that his aggressiveness made her uneasy. Father's answer was easy to predict.

"Not a young girl alone . . . he may walk his horse and accompany you and your brothers to our cottage on foot." Aine translated his reply to the waiting captain who seemed perturbed.

"Irish girls are surely watched with great care. Is it always so or just now?" he said with a wry smile. With that, he said goodbye to Aine, gave a curt nod to Father, and strode out with heavy steps. Liam was glad to hear his horse gallop away and hoped that maybe now he would stay in Ballinrobe.

Tomas strolled up. "I don't think that was his plan . . . to leave alone. He best learn about Irish girls and sooner is better." Neighbors who had acted guarded seemed relieved when the officer left. The next week passed without any visits from the captain.

After Sunday Mass in Partry, the Reillys hurried home to dig the first of the new potatoes, and in high spirits, they filled a creel and took them inside where hot water was boiling. It was early August – the time when some of the small, immature spuds were lifted early for their fresh taste. Liam missed Niall who relished more than anyone the eating of new potatoes covered in butter.

After the meal, Aine went out to feed table scraps to the chickens and piglets while Liam stood in the small front yard, enjoying the fragrant air surrounding the rose bush at the door. He took a deep breath and was admiring puffy clouds glowing lavender from the sun's reflection, when he heard the trotting of a horse and knew Lawrence was back.

When the captain spied Aine, he dismounted quickly, left his horse in the lane, and walked to meet her. Unseen, Liam watched as Lawrence laid her basket on the ground, held both her hands, and looking down into her face, moved closer. After listening a moment, Aine retrieved the basket and put it between them again.

Liam could no longer contain himself. "Captain Lawrence! Welcome," he yelled in English and waved. With that, Aine started for the door, and Lawrence followed, looking disgruntled.

Again surrounded by family, Aine seemed at ease and chatted. "Earlier this summer I noticed the white blooms on an elderberry bush near the glen, and yesterday I picked the berries, fresh and purple. May we eat some tonight, Mamai?"

"Yes . . . with milk perhaps," Mother suggested with a smile. The family enjoyed the tart berries, and although Liam resented sharing them with a member of the occupying army, he hid his feelings behind a pleasant mask.

"Any news?" Father asked. "We aren't in touch with the doings of the government as you are so what can you tell us?"

Lawrence paused and dabbed his mouth with his handkerchief. "Well, in the south of Ireland, there are reports of blight returning – even in Wicklow where they never had blight last year – but it isn't spreading much beyond."

"Still, that's worrisome," Father said. "Our potatoes are loaded with blooms and look hardy. We lifted new potatoes today, and they were delicious."

"That's good," he nodded.

"Tell me." Da leaned closer. "Is there any chance that the

government will limit the food leaving Ireland and let some of this harvest feed the starving here? That was what they did to avoid famine last year in Europe and once here in Ireland about fifty years ago."

Lawrence shook his head at Aine's translation. "Trevelyan is against it. Yet, Sir Routh, head of the relief commission here in Ireland, has called food exports a serious evil and says over 60,000 tons of oats alone have left Ireland since the first of the year. But Trevelyan is in control, and he says England must have cheap food for its factory workers, and to limit exports here would raise prices there."

Father leaned back and sighed. "God help us! Cheap food for the English and no food for us!" Aine did not translate his last remark.

"What did he say?" Lawrence asked Aine.

"He said, 'Yes, cheap food for the English.'"

Lawrence took a newspaper out of his coat and placed it on the table. "By the way, Aine, I brought a copy of the London *Times* for your English studies."

Suddenly from outside came a roll of loud thunder which caused Brighid to jump off the bench and stand on her tip-toes, peering out the window. "The sky looks black!" Another low rumble passed over the roof, and outside, the captain's horse neighed nervously.

Lawrence rose to his feet. "I enjoyed the berries and milk, but it sounds like I'd best be going since the weather is turning." Aine accompanied him to the door and thanked him again for the poetry book and newspaper.

"It's less than you deserve," he said and caressed her cheek with his finger tips. With what seemed like reluctance, he put on his hat and hurried out. His horse cantered into the splatter of rain now beginning.

From the open door, a damp gust rushed in and humbled the flames in the hearth, forcing Aine to slam it shut with both hands. Thunder shook the rafters and vibrated the thick walls. Silenced by the storm's fury, the family sat and listened as a loud crack of lightening briefly brightened the room.

"That was close," Sean said.

Father looked outside. "It was indeed and I just hope that it does not strike a thatched roof somewhere." Hard rain began clicking on the glass of their small window.

"I'm scared," said Caitlin.

Grandmother hugged her. "No reason to fear. The rain will drown any sparks, and we are safe here in our cottage."

Brighid sat up straight. "Sean and Da, please play music. I wish Niall was here too."

The family musicians took the fiddle and tin whistle from the mantel and drew everyone near the hearth. In lieu of a drum, Liam beat on a stool, and the rhythmic and staccato music distracted them from the howl of the storm.

The next morning, the sun came out, and puddles evaporated into steam. It was Liam's turn to fetch the cow and milk her, and carrying the pail, he picked his way back with care, trying to avoid the deepest depressions of water. His feet slipped and mud oozed between his toes. Looking up, he saw that things were changing as more clouds tumbled in from the west and shrouded the sun once again.

At the front door, he met Mother with a basket of new potatoes, and they chuckled at their matching feet, with mud to the ankles. After handing their loads over the half-door, they cleaned up together.

By afternoon the sky again grew dark and haunting. Birds

flew before the fog, and where they went, Liam did not know, but the stillness without a bird's song seemed deathly quiet. The temperature made a sudden drop of twenty degrees and chilled him when he stepped outside.

Just before dusk, the sky cleared, and bathed in a soft light, a beautiful rainbow arched in the heavens. Dinner again was new potatoes, and tasting such delicious white orbs coated with heavy butter made Liam fear blight more than ever. Liam, Sean, and Father walked out for fresh air and strolled up to the potato beds for reassurance. Water stood in the trenches between the rows, but the plants were a beautiful, lush green with white blossoms.

Da relaxed. "They look good, don't they?"

The next afternoon was hot and muggy with thickening clouds, and Sean complained of the heat, so unlike Ireland. "Where is this weather coming from? Africa?" They hurried to finish their chores, and since Grandmother always knew where to find eggs, she gathered them on the run. Liam pulled the cow to the shed and not a moment too soon. It became almost as dark as night, and lightning lit the fields in an ominous yellow. Loud thunder sent Caitlin and Brighid scurrying under the table, frightened.

Between rains, damp beggars came to the door, and Mother shared new potatoes. Their gratitude was overwhelming, and having survived this long, Liam hoped the beggars could make it. People everywhere were depending on this next potato crop, and it had to be bountiful.

That night a thick fog rolled in from the hills and hung over the fields. Liam tossed on his mat, threw off the blanket, and wished for a window, but finally fell into a fretful slumber. However, before dawn, he was disturbed by the cow's persistent lowing which sounded like she was complaining. He ignored it because the deep darkness in the loft told him that it could not be morning, but as he tried to go back to sleep, the sheep also began to bleat. What could be wrong with those animals? At last, soft light pierced through a crack and he realized dawn was nigh. From the room below he heard the hinges of the door creaking and realized that someone was slowly opening it.

Suddenly, from the yard came Mother's shrill scream! Liam bolted down the ladder and rushed outside to find her standing in front of the potato beds, wailing and wringing her hands. While his eyes adjusted to the dim light, a sewer-like, sulfurous odor sickened him and smelled eerily familiar. He slipped and sloshed through the watery ditches to get closer and saw that the plants, so lush last evening, were withering. A white, powdery substance covered leaves not yet black, and brown spots on the stems were spreading like sores. Panic gripped him.

By now the entire family stood in the potato beds, shocked and horrified. Mother rocked back and forth, moaning, and Father stood aghast. "Oh my God in Heaven! Oh, NO!"

Then he started shouting. "Liam! Sean! Get my knife and the scythe . . . Quick!" Feverishly, he hacked at the stalks, trying to cut out the sores, only to discover that the stalks were eaten through. He ran down the rows and slashed off the plants at the base. Dressed in his night shirt, water splashed as he slogged about, and mud speckled his legs.

"Sons, cut them down before it affects the potatoes underground! Work fast!" They did as commanded, racing from plant to plant.

"Seamus!" Grandda yelled out. "Check the tubers below!"

Father halted the slashing and dug down. He drew up a tuber that looked sound when he first opened his hand, but then with the slightest pressure, it collapsed inward and smelled like a dead thing.

Liam was in disbelief. No! He shivered with a paralyzing dread. How could these potatoes already be affected! His eyes were riveted on the decaying mass in Da's hands – the slimy potato oozing black just like what he had seen at the Sullivan's! Like a ghost, death stood at the edge of the field . . . waiting . . . silently waiting.

I 0

In Search of Hope

Daylight confirmed that the disaster was complete and that their fields of hope were now foul masses of black vegetation. Potato beds everywhere suffered from blight, and the sulfurous stench of putrefying fields filled the air for miles and sickened them. Neighbors and relatives wandered from cottage to cottage to commiserate with one another. Men slogged through the muddy rows, lifted withered leaves, examined rotten stems, and tried to comprehend what had happened. Women dissolved into each other's arms and wondered if God was angry to send such a punishment. What had they done to deserve this? Mothers wept and keened together in a high, sing-song wail while their children tried to console them, but as Liam watched his mother, she was different. Erin Reilly stood alone, staring at the ruin . . . stiff, lost, and communicating with no one.

Liam wanted to be strong for his family, but what could he do? Feeling helpless and scared, he swallowed hard and studied his mother through bleary eyes. Her anguish tore at his heart. Always before when Mother cried, it meant that everything was wrong, but now her strange, tearless silence puzzled him. Still standing in the same place that he had found her in the wee hours of morning, she stared at the fields and only wrung her hands.

Caitlin's small arms tried to reach around her mother's full skirt and hug her around the knees. "It's gonna be better, Mamai. The potatoes . . . they will grow back tomorrow." Brighid attached herself to Mother's other side, and Aine laid her head on Mamai's shoulder, but Mother was inconsolable.

"*Sin deireadh leis an dóchas* / Goodbye to hope," she whispered.

Uncles, cousins, and a few neighbors came to the yard to grieve together and seek ways to deal with the catastrophe. Like the disease-bearing fog, news spread that the entire Irish potato crop was in decay, and unlike last year, it was not partial. Forever they would remember the first week of August 1846, when, with lightning swiftness, it happened.

Each man pondered the same questions. What caused this blight? Was it the lightning? What would the English do in the face of total devastation? The British colonial system dictated that its territories send their produce to England for the use of the "mother country." It was the imperial plan that the mother country should profit at the expense of conquered people, whom they regarded as inferior and unworthy of rights.

"But they could *change* the plan, at least temporarily. Couldn't they? They have the power," Father said.

The only food which the landlord system permitted them to eat in a quantity that would sustain life was the potato, and the potato was gone. "Now the landlords will have to let us eat some of the grain we're growing. Won't they?" asked Cousin Eamon. Heads nodded in agreement as the men stood around in a circle in the yard with grave faces.

Uncle Padraig took off his worn hat and scratched his head. "Don't the British *have* to do something now? They are a Christian nation, no more than a day's sail away from our shores. They can't just turn their backs on us and let us die!"

Eamon's face flushed and the veins in his temples stood out. "They bribed people and forced us to join their union, an *unequal* union, at that! But doesn't that make us citizens and part of their nation, deserving as much help as any other part? If not, this so-called union is just a trick and a lie!"

Barra Fleming's deep voice resonated with emotion. "They take our young men, like my son, and sacrifice them in their foreign wars! Doesn't that give us any claim to their support?"

The men murmured "Yes" and gritted their teeth.

"It does indeed," Grandfather answered with that old fire in his eyes. "If only Daniel O'Connell can go before the Parliament and make them see. They say he's very sick and dying, but I know he'll try." Grandda's faith in "The Liberator," as he was called, was unshaken.

Listening to the men, Liam tried to think of something they could do, and an idea formed in his mind. "Da . . . ."

"Yes, Liam?"

"As I see it, we are trapped between blight and high rents. The blight has taken our potatoes, and the landlords will take our other food as rent, yes?"

The men nodded.

Liam spoke louder. "What if we went to Lord Sligo and asked him to temporarily reduce our rent and allow us to eat part of our oat harvest. We could give the rest to him, and then . . . ."

"But Liam," Father interrupted, his face flushed with alarm. "Lord Sligo would have to agree to that, you know. If we just hold grain back from him, he'll evict us, for sure. And it might make him angry if we even suggest that he take less."

Eamon yelled out: "He'd never give us permission! Landlords squeeze every bit out of ya down to the very last drop of your blood."

Barra Fleming held up his hand. "That's the truth, if ever spoken!"

"Listen." Liam stepped forward. "If he takes all our grain, we'll die, and he'll have no tenants to farm his land next spring. Why wouldn't he want to give us enough to survive? Reduce rent just this once . . . in this crisis. He would still get *some* rent! With all the tenants he has, it will be a huge amount, even if reduced." The men murmured among themselves.

Uncle Padraig put his hat back on. "Seamus, your Liam here may have birthed an idea. What do you think of it?"

Father crossed his arms. "Humm . . . to ask for nothing will get us nothing. If we assembled thousands of his tenants to go to him and beg for mercy, he might be moved. Liam is right. If he doesn't help us, we face starvation and he can see that! We have worked his lands faithfully for generations, so surely we have value to him."

Grandda Walsh smacked his gums, and his scratchy voice got louder: "He owes us! His fancy palaces – in Westport, in London, his hunting lodge in Delphi, and thereabouts – we built 'em with our rents, sure as you're born."

The men nodded.

Uncle Padraig shifted his weight. "So how would we do this, Seamus?"

Father began to pace and then stopped. "We can organize a peaceful march to his mansion in Westport. We need to tell as many of his tenants as we can about our plan, so start passing the word."

"When would we go?" asked Eamon.

"Let's give it about two weeks . . . should be time enough to spread the word to his tenants all over Mayo. We'll meet on the Post

Road to Westport at dawn on August 22nd."

Barra Fleming's face clouded. "Seamus, the British consider any petition or request from us to be a protest and an outrage. They could deport us to an Australian prison just for trying to talk to Sligo!"

Father turned to him. "It's a delicate matter, it is. We'll have to be orderly and respectful and not appear as a mob . . . dress in the best we have."

Fleming frowned. "'Tis risky . . . but . . . well . . . we *have* to do something! I'll go to Ballyburke and talk to tenants there." Eamon volunteered to go to Gorthbaum and Uncle Padraig to Killadeer.

"Good!" Father nodded. "But Sligo has many more villages than that. Tell everyone you see to pass our idea along to others like a chain, one village to another. We need to reach as many of his tenants as possible."

Sean looked thoughtful. "We best choose words to say in English because Lord Sligo does not speak Irish, I'm sure."

"Aine and I will write a plea in his language, and I'll practice the saying of it," Liam said.

Eamon grabbed him by the shoulder. "We're proud of you, Liam. What a head you've got on ya, and learning the *Sasanach* / English language too." With that, Eamon wandered home, energized by hope and a course of action.

Sean turned to Liam. "Maybe we can get aid from somewhere – Lord Sligo or the British government – but until help comes, we have to survive." Liam knew he was right. Each day would be a struggle.

Like priests all over Ireland, Father Mullen called for a special day of prayer that the government would respond with mercy and come to Ireland's aid. In a scene repeated across the land, Liam and most of the Reilly family went to Mass. When they arrived, the church in Partry was already full and people overflowed into the yard. The Reillys were forced to stand with the crowd outside its open doors where they listened to the sermon, recited the creed, and sang hymns. Father Mullen brought communion out to them as they knelt in the grass.

Even after Mass was over, people remained to pray silently. When the Reillys finally rose to leave, others reverently came to pray and knelt in their places, and it was evident that the candle-lit church would remain filled with worshipers through the night in a vigil.

As Liam, Sean, and Aine were climbing into the cart, Uncle Paddy hustled over with news. "Seamus, there's a big meeting on the green in Castlebar a week hence at noon! Men from over twelve parishes in Mayo are writing a petition to send to the Prime Minister, Lord Russell. All over Ireland men are writing and sending pleas for help. We should go!"

Father was eager for any action. "Yes, we should support the effort. We've got to make the London government understand our desperation. They must act quickly, and no half-way relief measures will be enough."

"Next week then," Paddy nodded.

On the way home, Da and Grandda talked about how most people felt helpless and hoped that those in authority would somehow come to their rescue. The optimism of Irish newspapers had most believing that the British would finally do something for the Irish. But Liam, recalling Niall's warnings and the reports from Captain Lawrence, was haunted by doubts. Clearly, this Trevelyan had few humanitarian tendencies, even sending away a ship filled with maize when people were starving. Liam could only pray that other British leaders would overrule Trevelyan's decisions, and maybe this petition would help.

Liam heard no talk of violence. People who had suffered blighted potatoes the year before followed by months of near starvation were too weak and passive to offer resistance. Having already pawned their coats, shawls, stools, tables, bedding, and even their manure pile, such families had little left and were barely hanging on. For these people, government help would probably come too late. But for people like his family, strong government relief programs could prevent starvation.

The following week, Da and Uncle Paddy left in the cart with Barra Fleming for the Green at Castlebar. When they returned home, Da was invigorated.

"I wish you could have seen it! Over twenty thousand people gathered on the green. The petition called upon 'The First Minister of the greatest empire in the world to take such steps as will avert the threatened calamity.' They used those exact words! The chairman, Richard Bourke, and James Conry, the Secretary, signed on behalf of the thousands of people who came."

Uncle Paddy, too, was flushed with confidence. "And since Great Britain is the richest and most powerful nation in the world, they can prevent widespread starvation if they decide to . . . the same way those countries in Europe did last year." Liam found their optimism contagious.

But in the days that followed, he saw Father's euphoria about the prospects for the petition slip away. Every day was a struggle to replace the potatoes. Although it was useless, he kept wandering among the withered plants – picking them up, examining them, and then tossing them aside in disgust. His thick auburn forelock hung over his forehead, and his eyes, which had always held a merry spark, now looked down, always down, making Liam feel shut out.

It was Grandmother who took the lead with a plan. She knew how to make boxty out of partially ruined potatoes and directed Sean, Liam, and Aine to gather into a creel any overlooked potato that was not totally decayed. Liam and Sean scraped and pounded them into pulp while Aine and Grandmother placed them in a cloth and squeezed them dry. Grandmother formed them into flat cakes and baked them till hard. By adding potatoes from last year's crop that were starting to deteriorate, the stack of boxty grew larger than anything Liam had anticipated. But he was troubled by the way Mother stayed apart and took no interest in the project.

In fact, she took no interest in anything, and her condition became a matter of great concern to the family. All her tears had stopped, and she hardly spoke. Occasionally, she would shake her head no . . . always no . . . to everything. The last words Liam remembered hearing her utter were "Goodbye to hope" as she stood in front of the blighted potatoes. With expression unchanged and posture slumped, she sat without moving wherever Da placed her.

It was as if she had retreated somewhere deep inside herself as a way to bear what seemed unbearable. Listless and withdrawn, she sat in the wall seat every day and stared into space. She ate little, and the small amount she accepted, had to be fed to her, almost forced.

Liam knew her depression alarmed the whole family, but everyone tried to act normally because if they spoke about it out loud, it would be real. Everyone suffered anguish privately, pretending her condition was not so grave and would right itself somehow. When someone would tenderly approach her with food or a suggestion, she would not acknowledge them. Not moving, hardly blinking, she seemed beyond reach and lost in her own bleak reality.

Only Da could get her on her feet, and even then, she moved like a mechanical thing, rigid and halting. Occasionally, he tried to take her on short walks around the yard, but she seemed unable to move normally and upon their return, she fell into bed. Several weeks passed with little change.

Scared, Liam was starting to give way to the strain, unable to sleep and consumed with anxiety. Maybe she would never be the same again. He had heard of cases where the hunger, the ruthless actions of soldiers and landlords, and scenes of death had broken people, and they had slipped into insanity. But not *our* mother! Each morning he studied her, hoping for even a small improvement, but she seemed to be drifting into a deeper hole. No longer saying "no," she said nothing at all, and it was like she was frozen in time, still standing before the blighted field.

The tension inside Liam grew so strong that he could no longer stand it. Somehow he had to find a way to fix her! He decided that maybe she might feel better if he took her to the glen . . . to a beautiful place. Leaning close to her ear, he whispered, "Mamai, I'll get the cart, and we'll go sit by the stream." If she heard him, she gave no sign. He tugged on her and tried to force her to stand, but her stiffness made her heavy and unwieldy. She seemed to be resisting his efforts. Exasperated, he grabbed her boney shoulders and started shaking her roughly as if to awaken her . . . to shock her . . . even to punish her!

Father jumped to his feet and intervened sternly, blocking him with his arm. "Liam, don't! Leave her be! Her melancholy might lift if we are patient."

Ashamed for venting his frustration, Liam bolted out the door and started running, running, until everything became a blur. This "melancholy," this sickness of the mind and heart, was more terrifying to him than even the hunger because he neither understood it nor knew how to combat it. As he stood by the gurgling stream under the glen's lush green canopy of rustling leaves, its comfort eluded him, and even God seemed far away. He trembled as he imagined Mother getting worse, still being alive, yet dead to them. Why could Father not see what was happening? He knew he was giving in to his fears, but he could not help it. He felt like he was spiraling downward.

As he walked home, his head throbbed and heart palpitated. Was he losing a grip on himself? Through the half door, he saw Da feeding his thin, hollow-cheeked Mother a few bites of food. Once inside, he stood watching, daring to hope, but she now clamped her teeth shut and refused more.

Grandmother murmured to Liam, "I fear this state she's in, this utter despair and misery. It's enough to drive her mad."

That night late, a wakeful Liam tossed and turned, but a warm glow from the loft's opening worried him, and he decided to investigate. Quietly creeping down the ladder, he found Grandmother, kneeling on aged knees on the hard flagstone. Her brow was furrowed and her lips moved silently. An open Bible lay on the table with a candle. He stood in the shadows, waiting, not wanting to disturb her, but when she labored to get up, she saw him and smiled.

"Liam lad, I didn't see you."

"Grandmamai, are you all right?"

"Ah . . . sleepless nights are God's workshop. Time to get up, light the candle, and listen."

"Listen?" he asked.

"Yes, it's a conversation, don't ya know. Alone in a quiet place, you read God's words, pray, meditate, and listen." Liam sat on the bench next to her and no longer feeling isolated, he talked about his own despair and shared the burden of Mother's condition. Comforted by her great faith, his fear subsided and he went back to the loft and slept.

The next day, Mother again sat in the wall seat, hunched over and staring like a stone statue. So afraid of what they saw, the family ignored her and tip-toed past like she was invisible.

Caitlin was sitting on a stool, looking at her sadly, when suddenly she began to whimper. "Why won't she talk to me? What happened to her voice? When is she going to be Mamai again?"

Once she blurted it all out, tears rolled down her cheeks.

Hearing this, Brighid began to cry. "I need . . . my Mamai! Is . . . is . . . she sick?" she asked between sobs. The tension and sadness of weeks poured out, and the little girls wailed uncontrollably.

Liam feared this outburst would make Mother worse, but instead, she stirred and looked at them. Then she raised both arms like wings, and the young girls flew to her, one on each side. "Now, now . . . it'll be better," she said softly and patted them.

Dumbfounded, the family sprang to their feet in amazement. At last she had spoken. Da's eyes brimmed with tears. With relief and joy, Aine hugged Sean and then grabbed Liam. Grandfather held up frail, trembling hands and cast eyes upward in thanksgiving.

An incredulous Liam could not take his eyes off her. Was it really true? She said something? No longer limp, she still held her little girls. Yes! She had responded to the children, and maybe soon she would relate to them. Liam thanked God and looked over in time to see Grandmother making the sign of the cross.

Little by little, Mother improved and no longer moved with stiffness. First, she took the heather broom and swept the hearth, and days later she started tending her garden. The next week she scrubbed clothes in the wash tub and even hunted for eggs. Each day she spoke to the family, a word here, a sentence there, but no one pushed. They waited patiently. With each meal, she ate something, and her appearance became less gaunt.

Liam was relieved that his little sisters could once again climb onto Mother's lap and was grateful to God that He had used their tears to pull her back. Yet, he was frightened by how close she had come to the edge and was haunted by the dread that something might trigger another siege of her melancholy. This fear and the threat of starvation were always lurking in his mind.

But as Mother continued to improve, Liam and Sean devoted

every waking moment to the ongoing struggle of finding food. The places where Irish were allowed to put in a fishing pole – places outside the landlords' preserves where a stream flowed through a village or crossed under a bridge – were overfished by hordes of hungry people. Once when Liam speared a frog with his sharpened stick, it became a celebrated addition to the table, and Grandmother boiled it in a soup with a little cabbage and a hand full of barley.

Mother's garden was more important than ever, and they guarded her cabbage, turnips, and onions by day, and hoped they would be overlooked by wanderers at night. One morning when picking turnips, Brighid reached for the leafy part and lifted it too easily.

"Look, Aine! The turnip is gone! Someone left the green top sticking up to fool us!"

The parents and grandparents always gave some of their food to the young, but despite their sacrifice, Liam was used to eating many pounds of potatoes each day and left the table hungry.

Father became irritable when the girls fed milk to Mittens. "She needs to find her own food in the fields." But Mittens was accustomed to handouts and insisted on them with persistent mewing. When Father tossed her outside, the little girls would wait until his back was turned and sneak bits of food out to her. Liam suspected that Da knew their intentions when they left to find her but disliked tearful confrontations with his daughters.

The most distressing time was meeting the beggars at the door. To see people who were far worse off than they were, and yet have nothing to give, made the Reillys feel guilty. Should they divide the little they had? Liam recalled the Irish proverb his family had recited for generations: "*An té a bhíos fial roinneann Dia Leis* / God shares with the person who is generous." Now what would God do?

A skeleton of a man came to the door with two little children and a toddler on his back, whose eyes were half-closed. The children's stick-like legs had no muscle and were so weak they had to lean against the cottage wall for support. Starvation induced a silence and a mind-dulling stupor. The voice was sacrificed as the body conserved strength, and thus, the children had no energy to talk or cry. Their hair had turned pale and had fallen out in large patches, yet additional hair had oddly grown on their cheeks instead. Liam had seen this in other starving children, and it was disturbing.

When Father explained that they had nothing to spare and asked for the beggars' forgiveness, they turned away without complaint and shuffled down the lane. Liam could not recall many times when his family had sent people from the door with empty hands, and he wondered, is it heathens we have become? Earlier he had urged his parents to cut back on the gifts of potatoes, and now when they did, he felt a profound sadness.

Caitlin and Brighid had looked over the half door into the children's eyes and were filled with pity, and now they ran and got some flat boxty from the basket by the hearth.

"Let us run after them and give them these . . . Pleeease, Mamai and Daidi?"

"Yes! Go!" Even though a similar fate could await his own family, Father answered without hesitation, and Liam was glad. Those faces . . . he could not get them out of his mind. He looked over the half-door as his sisters reached the family on the lane and saw the father bow deeply in gratitude.

When Caitlin and Brighid returned, their eyes were bright. "Oh, Daidi! You should have seen their faces! I don't think they had eaten anything in a long time!" Brighid said.

Caitlin put her hand on her tummy. "Starving must hurt!

Now they won't have to cry themselves to sleep because we made it better, didn't we!" The girls had done what everyone in the family wanted to do: they had eased someone's suffering and in so doing, they had found some peace for themselves.

The next morning his sisters wanted to hunt for nettles in the grave yard, mushrooms in the glen, and berries and crab apples along the roadsides. Liam decided to go along and took his long stick, sharpened to a spear, in case he saw a rabbit. His sisters carried their baskets in hope of good luck, but desperate scavengers had been thorough and had picked the countryside bare. Discouraged, they turned toward home, and as they rounded a curve where the ground inclined down to a gurgling brook, Caitlin searched for a rabbit among the weeds. A small animal scurried past her as she approached the stream.

"Ugh! Was that a rat?" Another ran through the grass. Then Caitlin started to bawl, and Brighid screamed, staring ahead in shock.

"Oh, dear God!" Aine covered her mouth. Alarmed, Liam followed their eyes, and sprawled by the brook with flies swarming over them was the family they had so recently fed! Their mouths were open, and their eyes stared without seeing. Arms as thin as broom sticks lay outstretched in the grass, looking frailer in death than life. Their twisted bodies spoke of agony. The English vicar's words to Maureen McGuiness rushed back to Liam: "Eat slowly. Only a little at a time!" Of course! The Reilly's gift of food had killed them!

Liam put his arms around his sisters and drew them away. "Don't look! Let's go. I'll come back to bury them."

All the way home, the girls wept. "Did we kill them? Did we?"

"Maybe we didn't give them enough!" Caitlin cried. Nothing

Liam said could comfort them, and he wondered what scars these memories would leave on his sisters. The family rushed out of the cottage when they heard the girls' crying.

"What happened?" Da demanded.

Liam explained. "They must have been ravenous and had no food for days. When we gave them the boxty, they must have eaten it too fast, and their bodies could not accept it. If only I had remembered and warned the poor father about the danger. I feel so bad about this." His shoulders slumped.

Grandda put his hand on Liam's back. "Don't blame yourself. The troubles in Ireland did not start with you."

With his brother and father, Liam returned to bury the remains. Rats were scurrying over the bodies, and they shouted and swung at the varmints with their spades. While Liam stood guard, Da and Sean dug a large grave where they gently laid the father first and then his children beside him. As the last shovel full of dirt fell, Liam remembered Father Henry in Castlebar and how he had feared his destitute flock would meet such a death – anonymous, alone, without the last rites. Perhaps these were from his parish. Liam fashioned a cross out of twigs and put it over them for a temporary marker. After the Reillys prayed over the grave, they started home.

Father sighed. "'Tis no way for human beings to die . . . in a ditch with rats . . . no family to mourn them nor clergy to bless them."

Sean's face flushed. "Are these the 'excess people' the British say they want to be rid of? This man and his children, Maureen McGuinness and her children, and how many more?" They walked in silence with thoughts they stifled to preserve their sanity.

Three afternoons later, Lord Sligo's agents rode into the yard and demanded to see Father. He emerged from the cottage, smiling and nodding like the agents were welcome guests. "Top of the morning to you, Mr. Wright, and may things go well for you!"

The agents ignored his greeting and conferred with each other as they sauntered around the yard. Liam resented both their rudeness and his Father's meekness. Did Da really need to act that way? With the potatoes rotted, they were making the rounds early to put the landlord's X on the grain, lest tenants be tempted to eat it, rather than save it for rent. Because their harvest had been unusually large, the Reillys had already hidden a small amount of oats and barley for their own use, and luckily it was stored in the house and out of sight.

The agents made notes in a small book as to the size of this summer's crop which would be due on November 2nd – the day called Gale Day when rent was paid all over Ireland. They also noted the little piglets which were usually offered as rent six months later on Gale Day, May 2nd. By then, they would normally be larger and fatter, but Liam realized that without potato scraps which usually fed the piglets, they would not be able to survive that long, much less fatten. To make certain the tenants did not sell them or the sheep for their own profit, the agents burned the landlord's X on their rump, and as the heated brand was applied, the piglets squealed in pain and the lambs bawled.

In broken Irish the agents stated their demands. "Mr. Reilly . . . a good harvest. November 2nd. Minus seed for next crop. Understand?"

Hanging his head submissively, Father nodded, and it was obvious he would do *anything* to avoid having his family thrown on the road, if he could. Liam had heard Grandda say many times: "All power is in the hands of the landlord and his agent."

That night by candlelight, Aine, Father, and Liam worked around the table on the words that Liam would say to Lord Sligo. Aine dipped a sharpened goose quill in blackberry juice and with a scrap of Lawrence's wrapping paper before her, she waited.

Father hunched over the table. "We must appeal to his compassion and say nothing that would sound like a demand."

Liam frowned. "I think we should be more direct and ask for rent reduction. Otherwise, he may miss the point of it all."

Father's eyes widened. "Oh no! We can't risk making him angry."

Liam argued. "If we ask, he can always refuse! To beg respectfully should not offend him."

Father's eyes widened. "Liam! I know more about landlords than you! The law gives them unlimited power over us, and you must trust my judgment."

But Liam could not let it go. "Sligo might ignore a general plea for mercy! It has to be clear. *Rent reduction* is the only thing that will help us. Let's act like men and stand up!"

Father's face flushed. "Enough! No more arguments! Are you saying I'm not a man!" He slammed his fist on the table, shoved the stool away, and headed for his bed in the side room.

Aine glared at Liam. "Why are you so certain you're right? A bold request might enrage Lord Sligo, and he could imprison you and Da as the leaders! Sligo is smart enough to realize that reducing the rent is the way to help us, without your having to point it out. I agree with Da." Liam was still fuming, but since Aine was better with the language, they wrote the plea in general terms, as she decided. Liam practiced it aloud with her until he memorized it with clear pronunciation and would review it many times in the week ahead.

The cow's milk was vital as never before, and Sean and Liam decided to take her to graze further up the hills where there was more grass. Halfway up, dark clouds started to tumble and twist overhead, and thunder rumbled in the distance. Not wanting to risk being caught in a storm with the precious cow, they turned back.

At first, heavy drops pricked Liam's cheeks and then the rain came in torrents – endless, magnificent, and almost frightening in its power. Engulfed in the downpour, Liam stood for a moment in awe at what nature had unleashed. Crouching and squinting to see through the dense curtain of water, he pulled the rope and led the reluctant cow forward until the cottage finally came into view. When Sean opened the shed's door to herd the cow inside, several wet hens scurried in after her with grateful clucking.

Soaked to the skin, the brothers sloshed through the yard. They saw Father Mullen's donkey next to the door tied to a rose bush whose flowers drooped with the water's weight. Sheets of rain poured off the thatch in a waterfall that dug into the earth. Inside, Liam and Sean hung their jackets on pegs in the wall, pulled up stools, and shivering in their wet clothes, they joined the semicircle around the hearth.

Grandda, nestled in his usual niche beside the arched fireplace, motioned to his grandsons. "Here, get in closer and dry off." Liam felt chilled by cold water dripping down his neck from his hair, and he scooted his stool forward.

Da sat in the opposite niche, stuffing his pipe, and a solemn Father Mullen perched on a stool with his hands raised to the blaze. His blue eyes had no twinkle and his ever present smile had faded into an uncommon look of worry.

He pushed his damp hair over to one side. "God help the poor souls, driven out by their landlords, who wander this day . . . hungry and homeless . . . in this weather . . . and with little children besides."

"Aye." They each answered with the same sad eyes.

"We should never complain," Grandda murmured.

"There's terrible news from England, I'm afraid," Father Mullen said. "On August 17 the Prime Minister, Lord John Russell, addressed the House of Commons. He admitted that the potato crop in Ireland was totally ruined." The priest's voice became exasperated. "But the most troubling thing is that it did not seem to matter! He announced there would be no food imports into Ireland this year and no curtailment of food going out! If public works jobs are started, they will be financed by Irish tenants and landlords. If the British Treasury decides to advance any money for these works, they'll be loans only, paid back with interest. Our Archbishop John Hale wrote a letter to Russell and said, 'If you aren't going to import food, you might as well issue an edict that all Ireland is to starve!'"

Da's face paled in shock, and he leaned forward. "Then the British government is going to do *nothing* to help us?"

The Priest nodded. "That's correct."

Da fell back against the wall, his mouth open. "Oh God! What are we to do! The Archbishop is right! By withholding aid, they condemn us to die! After last year, they *have* to know that! So why? Why?" There was a long and poignant pause as the men stared into the glowing fire.

Da clinched his jaw around his pipe and drew in. "Lord Russell is ignoring the many petitions we Irish have sent. So the only hope, then, is if the landlords reduce the rent."

Father Mullen shifted on his stool. "Ah, Seamus . . . now you're speakin' of what brought me here this wet day. I've heard the rumor of your plans, and is it out of your mind, you are? Do you know the danger you'll be bringing on yourself and your followers?"

"But we . . ." Da started to explain, but the priest cut him off.

"Listen to me! Just three days ago, a group of 300 starving men of Longford in Roscommon decided to walk to Mote Park, the seat of Lord Crofton. They just wanted to talk to him and beg his aid, but the British authorities sent two groups of dragoons brandishing weapons at a gallop through the town to force them out. They were treated roughly, like criminals, and never allowed to talk to Lord

Crofton. 'Tis a wonder they weren't arrested and sent to prison. Then where would their families be? All alone!"

Da's face sagged, and Liam could read his thoughts. Was he leading these men, who trusted his leadership, into a storm of British soldiers with weapons?

Finally Da spoke. "I appreciate your coming to warn me. You're speakin' the truth, I'm sure, but we *have* to try. It's our only hope, don't ya see?" Then he added gravely, "Pray for us!"

Father Mullen shook his head. "The soldiers have great hostility towards us, and the dragoons will seize any excuse to attack you . . . the slightest thing. But I will say a special Mass tomorrow as you make your march that God will bless and protect you. I'll see myself out." He stood and patted a sleeping Caitlin on the head and even stroked Mittens, curled up in her lap. From the window, he surveyed the sky. "Looks like the rain has let up so it's a good time to go." He nodded to Aine at the spinning wheel and to Grandmother, carding wool. As he opened the door, he glanced back. "May God go with you."

Liam was shaken by the priest's news. Had he been naive in urging people into action when it was hopeless? Even dangerous? He was glad now that they had written a less demanding speech. August 22 could be an historic day or a tragic one. Soon they would know what they faced . . . tomorrow.

I I

The March For Mercy: August 1846

Before dawn, Da climbed into the loft and shook them. "Sean! Liam! *Duisigh* / Wake up! Warm milk and oat porridge are on the table in your bowls. It's your only meal of the day." Liam's sleep had been fitful, but he was energized by the importance of this journey and threw off his blanket. Father instructed his sons to have smooth faces and wear their best Sunday clothes so Liam wore his frieze jacket and a white shirt.

Grandfather, Grandmother, Aine, and even Mother rose to tell them goodbye, and though they did not say much, their eyes looked worried and their hugs were strong. "*Go raiabh maith agat* / May it go well with you."

It was still dark when relatives and neighbors like Uncle Padraig, Cousin Eamon, Tomas, Barra Fleming, and Nic Flannery gathered in the yard. Joined by others from the Partry hills, the group quickly grew to more than two hundred, and Father had to stand on the stone fence to address them.

"Men, I'm glad to see you are with us. We must show solidarity today, but no defiance. The soldiers don't need an excuse to arrest us so we must be so orderly that it will seem remarkable.

In fact, I'm thinking we should march in rows, military style, four by four, all the way to Westport."

"Aye, Aye! As you say," the men called out.

"Follow me!" Father shouted. Leading off with him were Uncle Padraig, Liam, and Sean, and just behind was Tomas with Cousin Eamon and two neighbors. Everyone knew the goal and they fell into formation: four men side by side abreast and four such rows in each group.

Before sunrise they traversed a mile over the hills, and in the dim light beside the road, other farmers were waiting for them in silence. They nodded in the dark and mumbled greetings.

"Four by four, we march!" someone yelled, and without needing more explanation, they took their places. The chain of messengers had done their job, and these men were those who were convinced that an appeal had to be made and had come to stand with their countrymen – dangerous or not. In the villages and pathways of Mayo, Liam imagined groups of men standing and debating the merits of the march, and as more and more joined, he was heartened by their support.

Now dawn was giving a pink glow to the sky, and at the top of hills, men appeared, saw them, and broke into a run to catch up. When they got to the gravel post road, the crowds at roadside were even larger, and after waving to Father and the leaders as they passed, they took their places at the end. Liam wondered how far they had already walked before reaching this road. Many of the men were thin and boney, their best clothes were rags, and he feared that reduced rents would come too late to save them, but they wanted at least to help others.

He looked back at the long column behind him, and although he did not know their names, all these men were knitted together by history, land, language, faith, and the same desperation.

He recalled how Father had gone to one of the "monster meetings" of the Liberator, Daniel O'Connell, to hear him speak about Irish rights. Father had described how they marched military style to the meeting place and then stood shoulder to shoulder with a million Irishmen to hear the great speaker! It must have felt like this! As the proverb said, "*Ní neart go cur le chéile* / there is not strength without unity."

Amazed, Liam turned to Sean and Father. "I think there are almost 2,000 people in this march already! What do you say?"

"Since we're not even half-way there, I'm sure more will come. Let's hope our numbers will impress and move the Marquis to help us!" Father replied.

"What is he like . . . this Marquis of Sligo, and how did he get all this land in County Mayo?" Sean asked.

"In order to control Ireland and dominate our people, the English King granted titles and gave large land holdings to persons loyal to him. I'm not sure how the head of the Browne family found favor with the King, but by the 1700's he had placed him in a powerful position. Eventually the king made him the Earl of Altamont and sometime around 1800, he raised him to the rank of Marquis. Now his title is The Most Noble Marquis of Sligo, but call him "Your Lordship" when you meet him, Liam. He is one of the largest land owners in County Mayo with more than 114,000 acres!"

"And it's Irish land, he was given!" Sean grumbled. "I'll not use those fancy names, but Liam can, if he wants."

Da gave Sean a stern look. "You have reason to fear him because landlords can punish us whatever way they choose and answer to no one. The current Marquis inherited the title from his father last year and has a seat in the House of Lords. You're born into that group, not elected."

"I don't agree with this royalty stuff either," Liam said. "To my way of thinking, a pompous title doesn't make them better than us Irish or the common Englishman or Scot. The nobles and landlords assume such prideful attitudes and don't respect their tenants or ordinary people. 'Tis good luck that put them where they are, but to avoid his displeasure, I will call him whatever he wants."

"You should announce his title to the crowd," Father suggested. "*If* he grants us an audience, and *if* we can get past the soldiers patrolling the roads."

Father had no sooner said the words than dust could be seen on the horizon and all the men began murmuring. The answer was immediate as cavalry topped the hill, heading straight for them. Liam's heart quickened.

Upon seeing the column of 2,000 men stretched out before them, the dragoons broke into a gallop. An anxious rumble went down the rows of farmers, and Liam could feel the tension in the air. Father held up his hand for all to stop and wait while the cavalry rode up with rifles ready and stern faces. They reined in their mounts with an abruptness that made the horses neigh, jangle the bits in their mouths, and some reared on their hind legs.

"What goes here!" the angry officer shouted in English.

"He's asking our purpose," Liam whispered to Da.

"You'll have to talk to him!" Father said nervously.

The soldier rode closer. "What's going on here?" Liam could not see his face beneath the hat's bill, but the voice sounded familiar. Liam shaded his eyes and squinted up at him.

"Captain Lawrence! It is I . . . Liam Reilly!"

As Lawrence's spirited horse side stepped, he looked down at Liam and ignored the greeting. "Explain yourself. What is the meaning of this? Is this a protest?"

"No, sir. We go to Westport. We harm nothing." Liam then parroted the first two lines from his memorized speech, and it flowed without hesitation. "We ask for an audience with the Most

Noble Marquis of Sligo. We seek a remedy to avoid starvation and beg for help."

Lawrence looked thoughtful. He turned his horse around and, as he rode down the line of marchers staring them in the face, the men bowed their heads submissively and avoided his eyes. Then he galloped back to his troops and the second in command.

"They only want to lay their problems before their landlord, Lord Sligo. I know the leaders, and I'm inclined to let them pass, but we'll follow them all the way to Westport."

"Aye, Aye, sir." The second in command nodded acceptance.

Then Lawrence rode back to Father. "We'll let you pass, but we'll follow you and watch every move. Stay in orderly rows."

"Thank you, sir," Liam answered. The Captain frowned and looked displeased, but he seemed reluctant to drive them back. He ordered half of his men to take up the rear while the other half stayed with him near the front, riding on both sides. He looked straight ahead, avoided the Reillys, and said nothing more. Liam sensed that he did not want to appear friendly to Irish.

As they trod toward Westport, the August sun beamed down and thirst parched their throats, so Liam asked permission to draw water from the well of the torched village. Lawrence agreed, but instructed his cavalry to guard them closely as the groups approached, one row at a time.

A mile later, Liam heard a man moan and looked back in time to see him stumble and slump against the marcher to his left. When relatives carried him to the side of the road and hovered over him, Lawrence spurred his horse to a gallop, yelling, "Stay in line! Stay in line!"

Liam hurried to the man's side, and when he looked into his face, he could see every curve of his skull with prominent teeth barely covered by dry, stretched skin. To prolong life, his body must have consumed the fat of his lips.

Liam squinted up at Lawrence. "He's sick with the hunger and needs to go back."

Lawrence stared at the man and at last comprehended that he was dying. "Tell them to leave!" he ordered in an impatient tone.

Liam translated his words to the worried family. As Liam looked into the man's sunken eyes, he realized death was approaching. The man had given his last ounce of strength to this effort, but the journey's toll had been too much, and his family, haggard and thin, dropped out to carry him home. Despite their weakened state, they had attempted this long walk for the sake of their families and friends. For the sake of Ireland, they had tried. Their wasted bodies would have offered strong testimony to Lord Sligo for mercy and aid.

As the morning progressed, others collapsed and departed in distress. But though some were forced to abandon the cause, still more joined them until at least 6,000 persons were in the column, with more coming. Mile after mile of gravel road passed under their feet as the sun climbed higher on the horizon. Liam was heartened to see their numbers steadily growing as crowds waited on the hillsides to take their places at the end of the column.

At noon the petitioners entered the Irish section, five miles outside of Westport, and their countrymen gathered at the road, astounded by their courage in making such a strong expression of Irish unity. Liam could sense their stifled cheers which could not be voiced in the hearing of the escorting dragoons, and they made him more determined than ever to try to make a difference.

A priest, loping along beside them, asked where they were going, and when they told him Westport House, he pulled a young lad over to join the march. "He'll show the way," the priest said with a smile of support.

On the outskirts of Westport, Lawrence cantered ahead to confer with the commander stationed at the edge of the town. Soldiers on foot looked startled and perplexed at the huge numbers which now looked to be around 10,000 marchers.

Father leaned to Liam's ear. "By now, since Lawrence did not immediately disperse us in the beginning, he will have to justify his action by stressing our peaceful intent. Now he is forced to argue tolerance for us, whether he intended to or not." Lawrence evidently was successful, and the officers motioned them to pass without a confrontation.

"Just as long as they don't interfere or arrest us," Liam said. "These men *have* to see Lord Sligo after their exertion to make it this far."

The bustling town paused, and curious people stood astonished at the roadsides as the visitors shuffled past in what seemed an endless parade. Beggars, shopkeepers, and soldiers gawked and waited for the end of the column which seemed never to come. It stretched on and on for almost two miles – down roads, around corners, and through streets – yet more came and still more.

Liam was humbled by the great response to the call to march and honored to be their voice. He recognized that this march would be remembered for generations, and even if it did not result in the help they hoped for, it was a dignified and noble effort. His face flushed with pride for these humble tenant farmers who were peacefully demonstrating their great need.

The young lad from the Irish sector guided them through town until the estate of Lord Sligo and the spacious grounds of Westport House loomed in the distance. A cobblestone drive led to the mansion, and at one side, a river flowed under arching brick bridges. The grass was mowed close like an emerald carpet with trees planted in straight rows. Liam looked back at the column of men behind him which resembled a peaceful army, though ragged and barefoot. The guards at the gate must have been warned of their coming and did not seem surprised when Liam recited his request.

"We seek an audience with the Most Noble Marquis of Sligo."

The guards waved them through. When the road narrowed, one farmer shouted, "Stay off the grass," and out of respect and fear, they avoided the lawn with great care.

Straight ahead Liam beheld a breathtaking view. Around the side and back of the palace, a man-made lake, contained by high, brick walkways, stood like a mirror. The river which filled the lake flowed through and emptied into Clew Bay just beyond. In the distance, the holy mountain of Croagh Patrick was visible with a hundred islands in a sparkling sea. The setting for the palace was one of grandeur, and Liam was in awe.

The road now curved into the huge, cobblestone courtyard in front of the four-story limestone mansion. Here the men halted and gazed up at the roof where a British flag flapped in the breeze and two stone hawks with wings outspread perched on the corners. Men still filled the approaching roads for as far as the eye could see and stopped wherever they were when the marching ceased. Liam hoped the Marquis would look out a fourth-story window and see the column of marchers lined up for miles behind and be impressed.

The stairs leading to the high porch had stone banisters, flanked by statues. Opening onto the porch were three sets of tall double doors topped with gargoyles. Above the entrance was the family's coat of arms with a greyhound on one side and a stallion on the other. The elaborate facade was intimidating, and he hesitated, his mouth dry and his tongue thick.

In silence everyone waited for him to move until Father finally nudged him. "Liam, go on! Go to the porch!"

Liam patted his shirt for the paper with the printed speech, but it was gone! Taking a deep breath, he resolved to do without it and mounted the steps with slow precision. After he pulled the velvet bell cord, a servant in a satin coat opened one of the center doors.

To his relief, the much practiced words flowed out automatically. "We ask an audience with the Most Noble Marquis of Sligo." The servant, who seemed to be expecting them, nodded and disappeared. The wait seemed long, and through a crack in the door, Liam could see a long entry hall with a curved, vaulted ceiling, heavily carved with designs. A long, shiny floor made of different woods in a pattern led to a marble stairway between two pillars. Glimpsing someone descending the stairs, Liam stepped back.

First came the servant who pulled both of the center double doors open and secured them. Then he bowed deeply to a young man of no more than twenty-five years who stepped outside. His hair was tied back with a satin ribbon, and he was dressed in silk breeches, white hose, and a blue velvet coat decorated in braid with a tall collar. His features were handsome and his expression pleasant.

Remembering his father's instructions, Liam shouted: "The Most Noble Marquis of Sligo."

With that, someone in the crowd yelled "Kneel!" The throng of 10,000, which filled the courtyard and extended on to the roads, went to their knees and remained there. Liam was stunned at the gesture and glanced at the Marquis who also seemed affected. Liam proceeded with the speech he now recalled from memory.

"Your Lordship, we seek a remedy to avoid starvation. We have nothing to eat since the blight of the potatoes. Please have mercy on us and do not let us die. We, your loyal servants and tenants, beg your help."

Sligo stepped forward for his reply. "I deplore the terrible visitation that God has sent to this land. I will instantly go and describe your condition to Her Majesty's government in order to obtain relief and immediate employment for you. As to myself, I will go as far as any landlord in the country to attend to your problems. Although I do not intend to harass you about payment of rents, it is useless to talk on that subject because the time for collecting the rent has not yet arrived." He stepped back, indicating his statement was finished.

Liam nodded. "Thank you, your lordship, and with your permission, may I now repeat your message in Irish?" Lord Sligo motioned for him to proceed and stood waiting while Liam translated to the waiting crowd in a loud voice. Then Liam bowed deeply, wanting to win Sligo's favor.

The Marquis quickly retreated into the mansion, and his servant closed the tall double doors. When Liam heard a bolt lock slide into place, he turned to descend the stairs. Father was coming up to the porch with bright eyes and a spring in his step.

"Liam, did you hear it? The Marquis said he would do as much as any other landlord to help us and doesn't intend to harass us about the rents! Now, I feel hopeful."

"That's true, Da! So if some landlords decide to reduce rent, he promised to do the same."

Father stood on the porch and shouted instructions to the throng. "We must walk briskly. We still face the danger of arrest and will continue four by four." With that, Father led the thousands back to the gatehouse. He lined up with Uncle Padraig and the neighbors, while Liam marched with Sean, Tomas, and another cousin.

As they walked, Liam mulled over their situation. "Sean, yesterday when Father Mullen came to see us, he reported that the government planned to do nothing for Ireland. Yet today, Sligo promised to ask the government for help. Do you think he can persuade the Prime Minister to change his decision?"

Sean's eyes were smoldering and his face flushed. "Sligo just wanted to appease us with cheap talk and shift the responsibility of helping us to the government. He knows we need reduced rents, but he refused to talk about it. Why? Because his greed is greater than his generosity. You saw his mansion, and was it not magnificent? Most of these farmers marching here live in one room huts without windows and little furniture, while Sligo has more than 40,000 tenants paying him. He blamed the starvation on God and his 'terrible visitation,' but it isn't God that takes all the harvest out of Ireland! It's the British army and the landlords!"

"Sean! He *must* reduce the rents. Sligo can't let us all die!" Robbed of the optimism he had savored moments before, Liam's shoulders slumped. Had this great march to petition Lord Sligo been for nothing?

At the edge of the estate was a gothic stone building, and as they got closer, Liam could hear the ghostly groans of hundreds of people, shaking the iron bars of a large double gate and clamoring for admission. "Is that part of the estate?" Liam asked the young guide.

"No, that is the workhouse," he answered. "It's full and can't even take care of those it has already admitted. Since English rules say they may only feed people who are inside, many die on the grounds, and each morning, the staff comes out to collect bodies." Liam was sickened. The workhouses were a British invention, so why wouldn't they support them? It was puzzling.

Not wanting to think, he turned his body over to marching and followed the road through Westport, past the crowds, back to the countryside. More soldiers followed, unsmiling and watchful, but to Liam's disappointment, Lawrence was gone. He knew the captain's circuit regularly took him back and forth from Westport so he guessed that he and his cavalry had already returned to Ballinrobe.

The marchers still had a great distance before them, and with dusk approaching, Liam realized they would be on the road after curfew. The cold eyes of the soldiers convinced him that they would enjoy arresting them, yet, taking thousands into custody at once would tax the jails, and he felt confident that their orders this time were to be lenient. With each mile, the column of men grew shorter as marchers left the road to return to their villages.

When a convoy of food and livestock heading for Westport forced them off the road, a ravenous Liam eyed the eggs and oats with longing and imagined sinking his teeth into the large rounds of cheese.

Sean crossed his arms and his eyes glinted at the many bags of oats. "They would never miss one. If I was quick... maybe after dark."

"Forget it!" Liam was stern. "It's too dangerous! Why do you think they have a hundred soldiers guarding the convoy with cannon and rifles?" Sean shrugged his shoulders and said nothing more.

At a steady pace, Liam's legs moved in rhythm with the group. But like the others, he had not eaten since dawn and was weary. His parched throat burned with thirst and was so dry that he swallowed with difficulty. All he could think about was water, and he hoped he could endure until they reached the well.

At last, the burned village came into view. The soldiers allowed them to drink, one group at a time, and barked orders to move quickly. Liam's legs felt rubbery, and he continued drinking to fill his hollow stomach until a soldier shoved him with his gun barrel. "Out of the way!" he commanded. As Liam rested on the grass and waited for the lines to take turns, he wondered if the families driven out months before were still alive.

Too soon, he heard his father shout, "On your feet! We must push on!" Some men, overcome with weakness, had to be lifted and carried, and Liam himself felt lethargic and stumbled to the road. But when Tomas started to whistle a familiar lilting melody, new energy flowed. Soon other marchers took up the tune, and the music spread like a wave until hundreds were whistling to the same song. Stepping to a lively tune revived Liam's spirits and did the same for others.

He turned to see if Sean was whistling, too. Where was he? Had he gotten a drink at the well and joined a different group? In the approaching dusk, it was more difficult to discern faces. He turned his head and anxiously searched the lines around him, but his brother was not there. Recalling Sean's words upon seeing the bags of oats, "Maybe after dark . . . if I was quick," Liam's muscles tensed. No! How could Sean be that foolish! He dared not tell anyone what he feared. He had to behave normally and hide the panicky feeling inside.

Then the distant crack of rifle shots, several in succession, echoed through the air. The farmers stopped whistling. Suddenly alert, they marched in silence. Liam's apprehension grew and his breathing became shallow. Horses were galloping towards them.

With torches held high, cavalry rode up beside them, and the leader commanded, "Halt!" The men shuffled to a stop and looked straight ahead. An officer on horseback spoke English to soldiers who were guarding the marchers.

"We're hunting for a man who tried to take oats from our convoy. Find a man with a wound. There was blood on the ground, so we know we hit him." The soldiers rode up and down the column, scrutinizing the farmers, and selected some to step out for closer inspection.

One rider jabbed Liam with his rifle. "Jacket! Off!" Liam obeyed. The rider spun him around, but seeing no blood, the horseman, with a jerk of his head, sent him back into the group.

Liam's heart was pounding. Sean must be out there somewhere . . . bleeding! What should he do? He dared not leave the marchers to search for him lest he lead the soldiers to their quarry. One thing he knew: Sean would not hide in the column but would strike out through the fields alone and try to reach home, if he was able. The time the soldiers spent among the marchers delayed a search of the fields and improved Sean's chances of escape.

Finally the disgruntled cavalry allowed them to continue their journey. But the men, weak from not eating, plodded in their weariness and the pace was slow. Now energized, it was all Liam could do to keep from sprinting ahead, but because the escorting soldiers were observing them closely, he had to stay in line and pretend to be calm.

When Tomas glanced around and realized Sean was gone, he looked at Liam and raised his brows, but Liam put his finger to his lips, and Tomas kept silent. Both understood that no one must know who was missing and that darkness was an ally. Not even Father, who marched several rows ahead, was aware that the man for whom they were searching might be his own son, and Liam wanted to keep it that way until they got home. For now, all he could do was march and pray.

It was very dark when Father waved farewell to the remaining several hundred men who were continuing on to Partry and the surrounding hill country. Father walked down the lane to their cottage, still talking about the events of the day, when suddenly he stopped and looked around.

"Where in the name of God is Sean?" His eyes went wild and he grabbed Liam by the shoulders, shaking him, digging in his nails. "Tell me! Tell me!"

Liam blurted out all he knew. "He tried to get oats. I told

him it was too dangerous, but he slipped away. The soldiers were looking for Sean."

Father's eyes bulged, and he gestured wildly. "We must go back! But where? Where can we look for him!" Putting his hands to his head in despair, he cried out, "Oh, saints in heaven! Has this march cost me a son?"

I 2
Confounded

The cottage door opened, and there on the threshold, silhouetted against the gold light of the fireplace, stood Mother. "Seamus! Come! Come!" Hearing the urgency in her voice and seeing her flailing arms motioning to them, they ran to the cottage and stumbled past her. There on the oak table lay Sean, motionless with eyes closed, shirt off, and his shoulder bound in blood-soaked bandages. The fireplace shed a soft light on him and cast shadows on the rest of the family, standing solemn and silent.

Liam was shaken. His brother, white as death, was lying there like a body at a wake. "Is he . . . all right?" Liam asked haltingly, looking over the wound. Judging from the blood oozing through the bandages, the bullet had made a jagged path across his shoulder and chest.

Mother put her hand on Sean's forehead to check for fever. "The bullet grazed his shoulder and traveled across his flesh, but luckily, it did not lodge there and left his body. He lost a lot of blood, but I think he'll recover. Running home, he crossed fields and fences to avoid the roads. He lost a lot of blood and is exhausted."

Father examined the bandage. "You're a good nurse, Erin. Thank God he made it home." Father collapsed into his niche beside the fireplace and bellowed frustration. "What was he thinking? To protect those convoys, the British shoot to kill."

Stirred awake by father's scolding, Sean's eyes fluttered open. "Sorry, Da. Not even a bag of oats for my troubles! When the bullet hit me, I lost my nerve . . . dropped the bag and ran . . . too many guns."

Mother added another layer of cloth to his bandage as blood spread wider and saturated the dressing. "He needs sleep. The rest of you take boxty from the basket and go to bed. Morning will come soon enough."

Liam needed no urging. His own eyelids were heavy and his fatigue so great that his muscles ached as he climbed the loft's ladder, but before he went over the top, he looked back at her. Mother seemed stronger, somehow, and even with this crisis, she was not overwhelmed by the melancholy. Maybe it was because she saw a way to help. He could only guess.

The next morning Liam was the last to awaken, and had Caitlin and Brighid not played with Mittens so noisily, he might have stayed in the loft till noon. Sean spent the night on the oak table under Mother's watchful eye and now was sitting on the bench as she pampered him with a heaping bowl of the last new potatoes that remained. Mother had washed his wound again, changed the dressing, and put bloody cloths on the bench beside him in a pile.

The morning peace was broken by a loud pounding at the door. Tension filled the room and the family froze in place, wide-eyed and wary, knowing they could only open the door to the most trusted.

"Who's there?" Father asked anxiously.

"It's me!" Father recognized the voice, and when he opened the door, Tomas burst into the room. "They're coming this way! Soldiers and police! Just left our house and now they're at Eamon's

... searching for a wounded lad. Hide him quick!"

Father grabbed the bloody rags and shoved them under Sean's arm. "To the loft! Cover up in blankets and clothes!" Sean began a slow, painful climb, hoisting himself up the ladder, using only one arm and carrying bloody rags under the other.

The family frantically scurried about, trying to disguise telltale signs. Spotting a smudge of blood under the bench and another on the table, Aine grabbed Sean's bowl of buttered potatoes and smashed them into the stains. Liam, worried that there might be some they'd missed, scrutinized the floor from door to table.

Sean was still only half way up the ladder when Liam growled, "Sean! Hurry! Move along!

Grandmother was pale and could not stop trembling. In the wall seat by the fire, Grandfather pulled out his rosary and started to pray. Hearing horses trot into the yard, Liam peered through the small window and saw soldiers and police dismounting. "They're here!" With his heart pounding in his head and his muscles tight, he knew he could never let them take Sean without a fight. At last he was at the top of the ladder and crawling onto the loft's floor.

A fist pounded on the door, and a gruff voice demanded, "Open in the name of Her Majesty, the Queen!" Without waiting, a policeman kicked it ajar, and the men clomped in with heavy boots and jangling spurs.

Trying to be nonchalant, Father nodded and smiled. "Top of the morning to you."

Mother curtseyed in a manner aimed to placate, and her daughters copied her. The police ignored their pleasantries and treated all Irish with disdain. Liam hated this deference to soldiers, but now the curtsey served a purpose.

The lieutenant, his eyes darting about the room, remained focused on the task. "Search the house," he commanded in English.

A stout policeman with a heavy mustache nodded. "Aye, aye, sir, right away." With that, he looked behind the cushion in the wall seat and, before he threw it on the floor, ripped it open with his knife, causing feathers and down to float and drift in the air. Liam grimaced at the obvious harassment and took note of the man's Ulster accent. The English often recruited Ulster Protestants as constables because they were imbued with the same prejudice against Irish Catholics and often spoke both languages: English and Irish.

The policeman lifted the picture of the Holy Family off the wall and tossed it on the table with disgust. "Are all you Papists *here* in the house? Is anyone missing?"

Liam felt a slow burn. "We're all here."

The constable, serving as an interpreter, thumbed through paper on which he had made notes and glanced at Father over his spectacles. "It says here you have three sons."

Father gave him a blank stare and hurried to answer what was easy. "Well, one son named Niall sailed to Americay on a ship leaving Westport."

"Give me the name of the ship and the date of sailing," he demanded.

"The ship was *The Countess* from the Anchor Line, bound for New York the last week of June."

The details of Father's reply seemed to satisfy him, but he pressed on. "And you have two more? Where are they?"

"Well . . . here is my son Liam who is eighteen years old, and I'm hoping he'll be stayin' in Ireland so he can . . ."

The policemen, impatient with Father's slow replies, interrupted and whirled around. "We haven't got all day here! Get on with it!" Then he spied Tomas, sitting on a stool with his back to him and looking into the fire. "And that's the third one? All you men remove your shirts!" They lost no time complying. As Tomas pulled off his shirt, he caused his hair to fall over his face and the soldiers, looking for any sign of a wound, did not notice they had seen him earlier at his own cottage.

Father yanked off his shirt and, eager to distract them, he pulled away the curtain that separated the second room. "Here's a side room you can search where my parents and my wife and I sleep." With that, two soldiers swarmed in and examined clothing on hooks before tossing it onto the floor. "There is a shed in the back also," Father volunteered, "but what are you seeking?"

The Ulster policeman answered in Irish. "One of you marchers tried to steal a bag of grain from a convoy and got shot in the process, but we'll find him before we're done. We'll pay you well if you have any helpful information on suspects."

Since the lieutenant did not understand Irish, he was getting restless with so much Irish conversation. "What about the loft?" he asked in English to a soldier with a sword. The soldier went to the ladder and put a foot on a rung.

Liam's heart stopped. He had to think fast and speak in English. "My sister . . . there with fever. You say typhus . . . typhus . . . got it bad."

The soldier paused and stepped back down. "Did he say typhus?"

The lieutenant then turned to the plump policemen. "You! Get up there and take a look!"

The constable raised his eyebrows with obvious reluctance. "You mean me?"

"Yes, you! Get on with it!"

The ladder creaked with his heavy weight, as he made one step and then another as slowly as possible without stopping. Upon finally reaching the top of the ladder, he peeked over the loft's floor. "I see her. She's there, as he says." He backed down quickly, before the lieutenant objected to such a quick glance. Liam breathed easier, grateful that the man from Ulster was a coward and willing to lie to avoid any contact with the dreaded and highly contagious typhus.

Leaving disorder behind, the soldiers and police strode out the door without ceremony. The Reillys, weak in the knees from the close call, stared out the window until the gallop of the horses faded away.

Tomas heaved a sigh. "I was afraid they'd recognize me from the search of my own house and think I tipped you off! 'Tis why I kept staring into the fire and shook my forelock over my face. 'Twas quick thinking, Liam, to suggest typhus was in the cottage."

Liam's brow furrowed. "And 'twas lucky you were here to be that missing son! I think an informer may have named Sean as a suspect because he's young and bold. In these times, the offer of money would tempt a saint, but who do you think might take it?"

Grandda was grim. "Death to all informers who betray their own for silver, like Judas! They are the enemy, as sure as the English." In condoning retaliation, Grandfather no longer sounded like the follower of the nonviolent O'Connell.

Sean's face peered over the edge of the loft. "Everyone was drinking at the well, and I'm sure no one saw me slip off."

Father looked up at him. "You must stay out of sight until you're no longer bandaged, and never again go without your shirt. Your wound and later the scar are a brand they can use against you."

Liam hung the picture of the Holy Family back on the wall. "I can see now how the ribbon societies and other secret groups feel justified in acting against suspected informers. If someone named Sean, I'd see to it that they regretted it."

Mother swept the down and feathers into a heap for saving. "To rip the cushions was mean. He had no respect for us."

That afternoon Aine was studying the London *Times* which Captain Lawrence had given her a month before, and as she read, her face flushed. "This man's opinion is an outrage! How can he say such things!"

Grandmother paused in her mending, and Father sat up straight. "What is it they say?"

"An English lord blames the famine on the laziness of our people. Yet, the writer admits that the export of produce from Ireland to England has never been greater than now!" Aine looked up, exasperated. "Who does this English lord think worked to grow all that food, if we are so lazy? He does admit that the landlords in Ireland are getting rich from these exports and should, in turn, do more for their tenants. – Now *that* we agree with, don't we!

"Then the writer says that since the potatoes are gone, we Irish should eat *meat* now instead." Aine lowered the paper and frowned. "Now I ask you, where would we be getting *meat*? Tell me that! He talks like we *preferred* to eat only potatoes. Only at special and rare times could we ever eat meat."

"He's talking nonsense!" Father bellowed. ". . . just like the Duke of Norfolk when he said that the hungry here should eat curry powder from India mixed with water!"

Aine continued reading out loud: "Listen to this. He says the famines of today are unlike the ones of olden times when there was *no* food. Recent experience in India has shown that millions of people can starve even in the sight of full granaries. Their population is perishing even while ships laden with the produce of their fields are leaving their shores.

"Dear Lord!" Aine laid the paper in her lap. "Did you hear that? The British must be doing the same thing in India as they do here – creating famine by taking out food to England!"

Liam stared, incredulous. "Causing starvation in India, too?"

"Yes, and he goes on to say: 'The Irish should submit to their fate as God's will and not protest to the government!'"

Grandda jumped to his feet and shook his fist. "They want us to go like sheep to the slaughter, and most of the time, we are too weak to do otherwise! Old Martin of Ballinglass was right all along! For years O'Connell and our priests have preached against violence and turned us into lambs."

Liam began pacing the floor. "Before the blight, we existed by eating mainly potatoes, but the government knows they are gone now! So why won't it do more to help us? Surely they don't want us to *die*!"

"Just be patient," Father urged. "As time passes, the government and the landlords will finally realize the extent of this crisis, but until they do, we just have to hang on."

Despite their efforts, the Reillys had less food with each passing week. They guarded Mother's precious garden by day and covered it with straw at night. Sean had to stay home and out of sight until his wound healed, but Aine and Liam decided to walk to the coast for more limpets and sea weed. With Liam's sharpened stick, a fishing line, and a pail, they started off.

Along the roads, they saw the suffering up close. Liam thought the bodies lying motionless in the grass with mouths stained green were dead, but now and then, they moaned. Everywhere evicted beggars tried to cover ditches with brush and burrow into the side of embankments, but frequent rain made the holes soggy and unfit. Mothers and ragged children rooted through fields of stubble for diseased potatoes and dandelion roots, and in desperation they ate whatever they found and soon convulsed with violent vomiting.

One child with large, blue eyes and chalky, white skin, had the strength to chase after them. "Please, beautiful lady," he crooned to Aine. "Spare a crust for my little brothers and me. God will bless you with children and every joy of life. Please ... help us."

Aine wore Mamai's shawl and had hidden boxty cakes in its

folds for them to eat later, but she felt guilty for not giving them to this child and was weakening.

"Keep them out of sight!" Liam commanded. "I know it's hard, but stare the other way." Aine seemed torn, but obeyed.

From a side lane came a funeral procession which in normal times would have had at least a hundred people in attendance, but now it had only twelve. Frequent funerals had dulled the grief of mourners, and they walked like specters in a dream-like trance, barely alive and devoid of emotion. Their stark features and thin limbs showed they were gradually succumbing to starvation. Liam had had a nightmare in which the whole Irish nation in an endless procession was marching into a burial pit to be swallowed up. He shuddered at the resemblance of these stoic mourners to the ghosts in his dream.

People had no strength to dig new graves, nor was there enough land. Burial pits were left open for several days as bodies were added, with a sprinkling of sawdust or quick lime. The scarcity of lumber and the demand for coffins caused people to make a hinged door in the bottom so that coffins could be used again and again.

But this time the mourners were carrying a small old trunk that must contain a child. A young woman with tears sliding down her cheeks and her arms wrapped around the trunk moaned as she limped to the churchyard where a small hole was open. Liam was relieved that the young mother was spared the horror of casting her baby into a pit, and though the infant might be dressed in straw, he had his own trunk. As they passed, Aine and Liam crossed themselves and prayed for the child's mother who now was calling to God and the saints, inconsolable.

By mid-morning, they came to the ruins of Ballinglass. As Liam wandered down the same lanes he had strolled with Colleen, he felt an intense yearning. An eerie stillness now reigned over this once lively community, and the only sound was wind rustling through pasture. Grass had sprouted in the footpaths, and near a stone threshold someone's yellow rose bush bloomed unappreciated. He could clearly see the foundations and sooty hearth sites that once teamed with life, but now, no dogs barked or cows lowed . . . no fiddles, no laughter, no arguments, no prayers, no children at play, no calls of greeting. Like so many rural places once full of hardy people, Ballinglass was becoming an empty field of weeds. Sheep, scattered about the pasture, quietly munched grass, and for these, the people had been sacrificed. With heads low and hearts heavy, Aine and Liam walked on and pondered the fate of all the families who once called this place "home." Ireland was falling silent.

When they reached the ocean, alive with energy, Liam welcomed its roar. Water surged forward and scurried up the sandy incline, complaining loudly as it pushed to shore, but whispered as it retreated, pulling sand and small shells back into the infinite well which filled the horizon. Liam tried to drown his heartache and lose himself in the sea's hypnotic repetition as he caressed the sand with his bare feet. Would he carry this longing his whole life?

Aine wasted no time beginning the search for dillisk and waded to her hips in the cold current, but soon she stood up, perplexed. "There's none here so I'll try further down shore."

Liam hunted between rocks and boulders but found only empty shells littering the sand. Then he had a sinking realization. Of course. The hungry had swarmed to the coast and already taken everything edible.

Aine's basket held only a trace of seaweed, but she was stubborn and kept trying.

Liam called to her. "I'm afraid we're too late."

"No limpets either?" she asked.

Liam heard anxiety in her voice and was loath to answer,

but finally managed a reply.

"None."

"We have to catch a fish then. We can't go home empty-handed."

A seal, protected from hunters by tricky currents, jagged boulders, and deep water, slid onto a sandbar fifty feet away, and his shiny coat glistened in the sun. Liam wondered if seals ever came in closer . . . what a dinner he would make! The fragile, lightweight boats of fishermen were abandoned on the rocks, and wondering why, he waded back to see if they had oars. There must be schools of fish out there which fed the seal, and with a boat, he could go out beyond the sand bar and find fish.

A stooped figure limped toward them on the beach with shoulder bones protruding from his torn shirt and sagging skin showing the effects of years in the sun. Seeing Liam by the boat, he read his mind. "It takes a boat to get past the sand bars and skill with the oars to avoid the rocks. You're not a fisherman's son, are you?"

"No, but I'd like to try it."

"Don't. In the rough seas of our coast, it takes several strong men to control lightweight boats like these. The currachs here are abandoned because the owners are too weak to handle them and get them past the breakers. The hunger . . . don't ya know. We used to catch herring about ten miles out with nets, but people have sold their nets for maize."

Liam nodded. "No fish in closer?"

"Not many . . . especially now with people scouring the shore everyday."

Aine had put a bit of seaweed on the hook and waded out to her shoulders, hoping for a bite. Liam worried about undertow and was about to call her back when she started to holler. "Help me!

I've got something!"

Liam struggled through the current. "Lean back! I'm coming!"

Aine held the pole with an iron grip but was afraid to move, so Liam grabbed her around the waist to pull her in, fish and all, rather than risk taking the wet pole and losing it. Trying to break free, the fish jumped out of a wave and flipped in the shallows. Elated to carry the fish home, they gleefully scooped seawater into Liam's pail.

"Well done, Aine! About twelve or thirteen inches long, I'd say."

The fisherman tottered over. "It's a rare day and it's lucky, you are!" His hollow cheeks and taunt skin made his head look like a skull on a pole. As he wandered away down the strand, he waved goodbye.

Liam decided to avoid the painful memories of Ballinglass and take a longer route home. On the more traveled road, they rejoined the suffering humanity which flowed toward towns to beg, to pawn, and to seek work where there was none. By necessity, Ireland had always been a land of walking feet, but now in this crisis of evictions and blight, they wandered the roads as never before. A passerby looked hungrily at the fish they carried in the pail but smiled at their good fortune without envy.

Coaches with gold designs on their doors clattered past, covering them in dust. Through the windows, Liam glimpsed gentry dressed in satin with fancy hats decorated with feathers. A young boy on the road darted toward a coach with hands outstretched to beg a coin, but when the occupants ignored him, he leaped onto the running board. The driver cracked his whip on the child's back and threw him to the ground, whimpering.

"Out of our way!" the coachman yelled. "Gentlemen and

ladies are passing!" Liam heard shrill laughter as the men amused the female passengers. When a person in the second coach tossed a pear core out the window, people scrambled to find it in the grass.

The coaches crossed a bridge and carried the passengers through the gatehouse to a gray stone castle. Liam heard the distant strains of music as an orchestra on the lawn played a welcome for the guests. Its gardens were barely visible through the gate, but Liam knew the high stone walls hid an opulence he could barely imagine and hid the noble gentry from the eyes of common people.

"Their way of life goes on unchanged," he muttered.

Aine shook her head. "I just can't understand it . . . not having pity. They probably discard enough food after their banquets to feed many of us." She looked down into the pail at the one fish. "The walk to the coast was too exhausting for only this."

Liam gripped his spear. "I need to get a rabbit, and there are plenty in the hunting preserves. I wonder if rabbits know when they cross the boundary. If not, an alert lad could get one before the creature ducked back in." With that idea in mind, Liam walked the road, watching along the fence with his spear ready.

Miles later in late afternoon they heard a large party of aristocrats coming toward them in long flat wagons pulled by horses. Laughter and jovial chatter were carried on the wind, and some sang to a strumming mandolin. Many hares and grouse dangled from high poles on the wagons and swung back and forth with the motion of the car. The hungry people at roadside stood transfixed, staring at the game.

Liam's attention was caught by a young man in handsome hunting clothes who was scratching the ears of his greyhound affectionately. When the dog sniffed at a grouse just out of reach, a companion of the man jerked the grouse off the pole and tossed it to the dog who devoured it with gusto.

The young aristocrat laughed and stood up. "Look how hungry he is! The glutton! My keeper fed him well this morning." Without a glance, he and the others in the hunting party ignored the gaunt faces with gaping mouths as they passed.

Liam loathed the callousness of the noblemen. "Aine, see how they lavish food on their dogs? The truth is, the landlords care more about their animals than their tenants. Niall said the British government supplies ten pounds of oats every day for each horse quartered in Ireland with the army."

Aine became thoughtful. "Brother, you've given me an idea."

"What is it?"

"The horses don't need that much! What if I asked Captain Lawrence to get a bag of oats for us? He's a cavalry officer and would have ways to take some out."

Liam pondered the suggestion. He distrusted Lawrence, but should he? After all, he gave Aine the poetry book and helped them on the march to Westport. If he were to give us a bag of oats, it would be worth letting go of pride.

"It's worth a try, Aine."

"I want you to go with me . . . tomorrow."

The thought of oats cheered Liam. Bringing back only one small fish was discouraging and once they arrived home, they explained the futility of their walk to the coast and apologized. However, Mother praised them and stretched it by making a soup, putting their fish with a little onion, turnips, and cabbage in boiling water.

Da was in high spirits and showed them with a copy of the *Mayo Constitution* to which he had subscribed last spring. "Some landlords are starting to help us tenants! It says here that the Duke of Devonshire is giving rent reductions of 33 to 50 percent! I hope this will inspire Lord Sligo to do the same, as he promised he would. With nearly 40,000 tenants, Sligo could spare us enough to live. Charles Cromie of Annefield House has told his agents to grind oats and give them to his farmers. Sir George Staunton of Clydagh, County Galway, is absentee and yet he has forgiven the next rents." Father seemed so hopeful that Liam did not have the heart to tell him what he had seen of aristocrats this day. These generous landlords made welcome news, but he decided they were the exception.

The next morning, he and Aine left early, took the pole as if they were going fishing, but walked instead to Ballinrobe where Lawrence and the cavalry were garrisoned. As they approached the town, they met a hunched old woman with a cane and asked her the location of the soldiers' barracks. She peeked out of the shawl drawn over her head and stared at them with a look that questioned their sanity.

"*Go Saora Dia sinn.* / Good Lord, deliver us! What do you want with soldiers!" She frowned. "Tell them nothing and keep your distance!"

Feeling upbeat, Aine smiled. "Don't worry about us. We have nothing to tell but only wish to ask a favor."

But the old one continued her cautions. "Soldiers don't give favors to Irish. They may *take* a favor, but never give one. Surely you have not forgotten that old Irish proverb: 'Beware of the horns of a bull, the heels of a horse, and the smile of an Englishman.' We Irish have had centuries to learn that!" Finally, with great reluctance, she gave the requested directions. "You'll find the barracks down this road. Take a turn to the left just outside of town and you'll see some fine and costly buildings. The only thing the British build in Ireland is quarters for more soldiers!" She wagged her head in disgust as she hobbled away.

They found the garrison as directed. A special road led to

a group of three-story brick buildings inside a gate and surrounded by a stone wall. Stables were in the rear, and the harsh sound of a blacksmith's anvil clashed with an iron horseshoe. Additional quarters were being built, and hammering added to the noise.

Aine stopped beside the wide iron gate that opened into the cobblestone courtyard. "I think it's best that I go alone so you wait here, Liam." Not wanting to hear her beg, he willingly agreed. Sitting on the grass, he watched from the shadows as she strolled across the yard. Horse hooves clopped on the cobblestone as cavalry returned from patrols. The smells of harness, smoke, dust, and horse dung mixed in his nostrils.

Liam felt uneasy as he noticed soldiers casting admiring glances at Aine, especially with the old woman's warnings fresh in his head: soldiers only *take* favors. Three soldiers approached and surrounded her, laughing, flirting, punching each other's shoulders, and reaching for her shawl, her skirt. Aine twisted away and seemed persistent in her request. Liam wanted to confront them but held himself back. After some bantering, the men finally disappeared into the barracks while Aine waited outside and peered up at the large structures nervously. She has courage, he realized, as more soldiers came up to tease.

Why was Lawrence not coming? The wait was long, and Liam worried that he might be away on patrol to Westport and their tiring walk would be for nothing. Then the door opened, and Lawrence stepped out. At the sight of Aine, his face brightened. When he called to her, the soldiers of lesser rank quickly backed away.

He put his arm around her and led her to an alley between buildings where there was shade and some privacy. Leaning close, he stroked her blond hair as she talked and looked down into her eyes with a boldness that had always annoyed Liam. When Aine finished talking, he took her hand in his and kissed

her open palm. Liam could see that Lawrence was telling her
something, as he pushed her hair back and tried to put his mouth
to her neck.

Aine stepped away, jerked her hand from his, and bolted
from Lawrence. Without pausing, she ran past her waiting brother
and back down the road.

Liam chased after her. "Aine, wait! What happened?" He
caught up with her. "Is he going to get the oats?" Now having
slowed to a brisk walk, she was crying so hard that her breath came
in jarring gasps, but in reply she shook her head no.

Liam was perplexed but said nothing more. He matched
her fast pace till they were well past Ballinrobe. After several miles
her emotions ebbed, but tears still flowed down her cheeks in little
rivers. Liam decided to wait until she was ready to talk and not
push. They walked without speaking for several miles, and then
slowly it came tumbling out, bit by bit.

"Liam . . . friends will help you without asking anything . . .
in return. I thought Captain Lawrence was kind and our friend, but
he's selfish . . . and . . . and . . . ." She started to weep again.

Liam put his arm around her. "What did he say? What did
he want?"

"I . . . I . . . told him how much our family needed food. I
thought he would just want t-t-to help." She bit her lip. Again,
tears came rushing, and she could say no more. Liam did not press
her because he now realized that his earlier suspicions about the
captain evidently had been correct.

Liam seethed inside, and his hatred for Lawrence was
intense. How could he insult and humiliate her! Did he think
he could treat her this way because she was Irish? Even though
Lawrence had once conceded that Aine was very intelligent, Liam
now recalled how he had referred to her as one of "the peasant

class." Could he not see that she deserved his respect! Liam hated the assumed superiority and pompous airs of the English.

At home, Aine's eyes told Mother of her distress. She refused to eat the bits of cabbage, climbed to the loft, and collapsed on her mat when it was still light. Liam hoped the rest would heal her broken spirit.

When he went to the yard for fresh air, Mother followed. "Aine is very sad so tell me what happened today." Liam confessed their plan and how Lawrence had reacted.

She lowered her head. "I'm sorry our desperation drove her to ask him. And Captain Lawrence! We welcomed him as our guest and shared our food! I'm surprised he forgot our hospitality."

Liam gritted his teeth. "Aine's a gentle creature . . . full of kindness to everyone and suspects no evil in others. I should never have let her go. I distrusted him from the first day he followed her at the turf cutting in June, but I had hoped I was wrong."

Before they went inside, Mother whispered, "Let's not tell the family of this. Best they not know."

Liam nodded, but the storm inside him continued to rage, unabated. His emotions alternated between self-criticism, desire for revenge against Lawrence, and anxiety for his family's survival. When, at last, he climbed to the loft, everyone was asleep, and except for the creak of the ladder, the cottage was quiet. On his mat, he tossed like a man tormented. Niall must be in America now so why had he not written? He longed for him and his advice and wondered if his brother knew of the second blight.

Then a sound like the clop, clop of a horse distracted Liam, and he listened, instantly alert. When it stopped, he decided that he must have been mistaken. All was again silent. Then it began again and turned into a canter . . . de-clop, de-clop, de-clop.

He threw off his blanket and crept down the ladder. Lifting

the small curtain, he peered out the window, and in the empty yard, he saw only the moon's silvery rays atop the stone fence. Still curious, he opened the door and stumbled over something low in the shadows. The dim light from the fire revealed a heavy burlap bag on the threshold. He dragged it into the room and, as his eyes adjusted, he read the English inscription: fifty pounds – oats. He was surprised and confounded.

I3
Christmas in Crisis

By the first of November 1846, the weather became cold, with six inches of snow in County Mayo and in the drifts, even deeper. Usually a strong but mild wind blew across Ireland from the west, but this winter an icy gale came from the northeast across Russia. Grandda said that never in living memory had winter come so early or been so severe, and Liam could not understand why Mother Nature had also turned against Ireland.

On the second day of November, Sligo's agents came and collected the grain as though there had been no blight at all, leaving only enough seed to take care of the spring planting.

Liam was bitter. "A curse on Sligo and his hypocrisy! He said he would not harass us about rent and would do as much as any landlord to help us! Remember how we knelt and begged for his mercy? Now that Sligo is evicting and clearing away villages, he condemns George Moore and other kind landlords because they embarrass him and bother his conscience."

Father gave a deep sigh. "At least he did not drive us out to make pasture of our home." Since being homeless hastened death, Liam understood why eviction was Father's greatest fear, but just as dire was hunger.

With dread Liam watched their food stores shrink. Before the onset of winter, his sisters and mother had gathered edible weeds such as nettles, sorrel, and charlock, but now these were gone, as were vegetables from the garden. As the supply of boxty dwindled, Liam felt a reluctant gratitude to Lawrence for the oats he had left at the door. The pigs which usually fed on potato skins had to be slaughtered because no scraps left the table uneaten. This smoked pork provided food for a while, but because pigs paid the spring rent, Liam worried about that next Gale Day. To feed the chickens, the girls scrounged for seed and berries. One night, a chicken was stolen and its head left in the shed so Liam built a pen, and thereafter they kept the two hens and rooster in the cottage at night.

Sometimes Father bled the cow from her neck and closed the opening with a stitch made with the hair from her tail. Da disliked the bleeding because it made the cow weak for a time, but mixing blood into the milk, or cooking it until thickened into a blood pudding, was a way to enrich their diet.

The harsh winter of 1846 magnified the suffering in Ireland. By October people usually had a new harvest of potatoes, and since no outdoor labor was necessary until spring, people normally stayed inside the thick walls of the cottages around the fireplace during the coldest months. The poorest families managed with a coat for only the father, but with the blight, many fathers pawned that coat to buy Indian maize to feed their families. A profound, numbing sadness gripped Liam when he witnessed the suffering of homeless families as they shivered in rags and huddled in ditches beside the road to escape the wind's icy sting. Evicted people often walked ten miles to a workhouse, and when they were denied entry, lay down outside the gates to die.

The director of Irish relief, Charles Trevelyan, vowed that relief money had to come from the Irish themselves and not from the British treasury. To get more money for the workhouses, the British were sending police and soldiers to confiscate goods from tenants. Father had paid his poor tax earlier, but now the guardians of the workhouse imposed a new one, and he was irate.

His voice became shrill. "Absentee landlords can easily avoid paying the tax, and even those who live here aren't *forced* to pay."

Liam, too, was indignant. "Lord Lucan is starving inmates at Castlebar and is behind on his support, yet the government shows lenience to him. Then they squeeze it out of us tenants at gunpoint when we are barely surviving." Liam scowled. "Let's hide the little we have now before they get here!"

Father shook his head no. "They will take something, regardless, even clothing. You can't hide *everything*. It's no use."

Afraid that he could not control his angry sons, Father sent them on a hunt to the bog on the day he knew they were coming. By the time his sons returned, police had seized the donkey, the cart, the lamb called Curley, and the ewe Shelby. As a child Liam had adopted Shelby as his pet and even now when he came into the yard, she nuzzled up to him for an affectionate pat. When Liam strolled into the yard, he missed Shelby's presence immediately and was furious when told she was gone.

"Had I known, I would have hidden her in the glen!" he yelled.

Father seemed oddly passive and shrugged his shoulders. "At least they . . . they did not take the cow." His words had a slur, barely detectable, but Liam still heard it and wondered a moment before he resumed his raging.

"I couldn't have stood by and let those soldiers drag all that off!"

Father looked into the fire. "That's why I sent you away. I didn't want them to take my sons, too . . . or cane you until you were senseless and broken because you dared to protest."

Still distraught, Liam and Sean set off for Partry to check for mail. Da's subscription to the *Mayo Constitution* had six more months and a November issue had been delivered to the post office. It was full of stories about police and British troops evicting villages all over the island. Liam read aloud the statement by Charles Trevelyan of London's Treasury: "It quotes him as saying 'The right course is to do nothing for Ireland and leave it to the operation of natural causes.'" Liam fumed. "Are the landlord's evictions natural? Are the convoys taking out food to England natural? No! These are decisions made by men!"

Sean frowned, perplexed. "It's as though Trevelyan is just watching and waiting . . . but for what? What could be his goal?"

The Christmas season was now upon them and though usually a merry and spiritual time with special traditions, music, prayer, and decorations, Liam fretted . . . what now? Has Christmas been starved out of us? Is our culture gone forever or just postponed?

On December 23, Father went to Partry, hoping for a letter from Niall, but brought back a December issue of the newspaper instead. Da smoothed it out and read, first in silence and then aloud. "Hear this now." His voice grew hoarse. "In Belmullet in Erris, Mr. Walshe, a judge and landlord, evicted three hamlets ten days before Christmas with the help of the 49th Regiment. The bewildered people made shelters from the ruins, but the troops returned and tore these down. The people begged to remain even in the ruins till Christmas since it was so near, but they forced them to head into a night of hail and high wind."

Liam clinched his fists. "The government supported those evictions with the same regiment used at Ballinglass! You know what people are starting to say! It's the destruction of the Irish people they're after."

Father continued. "At least 102 families lived in Mullaroghe and more in Tiraun and Clogher. People heard the wailing from a great distance. A Poor Law inspector said most had no place to go and died of exposure and hunger in a short time."

Father crumbled the paper and his face flushed. "Everywhere ... extermination." A silence hung over the room. His eyes were steely as he tossed the paper into the fire where it flared and crackled. The sleet hitting against the glass of the window sounded loud, and the wind occasionally howled and whistled as it blew under the door.

Father's mood was dark, and the family tiptoed around, not sure what to say or do. He slumped in his wall seat across from Grandda, and both stared into the fire. Then Da retreated into the small sleeping room and pulled the curtain. Mamai and Grandmamai were also there, and Liam wondered – had they gone to bed too?

The next day was *Oíche Nollag* / Christmas Eve. Sean, Aine, and Liam looked at each other and realized they had to lift the gloom. When Aine suggested they go cut the customary holly for the season, the brothers gathered two large creels, knives, and their coats. After Aine wrapped herself in Mother's wool shawl, she borrowed Grandfather's boots and pushed rags into them to make them stay on. Ready for the weather, they slipped away.

Outside, the bare branches of the lilac bush arched gracefully with the weight of the snow, and the smooth blanket which lay over the gentle hills sparkled in the light. Smoke rose from their nostrils and mouths as they breathed out in the cold air, and in the white world outside, they soon found green, holly bushes full of bright, red berries. They cut branches, shook them free of snow, and stacked them high in the baskets.

When they entered the cottage, Caitlin jumped up and down and squealed. "I'll help ya!"

Brighid rushed over to the baskets. "Me too!"

Aine took charge. "Lay these in the window sill, Cait. Brighid, stand on a stool and put holly on the mantle." The glossy greenery soon hung above the door, on the coat pegs, wound around the sides of the loft's ladder, and transformed the cottage with cheer.

The brothers, taking a slingshot and the sharpened stick, now set out again, this time to the bog. With some luck, they might find a whooper swan or a white-fronted goose for Christmas dinner. Liam wore Father's soft hat pulled down over his ears as far as it would go, and Sean took Grandfather's. The snow was coming down hard now, and the roads were filling up and disappearing. They needed to note their bearings as only the stone fences showed above the quickly growing drifts.

Sean shivered. "No time to get lost."

As they approached the bog, Liam squinted in the bright white and found it hard to discern where it began in the snowy landscape. "Maybe the birds are distracted by the weather and conserving warmth by being still. Perhaps we can sneak up on them."

Sean pulled up his collar. "It will be hard to see a white swan, but the goose has more black. Let's meet in an hour or two at the stile over the last fence." Then they separated.

Liam made the sign of the cross. To go home to a Christmas table with game would be cause for celebration. To find none ... well, he must find something! He moved forward ten steps, then halted. He listened and looked. Then ten more steps. The wind blew in his face and stung his cheeks with tiny sleet droplets. Then he saw a black spot in the white expanse of snow ten feet away. Could it be a swan's beak? Moving forward slowly, he took hope. He crept closer. Now he could see the swan. Its eyes were closed against the wind which ruffled its feathers.

He dared not delay, but to rush might alert the bird so he took one step at a time, followed by a pause. Coming from behind, he gradually inched forward until he was within reach. Taking a deep breath, he thrust the sharp stick into its side with all his strength. The swan whooped in alarm and red blood oozed on white wing as it tried to flap away. Liam lunged for the bird before it fluttered out of reach, and then he broke its neck. Slowly the swan ceased to struggle and grew limp. As Liam walked back to the stile, he dragged it behind him, leaving a red trail in the snow.

Overhead the haze hid the sun, and Liam couldn't tell how long he had been waiting at the stile. His feet were numb, and he put both hands underneath the swan for warmth as he cradled it on his chest, careful to avoid its wound. Then he heard his brother crunching through the snow.

"Liam! I got a goose! We'll have a dinner!" Sean stared at Liam's swan in disbelief, wide-eyed with snow clinging to his lashes. "A big swan as well? After finding no game for a month, we have two! The snow brought us luck."

"No," Liam said. "God did. Merry Christmas," he grinned, and they trudged home before dusk could engulf them. As Sean and Liam stomped the snow off their feet, Mamai opened the door. At the sight of the game, she threw up her hands and cheered, drawing the whole family to the door. When the hunters strode in and flopped the large birds on the table, even Grandfather, who had been very quiet of late, became animated. "Well, an answer to prayer!"

Da patted the game with great satisfaction. "Roast goose tonight and the swan tomorrow! We'll invite Uncle Paddy and Cousin Eamon to share our good fortune. I'm afraid we can't go to Christmas Mass in Partry since the roads are impassable, but we'll have our prayer and traditions here tonight."

Mother hugged Aine, and each son, in turn. "Thank you for decorating!" Grandmother and I slept late this morning and then awakened to such a joyous scene."

Brighid looked puzzled. "Liam, I had never seen them both sleep at the same time, and I was worried. Then they came out, and we yelled surprise!"

Grandmother put her arms around Caitlin. "It's almost time for you to light the candle in the window. You know . . . the one that guides Mary and Joseph to our house? That honor goes to you, as the youngest child."

Caitlin frowned. "Grandmamai, it's Brighid's turn. I've been the youngest for a long time!"

Mamai looked pleased at Cait's unselfishness. "Well, Brighid it is!" Brighid's sweet smile at Cait said thank you and her flaxen hair glistened in the light from the fireplace. A fitting Christmas angel to do the job, Liam thought.

After Father dressed the goose and put it on the post for roasting, the hungry family stood around the hearth, transfixed without conversation. That morning they each had had only a cup of milk with a single egg stirred into the pitcher, but they still suffered patiently through the long wait for the bird to be done. The fire smoked up toward the meat, and each anticipated how it would taste. Mamai rubbed butter on the skin, making it shine and turn golden, and the aromas that filled the cottage caused their mouths to water.

When at last it was cooked, they rushed to their places at the table and sat tall, all eyes on the golden bird. They bowed their heads and said grace in unison with heartfelt thanks, but quickly. As Father began slicing, they held up their bowls toward him to catch the precious morsel as it came their turn. In her haste, Caitlin stuffed a bite in her mouth and then cried in pain as she burned her tongue.

"Easy, Cait!" Liam cautioned, but it was hard not to swallow it whole. Yet, when Grandda put half his portion back on the platter, Liam observed his rail-thin frame, and wondered, when did he grow so thin? "Grandda, what are you doing? You need to eat!" he insisted.

Grandfather looked sheepish at the scolding. "It's not right . . . not the proper order of things for the old to take food from the young. I don't need all this."

Liam noticed that Grandmother had moved half her portion to Brighid's plate. How long had she been doing this? Her arms were hidden by a sweater, but her wrists and hands were boney and the vessels stood out. Yes! They were starving themselves for the sake of their grandchildren.

Father, too, was alarmed. "You must not refuse food, or you'll grow sick!"

Grandda leaned over his plate and looked up out of the corner of his eye at his son, his jaw set, and though he said nothing more, Liam read that look: I'm old and no one can tell me what to do. The only hope was to try and change his mind.

After dinner, Father took the Bible off the shelf and retold the story of Bethlehem. At the point when the innkeepers turned the holy family away and said there was no room in the inn, Brighid stood on a stool and lit the *coinneal mór na Nollag* / Christmas candle. It would shine every night for a week as a beacon to those needing shelter. They left the door cracked as a sign of welcome for travelers and wanderers, and according to this tradition, no one would be turned away. But this night, due to the frigid air, they only left the top door slightly ajar.

In the dim light of dawn on Christmas morning, Liam heard his little sisters whispering excitedly and scurrying across the loft to descend the ladder. What were they thinking? No Christmas surprises this year! By expecting them, they would make their parents sad, but before he could grab them by the ankles, they were on the ladder.

Excited giggles from below confounded Liam for it was not disappointment he was hearing. Mamai and Grandmamai were joining in, and delight was filling the room.

"Look at MINE! It has a lace collar!" Caitlin bragged.

"This one has a lace apron! And yarn hair!" Brighid countered.

"Grandmother, where did you get the hair for mine?" Caitlin asked.

"The cow's tail! It looks real, does it not? Your Mamai's idea."

Hearing the talk, the curious siblings in the loft came down, and the little girls proudly held up their new rag dolls.

Caitlin introduced hers. "This is Colleen Reilly. Isn't that the name of the pretty girl from Ballinglass?" Then she bent the doll to make her curtsey.

Liam froze and his spirits sagged. Yes . . . dear Colleen! What kind of Christmas could she be having? God, help her!

Aine turned to Mamai as she admired Brighid's doll. "When did you make these? They're wonderful!"

Mamai's eyes twinkled. "While you were all decorating and we were sleeping late in the next room!"

Caitlin pursed her lips. "I wondered about that! You *never* sleep late."

Yesterday Mamai had sent Sean to Uncle Paddy's and Cousin Eamon's with the good tidings: we killed a swan, large enough to share. Come for Christmas dinner. When Sean returned, he reported that the gloom of their relatives' houses turned to elation. Aunt Una wanted to add to the table and was baking bread from the last of their barley, and Cousin Eamon was bringing a special soup.

Father had dressed the swan yesterday, and now it hung over the fire and sizzled as the drippings fell. Mother rushed over and set a cup under the fat to catch it for eating later. Like yesterday, everyone watched the roasting with mouths open, and it was a torturous wait. When the outside skin got crisp, Da took his knife and trimmed off a few morsels to abate each person's intense craving.

Even the skinny cat Mittens got a bite, but she continued to mew and beg for more. Father became irritated and tossed her outside in the cold. "We can't feed a cat when people are hungry." Caitlin whimpered and retreated to the loft for to her, the cat *was* a person.

It had been weeks since Liam had seen his cousin, and when Tomas walked through the door, he was startled. He could see the famine's toll in his sallow complexion, haggard look, and dark circles under his eyes. His shirt could not hide his thin arms and chest of protruding ribs. Liam wondered . . . is my own family wasting away like this but less noticeable to me because I see them everyday?

When they talked, Tomas confessed his suffering. "I can't bear to eat when my parents and sisters are hungry so I always take less. I've got to do something, and I'm thinking of stealing a lamb from the pastures at Ashford Castle. That landlord has so many that he wouldn't miss one. Besides, I don't want to take food from my own neighbors. If I get away with it, my family will eat for a while. If I'm caught, they'll transport me to Australia, but at least they'll feed me. Don't ya know that some people are deliberately breaking the law because prison is better than dying of the hunger?"

"Tomas! What are you thinking now!" Liam growled. "It's a long walk to Ashford Castle, and the landlord's herders guard the sheep with guns! It's *dead* you may be, or in an Australian chain gang with cruel men as task masters. You're too young for the likes of that."

Tomas shrugged his boney shoulders. "What faces me now is worse so I'll take my chances." It was a terrible choice, and Liam had no answer.

The table was crowded with aunts, uncles, cousins, and even Granny Walsh, the mother of Aunt Una. These, together with the Reillys, all squeezed onto the benches or stood at the board. Each child was welcomed onto a loving lap. As Liam looked around the table, he felt heavy-hearted because he feared that by next Christmas, many would be gone. The grace in unison was beautiful to hear – one prayer, one faith, one family, one heart.

"And may God hold Niall in the palm of his hand," Father added, looking worried.

"Amen." For Niall's sake, Liam was now glad he had left for Americay, but why no letter?

The swan was large and fat, maybe thirty pounds, and as Da carved the bird, Aunt Una exclaimed, "What a blessing!" The barley bread was enough for everyone to have a taste. Cousin Eamon and his family brought a soup of frog and lizard and what else, Liam was unsure, but it was flavored with dried onion and herbs which had been salvaged from the fall garden, and it was food.

"Everyone, please pray for my brother Colm!" Aunt Una said. "He's gone and taken the soup! Desperate to get some food, he went to live with Edward Nangle, that Protestant preacher on Achill Island."

Shock interrupted everyone's eating. "He wouldn't!" Grandda croaked. "The same preacher who even ridicules the sacred host of Communion?"

"Yes, he is the one! Colm has gone and joined Edward Nangle's church, but I pray he'll come back to us after *an droch-shaol* / the bad times have passed, if they ever do."

Sean's eyes widened, and he looked stunned and incredulous. "You mean he's become a *souper* . . . denied the faith of our fathers?"

"I'm afraid so. To be given soup, don't ya know, you have

to join his church and toil on his farm like a slave. He isn't like the Quakers who give charity to a needy person, regardless of his religion. By the way, I heard that Quaker people are coming from England to try to help us, God bless them."

Aunt Una picked up her spoon and tasted Cousin Eamon's soup. "This isn't bad. Now what did you say was in it? A lizard and a frog?"

Eamon chuckled. "If you like it, eat it, and don't be asking."

His ten-year-old daughter Ailis watched her with a glimmer in her eye, and when Una was almost finished, she announced, "Da put grub worms from the stream bed in it!"

Una half choked on the soup still in her mouth. "Grubs, you say? Eamon, you should have told us your recipe before we ate!" Most were amused, but Caitlin, Brighid, and Ailis bubbled over with mirth and giggled out loud.

Eamon stirred his soup vigorously. "All the stuff in this is nourishing and you'll be the stronger for it. In times like this, we have to be creative."

After dinner they gathered around the hearth for carols. Tomas and Sean played their tin whistles with a tone as pure as a nightingale's call. Aunt Una, with harp in her lap, strummed harmonious chords. Father's violin, Uncle Paddy's mandolin, and Cousin Eamon's bodhran softly joined in. For the first time since the blight, they were together and felt the joy of a close family, a warm cottage, a full stomach, and the music. Aine and Mother, both with beautiful soprano voices, sang a duet of *Oíche chiúin* / Silent Night, and after the first verse, they signaled for all to sing along. With hearts full, every soul sang the ending lines: *Críost a theacht ar an saol* / Christ is coming into the world. Liam knew this moment would be a precious memory of Christmas forever more.

Enjoying the euphoria, no one remembered the curfew until Mother glanced out the window and saw the setting sun in the hazy winter sky. "It's dusk. Must they leave?" she asked Father. He looked questioningly to Paddy.

Uncle Paddy frowned. "Surely the soldiers are not patrolling this snowy, Christmas night! They must be having carols themselves and a dinner with all the trimmings, paid for by the government." Deciding to take their chances since they lived closeby, the relatives sang more Christmas songs and went home late.

A week passed and the Reillys often went to bed hungry. The chickens' feathers could not hide their boney skeletons, and they stopped laying eggs. Although they clucked hopefully, the sisters had little to give them except holly berries. Finally, Mother killed one for the pot; then several days later, another. Concerned, Liam noted their shrinking supply of food, but said nothing.

One afternoon Uncle Paddy burst through the door, wild eyed and hysterical. "They caught Tomas with a stolen lamb! He's in the gaol at Castlebar." The news took Liam's breath. Paddy closed his eyes and groaned. "My only son!" Father's eyes brimmed with tears as he put his arm around his brother's shoulders. Da was not only Tomas' uncle, but his godfather and had helped raise him from an infant.

"My Una is lost to sorrow, and she'll never recover. Tomas is only fifteen, and if he's sent to the chain gangs, they'll beat all the spirit and life out of him." Paddy laid his head on his arm and shook with violent sobs.

Liam was desolate. Tomas was always bright and jovial, and he shuddered to think of him crushed by cruel overseers. He wished he had warned Uncle Paddy of his intentions, but Tomas believed he had no choice, and since he was always so nimble and fast, Liam believed he wouldn't get caught.

On the appointed day, close male relatives who were strong enough and had coats and shoes proceeded to Castlebar to attend the trial. But due to the poverty of Ireland, children and women generally had no shoes, so only his devoted mother, Aunt Una, walked in the snow to Castlebar with her feet wrapped in rags. At all costs she would go because it might be her last chance to see her only son.

At the entrance of the courthouse, Sean saw a poster nailed to one of its tall, round columns and gestured for Liam to come read it.

"We the undersigned Magistrates offer the following rewards:
- For prosecuting to conviction any person guilty of writing, posting, circulating illegal notices, 30 pounds,
- To any person who gives information on possession of concealed arms and ammunition, 100 pounds,
- To any person giving information of persons unlawfully meeting as a committee, 50 pounds . . ."

Before Liam could read more, Father nudged his sons. "The trials are starting."

Liam was appalled. "Da! Read the size of these rewards! Some are more than most men could earn in a lifetime! How can they know an informer is telling the truth with such a large bribe in the offing?"

"They can't, and I doubt they care," Father said with disgust. "These aren't trials with a jury. Since Parliament passed the Coercion Act last February, the magistrates have great power and can decide guilt or innocence on their own. Great Britain profits from convict labor. There's no profit in mercy, so expect none.

They mounted the stairs to their assigned courtroom on the second floor. The chamber had high ceilings with tall windows containing numerous panes. The Reilly family slid into the smooth, wooden benches and spoke to each other in whispers. Soon the room was packed with anxious and grim relatives. Most of the many bodies were visibly shivering and lacked coats.

Next to the wall in comfortable pews with cushions, the despised witnesses waited to testify against their countrymen for a fee, and if looks could kill, they knew their lives would be short. They stared at walls and ceiling to avoid the eyes of neighbors, but the monetary reward for testifying would compensate them well for the hostility and ostracism they would soon face.

In the front of the room where the magistrate would sit was a high, wide desk, equipped with reference books, a quill and ink, and a polished wooden gavel. A British flag hung from a pole stand nearby. When an officer of the court came in and commanded all to rise, they stood and solemnly waited.

From the hall a magistrate wearing a white, tightly-curled wig and a black robe entered the room. His eyes glowered from beneath bushy black and white brows, and his mouth was in a permanent pout with jowls. He sat in the high seat where he looked down on the proceedings, and loose skin beneath his chin wagged with any movement. Taking his time, he put small spectacles on his nose and around each ear and peered over them at the spectators. "Be seated. Court is now in session," he announced as he clacked the shiny gavel.

The first man on trial, Paddy Stephens, was accused of writing a threatening note to his landlord, and the prosecuting officer read the note as evidence: "If ye or your agents take any tenant's cow, your barn will burn. This is a warning."

The landlord's agent, a hulk of a man with a roll of fat around his neck and small eyes without brows or lashes, spoke next. He related the time and manner in which the note was found. When the informer took the stand, he claimed he overheard a conversation in which the accused had cursed the landlord for seizing the villagers' pigs. Furthermore, he said that he saw the man fleeing from the manor house on the morning of the note's delivery.

Finally, they allowed the accused to speak for himself. "'Tis true I was angry. My neighbors and I had paid our rent with grain. Then the agent came and took our pigs, too, even though they were not due till spring rent. But, your honor, there's no way I could have penned the warning because I can't read or write! I was nowhere near the manor house on that day! It was the same day that my small son Brian lay dying of the fever, and I never left his side till he passed, I swear it." His voice grew louder, and he trembled. "It's a lie he tells to get the thirty pounds!"

When Stephens heard his wife start to whimper, anguish contorted his face, and he twisted about in his seat to find her. She held an infant in her arms, and two other wee ones clung to her ragged skirt. A loud sympathetic murmuring rose from the crowd, causing the magistrate to pound his gavel.

"Order here! I will tolerate no outburst!" He cupped his hand over his ear and leaned sideways toward an interpreter who stood beside the table. The interpreter spoke English into his hand for several minutes after the accused had finished, and the magistrate nodded that he understood. Then he stopped and drank water from a glass and swished it about his mouth before he swallowed. The courtroom was expectant and tense as he adjusted his spectacles and referred to a document.

When he cleared his throat, the people knew he was ready to give the verdict. As he spoke, the translator echoed his words in Irish. "After hearing the facts of this case, I hereby sentence you to be transported to Norfolk Island in Van Diemen's land for twelve years, followed by two and a half years to the road gang. Thereafter, you may work under supervision, and if your deportment is

acceptable, you will be granted a ticket-to-leave the work camp."
His gavel's solid clack concluded this trial.

As the wife stretched her arm to him across the room and wept, her legs buckled under her, and relatives held her up. The man slumped over, but soon constables dragged him from the chair to the door.

Liam felt a rising anger. "Where are they sending him?"

"It's a prison island south of Australia." Father gripped his knees till his knuckles turned white. "If he's docile, maybe fifteen years from now he can work there as a free convict, but any rogue guard can change his fate for the worse. Cian O'Gorman, a twenty-year-old man from Killadoon, died of a vicious flogging while on Norfolk Island. Word was sent back by Irish who had passes to work in a nearby town."

Next, a parson's wife from the Anglican chapel in Castlebar testified that her purse was snatched by a seventeen-year-old lad, Siles Farrell. Once on the stand, he appeared confused and his feelings were blunted, like Liam had seen before in other persons who were severely malnourished. He doubted the lad would survive transportation to Australia, but the penalty might work in his favor since he would surely die if turned back to the streets. Perhaps this was one of those intentional offenses that Tomas had talked about . . . going to jail in return for food. But when the magistrate also sent him to Norfork Island, the harsh sentence for his offense caused angry groans to fill the chamber. Clearly, the judge wanted to discourage others from following this example.

Then the bailiff brought in Tomas who was shaking and pale. Uncle Paddy and Aunt Una sat tall in their seats and tried to support him with their eyes. Liam suffered with him and knew that Tomas now regretted his decision to steal. He bit his lip and looked down during the testimony of the pasture guard who recounted how he had seen Tomas take a lamb. A chase ensued, and the guard captured him just off the property, hiding under a bridge.

When it was his time to speak, Tomas turned to the magistrate, tears in his eyes. "I never stole before sir, but I was desperate. My family was starving, all the work houses were full, and I didn't know what else to do! Ple . . .please put me in an Irish jail!" His voice broke.

The magistrate, with cupped hand, again leaned toward the interpreter and kept nodding. His face was impassive, and having seen so much hardship, he seemed inured to the grief around him. Liam realized that this was a crime against property – a landlord's property – just what the coercion law was meant to protect. Recalling Da's words about how Britain profited off convict labor, he expected a harsh sentence. They waited while the judge took a swig of water, pushed his spectacles back up on his nose, and reached for his gavel. Clack!

The judge spoke in a monotonous tone by rote, and the translator imitated his manner of delivery. "I hereby sentence you to fifteen years transportation to Norfolk Island in Van Diemen's Land at hard labor . . . ." Although that was not all of his punishment, Liam could not bear to hear the rest which became a hum in his ears.

Aunt Una shrieked and buried her face in her shawl. "No! No! He's too young! Have mercy . . . mercy! Our only son!" she sobbed and cried. Uncle Paddy guided her to the hallway outside where the sound of her grief echoed in the stairwell. Liam felt a lump in his throat and bit his lip hard. Another trial was about to begin, but he had seen enough of this English justice so with Sean and father, he left the stuffy courtroom, passed down the stairs, and through the double doors into the gray afternoon.

In front of the courthouse on the large grassy mall lay a

number of boney bodies who were either sleeping, unconscious, or worse. From the maze of cobblestone streets converging on the square, half-starved, ghost-like figures silently limped along the sidewalk, too weak to beg. For Liam, the scene was unreal and nightmarish. This should not be happening – not to Tomas, not to Ireland.

Some of the prisoners already sat shackled in the wagon, and Tomas was soon brought out to join them. With all hope gone, he now looked like he would welcome death. Liam winced as he watched police clamp heavy, metal ring bolts around his raw thin ankles, already abraded and scabbed from the jail. Thick chains were attached to them, linking one prisoner to the other, and Tomas' ankles began to bleed.

The horses waiting to pull the wagons away seemed impatient and shook their harness. Soldiers with stony expressions stood guard with bayonets attached and kept family at a distance from the convicted. Only the priest was allowed in close to pray with each man and to bless him, but as time grew short, he too was forced back. Realizing that he was the friend of Father Mullen, Liam approached him.

"Father Henry? Can you tell me where they are taking them now?"

"Yes! . . . Oh, you were at my house!" He gripped Liam's hand and blinked in a look of compassion. "Well, they're going south to Cork where they'll be kept in the Spike Island Depot in the harbor until there are enough prisoners to fill a ship to the South Pacific. They won't ever return. I'm sorry. A relative?" Liam nodded and hurried back with the information to Uncle Paddy.

Everywhere families were weeping, cursing, moaning, and hovering. The wife of the first prisoner held up her baby for a last kiss from his father but was unable to bring him close enough.

When the driver lashed his whip and the horses lurched forward, the husband twisted his neck to glimpse his wife's tear-stained face. As the loaded wagons began to move away, wives and mothers tried to walk with the column and begged the police to permit them a last, tearful exchange. Aunt Una skipped beside the wagon and reached in to grasp Tomas' hand, and they shared a mournful look before a guard pushed her away with his gun barrel. Children ran after the prisoners even after the adults had given up.

Liam felt torn apart inside and, trotting after the wagon where Tomas sat, he shouted, "Be strong! Live! . . . Damn them all! Live Tomas! Show them and *live!*" He slowed and fell behind when distance and dust eclipsed Tomas' tearful face. Agitated, he stood in the street, opening and closing his fists, with tears of anger and grief standing in his eyes. Tomas was like a little brother, and being older and stronger, he wished he could take his place.

Sean put a hand on his shoulder. "Who knows, Liam . . . he may end up being the fortunate one, rather than us." They continued watching the wagons until they turned a corner and were gone from sight. On the way home, Liam was flooded with memories of their cousin from childhood: the games and competition, the antics and jokes, the shared confidences and hopes, fishing and swimming in the glen.

Sean, too, was remembering. "Liam, do you recall the Christmas when Tomas got a tin whistle?"

"Yes, and astonished us with his talent. But now he'll be at the mercy of cruel masters on the chain gangs. Tomas is so young, and none can endure that form of slavery and remain unchanged." Absorbed in grief and worry, the brothers became quiet, and the walk home seemed a blur.

Finally reaching the lane to their cottage, Da left his brother and Aunt Una and caught up with his sons. As they shuffled through the door, drained and depressed, the family encircled them. Mother laid the pants she was patching aside and hurried to Father.

"Did they send him to Australia?"

Father nodded weakly and went to the bucket to scoop a ladle of water. "It was terrible to see . . . Tomas dragged off in chains. I only hope that somehow he can survive what faces him."

Mother tried to comfort Da with a tender hug. "We'll pray for him every day." Then she touched something in the pocket of her apron. "Seamus, since Barra knew you couldn't go to Partry today, he brought the mail back for us." Her eyes gleamed. "I have what we've wanted . . . for a *long* time."

Da looked incredulous. "It was there?"

"Yes!" She smiled and held up an envelope.

Father's eyes sparked with jubilation. "Oh! What did he say? Tell us *now*!" Their hearts leaped! At last, a letter from Niall.

I 4
The Struggle to Survive

Mother held the crumpled envelope from half-way around the world like a precious document. With Caitlin squirming onto her lap and the family hovering around her, she slowly unfolded the letter and began reading aloud.

"Dearest Mamai, Da, Grandda, Grandmamai, Sean, Liam, Aine, Brighid, and Cait: I cannot describe my distress upon hearing that a second blight has struck the potatoes of our oppressed country, and I pray each day for you. I'm serving in the American army in Mexico as the United States is at war with this nation to their south. As soon as I get some money saved, I'll send it home to buy food for you there or bring some of you to Americay. Many Irish lads are in the army with me, as recruiters grabbed us when we landed and promised citizenship if we served.

"The grub they give is good – that is American for food – and Mamai would like the blue uniform and boots I wear. Wearing the boots is new to us Irish, and our calloused feet are often remarked upon. I'm in good health and hope to survive all battles still ahead. Although some American officers are hard on us Irish lads and tempers flare, I'm determined to keep mine and not endure a vicious flogging. This harsh treatment and the army's habit of stabling horses in the sanctuary of Catholic churches here outrage us. For these reasons and because Mexico is a Catholic country, some Irish have switched sides and are fighting for the Mexicans. These Irish units call themselves the Saint Patricks and are fighting us under a flag that says the "San Patricios," which is Spanish. I hate fighting against other Irish, but I must if I want to be an American citizen.

"In New York City, I left the Murphys all in one room on Mulberry Street. The places are far worse than Ireland, full of bad smells, no water, and foul air. Irish speech fills the neighborhood streets and hallways, with accents mainly from Sligo and Cork, and most people help each other just like in Ireland. Sean and Aine, there's one thing I know. Maire and Brian are sick at heart with missing you. If you haven't a letter from them yet, it is for the want of a stamp and will come soon.

"My love I send to all of you. At night when I try to sleep, I remember each turn in our lane, the worn threshold at the door, your laughter, the music, and the view from all corners of the yard.

Your loving son,
Niall Seamus Reilly

Also, tell Cait that I have her holy card of St. Patrick in the pocket close to my heart."

Caitlin's face brightened at the words. "I'm glad I gave him that. Aine told me to, and at first, I said no." Liam smiled at Cait's appreciation of her own generosity, however reluctant.

He longed for his elder brother and took the letter aside to read again to himself. Although Niall was generous, it would take him many years to earn passage money for the whole family. Liam would never leave his parents behind in Ireland so the truth was . . . he'd never see Niall again.

A loud rapping at the door disturbed his thoughts, and the family stood quiet and alert, still worried about police and searches. Even though the wound under Sean's shirt had healed, the path of the bullet had left a long, red, tell-tale scar that would condemn him. The knock came again, insistent, and they exchanged anxious looks. Da peered out the window and cautiously opened the door.

Three men in dark coats, white shirts, and tall hats stood in the snow and were escorted by an Irish man who asked, "May we come in?"

Father nodded and stepped aside. "Take yourselves out of the weather. My house is yours."

The men stomped their boots and removed their hats. The Irishman spoke first. "My name is Tomas Fitzmaurice from Ballyhaunis. These are Quaker agents, Mr. William Forster and his son Edward, and with them is James Tuke. They're here in Mayo to determine the extent of the hunger."

Father shook their hands. "Welcome."

Liam carried three-legged stools to the hearth and motioned for them to sit, and through Fitzmaurice who acted as an interpreter, the men talked in a friendly manner. "We hope to relieve the distress in some way and are surveying the needs. How many have you here and what food remains?"

Father sat in his wall seat beside the fire. "We have no potatoes and have eaten the last two chickens. We killed and smoked the two pigs in October. Soldiers came and seized the sheep, donkey, and cart for the workhouse tax, and only the cow remains. We hunt for scarce game but are usually disappointed since the competition is great. We have some oats and barley left for the spring planting but dare not consume them or we face eviction."

The men wore grim expressions and nodded as they made notations in a small, black book. "And clothing?"

"Soon we'll have to pawn clothing and furniture to buy some of that Indian maize which Peel imported last year from Americay."

Forster lit his pipe. "The maize sells for only three shillings in New York, but if you can find it in Ireland, they sell it for nine shillings at a great profit. So I warn you, your goods will buy very little."

Da opened his arms. "What choice do I have? We must have food or die!"

Mr. Forster glanced around at the faces encircling him. "I count nine people here?"

"Yes . . . my parents, my wife, and five remaining children."

Forster's expression was sympathetic as he scribbled in his book. "Soon, in the town of Ballinrobe, we're going to have some caldrons in which we will prepare stirabout. If you can get there with a pot on the appointed day before the supply is gone, you can carry the thick mush of corn meal home to the family. If we can get a little meat or rice, we'll add it and make it as hardy as we can."

The younger Forster shifted on the hard stool. "We Quakers intended to add our aid to that of the British government, but I fear that our efforts will exceed theirs . . . even though we are a church and they are a rich nation. We thank God that Americans are generously supporting us with donations or we could never feed as many as we do. Soon perhaps, the government will allow American ships to bring food directly to Ireland, without first stopping in England to pay a duty and then transferring to British boats. The whole world is shaming them for doing so little themselves and even making it hard for other countries to help."

Father frowned. "You mean they *still* have not changed that law about the boats?"

"No, they have refused so far. We disagree with Trevelyan and his cohorts who claim that this famine is sent by God as a punishment to the Irish and should not be interfered with. At first, he even discouraged the formation of a charity to solicit funds for Ireland, claiming English people have no sympathy for Irish and would not give. But evidently, reports in the newspapers have moved the hearts of many in our country."

Father leaned forward. "They've made collections for us in England, have they?"

"Yes, there is a charity called the British Association for the Relief of the Distressed of Ireland and Scotland. Irish soldiers in the British army all over the world have given, with £14,000 from Calcutta alone, and even Queen Victoria gave money. The island of Mauritius off the coast of Africa sent £3000, and I'm guessing that in earlier times, Irish were forced to go there as slaves to work on English sugar plantations. The Choctaw Indians of Oklahoma collected over $700 for Irish relief, and the Cherokees are also sending aid. Your Catholic pope gave 1,000 Roman crowns."

Mr. Tuke cleared his throat. "Trevelyan doesn't openly oppose the charity and even gave a donation, but he still interferes with various plans of the charity's leaders to give things directly to the needy. He disapproves of all gifts of food, seed, and clothing and wants to rely on the workhouses, which are underfunded and dismal failures. Despite Trevelyan's objections, Count Strzetecki, a Polish man who is leading the Association, has plans for direct aid, but I worry about the future. Trevelyan wants to control the charity's funds himself, and I predict that, little by little, he'll take over and the flow of aid will dry up."

Edward Forster stood and lit his pipe with an ember from the fire. "Even the Prime Minister, Lord Russell, wants to distribute seed to landlords to give their tenants, but Trevelyan is blocking it on the grounds that it would displease the seed merchants! He even returned a donation from a Turkish sultan, saying that it was more than Queen Victoria's gift and might embarrass her." Forster shook his head. "It's hard to understand."

Liam listened intently with rage churning his insides. It's *they* who are punishing us, not God! He had hoped and prayed that other persons in the British government would overrule Trevelyan and his circle, but evidently many support him. But somehow, with the help of these good Quakers and the Americans, he hoped his family could survive.

As the men rose and were putting on their coats, Grandda lifted his hand and was struggling to get to his feet when Mr. Forster intervened.

"No, keep your seat, sir. We can see ourselves to the door."

Grandda slumped back, exhausted by the brief effort, and his voice faltered. "I . . . I . . . want to thank you for helping Ire . . . Ireland."

Forster's face was full of compassion as he leaned over and clasped Grandda's trembling hand. "Don't mention it. It is but our Christian duty."

After the men left, the family was quiet with long faces. The Quakers' questions had forced them to confront the reality of their desperate situation. Except for the cow, they were out of food.

The silence was broken when Mittens began a shrill mew, pleading for a cup of cream. Her cry was insistent, and she looked up at Caitlin and Brighid with questioning eyes.

"Put out that cat! I can't stand its begging!" Father demanded, and grabbed his coat off the peg. "I'm going out to hunt, and I'll not come home till I have something!"

"We'll go with you, Da," Sean volunteered.

"No. You and Liam go along the road to Castlebar. I'll go south alone, and maybe one of us can find some game, but stay clear of all hunting preserves and landlord pastures. I couldn't take more trials! May God help poor Tomas this day, wherever he is." He slammed the door behind him.

Before leaving, Liam looked back to see Mother helping Grandda stand up and return to his bed to rest in mid-day. Both his grandparents were aging before his eyes, years older in just weeks, and Grandfather, no longer his peppery self, seemed flat, withdrawn, and passive. Then Liam recognized the symptoms of starvation. Vowing to find food and *make* him eat, he grabbed Grandda's hat and set out with new determination to bring back game.

Sean picked up the cat and carried her out with them. "Maybe she can find a mouse or such outside." They put her down past the yard in hopes she would become a hunter if she left the walled areas, but she followed them, wanting their company and mewing. As her feet sank into the snow, she stopped her pursuit, and they left her, sitting in the lane, shaking her paws free of the white powder.

Sean shook his head. "Look at her! She's a prissy one and doesn't like this snow much . . . just wants the milk and food set before her. Spoiled, she is."

"'Tis true and we can't spare it."

First, they headed for the tall trees and water in the glen

since it was close and not part of a landlord's preserve. Liam raised his shoulders to lessen his neck's exposure to the cold wind. "Let's check the stream because it's almost time for the salmon to run."

As they neared the glen, Liam noticed thatch from the Murphy's scalp strewn in the grass and wondered what had happened. Where was the evicted family? He had heard of people finding victims still in their dug-outs, dead and half-eaten by rats, and he did not want such a memory to haunt him every time he closed his eyes. But they had to know and loped down the incline, seized by a clammy dread. The scalp was now a tangle of thatch and wood. Landlord's agents must have discovered the family and caved in their hovel by collapsing the supports. Liam peered into the dark corners and was glad to find no human remains.

Sean moaned. "They drove them away into the snow . . . even denied this hole. I can almost hear the cries of their young children."

As Liam surveyed the wreckage, despair oozed from the moist soil, and the wind sighed through bare trees. Not wanting to think about the fate of the wandering family, he shut it off and studied the stream for the glint of silver scales, but it was icy and empty. As they slowly climbed the hill, snow flurries started to drift down.

Then Sean stopped. "Is that a badger waddling away from us?" It was awkward and slow enough to be overtaken, so Liam gripped his stick and moved smoothly toward it. Sensing them, the badger's short legs ran faster and as suddenly as it came into view, it disappeared. They searched the ground and found his hole, but he was home.

Sean peeped inside the dark opening. "If we put our hands in there, he'll claw us to shreds, so let's wait behind the hole and maybe he'll come out."

They watched the opening until the sky turned purple and they were numb. Liam shivered. "He's in for the night, so let's come back tomorrow. Maybe Da got something." Sean agreed. With cold, darkness, and curfew, their chances were not good, so they reluctantly walked home, empty- handed.

When they saw Father in the side yard, dressing a small animal, Liam was relieved.

"Da, what have you?" Sean called out.

Father did not even glance up. "A rabbit," he muttered. Liam thought he discerned a tone of bitterness and understood: his burdens were heavy and the rabbit was small.

Inside, Liam crouched next to Grandfather who was again sitting in his seat at fireside. "Grandda, Father got a small rabbit, and I want you to eat some of my portion tonight. You're not doing well."

Grandfather didn't respond but kept looking at the fire. Liam tried again. "Did you like the Quaker men, Grandda? They were kind, were they not?" Grandfather weakly nodded in assent but offered no comment. How unlike him. The will to live seemed to be draining away.

Grandmother, too, said little and as she watched her mate grow weaker, Liam feared she was not far behind. At least, the cooking pot would not be empty tonight. In with the cut-up rabbit, Mamai threw a handful of oats and some hard berries.

Fretting about their pet, Brighid and Caitlin kept opening the door and peering into the darkness. "Mittens! Where are you? Here Kitty."

When Brighid closed the door, her face was in a pout. "She should not have gone out in this weather. Do you think a fox got her? Her black fur would be easy to spot on the snow."

Mamai moved her away from the window. "Don't worry. Cats wander, but they come home. She's found a nest of mice and is having herself a feast, that's what!"

Aine added her own optimism. "She'll be crying at the door by morning, wanting in. Just you wait."

Despite these predictions, the mood around the table was somber. Grandfather left his bowl half full and pushed it away, but Liam scooted it back. "Try to eat a little more . . . just a few spoonfuls."

He shook his head. "Not good like potatoes and butter." The others ate the stew without questioning the gamey flavor, and the wooden spoons clacked on the bottom of their bowls as they scraped for every last drop. But the distress of the little sisters affected them all, and Father was especially touchy and gruff.

Soon Caitlin began to whine again. "What if Mittens never comes back? What will we do?"

Brighid joined her. "She was our only playmate since our lamb was taken by those mean soldiers." Tears stood in her eyes.

Father tossed down his spoon with a clatter and bolted for the door. He overturned his stool, leaving it on its side, and stomped out the door into the frigid air without a coat. The family was stunned.

Mother tried to explain. "Maybe he's gone to hunt for Mittens. Let him be."

When he had his chance, Liam strolled over to the window and looked into the yard. His Father was sitting on the wall, staring at the cold landscape – not hunting for the cat – but brooding. Liam wondered if the starvation was forcing cruel choices on his father but kept his suspicions to himself.

As the night grew later, the family gradually went to bed, until only Liam remained at the table. Father was no longer slumped on the stone wall, and despite Liam's repeated searches out the window, the moonlit lane and yard remained empty. Where *was* Da? The fire burned low, and still there was no sign. His coat hung on its peg, and Liam fretted that without it, this weather could make him ill.

Finally, the door slowly opened, and a gust of cold wind displaced smoke seeking the chimney. Father stood a moment, then haltingly turned and closed the door. As he crossed the room to the arched fireplace, his gait was awkward and his balance unsteady. Slowly he lowered himself and fell into his seat, clumsily and hard. Upon noticing his son, he nodded and smiled in a jocular manner. Liam could see that his mood had turned decidedly mellow.

He recalled the feast of departure and going with Father to retrieve the jug of poteen for toasting from its hiding place. Apprehensive, Liam wondered where that jug was now. Unwelcome memories of Father's youngest brother intruded. His problem with drink had started small and grew till he pawned everything and would go missing for days. Liam could still see the worried faces of cousins at the door, searching . . . still feel their pain. His own family did not need that kind of trouble.

He anxiously watched Father whose presence usually gave him security, but now Da seemed unavailable . . . somewhere else with eyes glazed and not seeing. Da leaned against the wall and nodded off, and Liam, not wanting to deal with him, left him there and went to his mat in the loft. By early tomorrow he had to return to the glen and the badger's hole.

At dawn the next morning Sean and Liam rose to resume the hunt. Liam was sharpening his stick, when Caitlin, eyes bright with hope, came down the ladder.

"Aine said Mittens would be at the door by morning." A cold breeze lifted Caitlin's copper hair as she opened the door, leaned over the threshold, and looked to both sides. When the cat was not there, she turned around with head bowed and began to whimper.

She clamped her little mouth shut against a flood of tears.

Liam could not bring himself to give false hope. "Caitlin, be a big girl. I'm sorry about Mittens, but you must be brave and not cry." The stern scolding made Cait hurry to the loft with loud sniffs and once there, she burst into a wail.

Perturbed at being ignored, Liam yelled up to her: "Yes, I guess a fox got her for sure! So be strong and don't make our parents sad with your bawling!"

Aine must have overheard and flew down the ladder, her green eyes blazing. With hands on hips, she yelled at Liam. "How cruel you are! You know how much she loves that cat!"

Liam continued sharpening his stick with the knife. "I know her grief is real, but she has to get over it."

Aine looked at him quizzically. "Why? It's still early, and Mittens may yet return . . . so do you know something that I don't know?"

Liam avoided her eyes and motioned to Sean. "It's getting late and that badger will rise early. Let's get going."

The brothers put on coats, pulled the caps borrowed from Grandda and Da over their ears, and hurried out the door. With their breath fogging the air, they walked briskly to keep warm and get there while the sky was still pink. Without talking, they took positions downwind from the badger's hole and waited, hoping he was still inside.

They had crouched motionless for the better part of an hour when just below them, a full-grown badger poked its head out and sniffed the air. Content that it was safe, it crept into the open, scuttled across the snowy grass, and headed for the stream. Liam sprang forward and with all his strength, drove his makeshift spear into its furry side. True to the badger's reputation for fighting hard, it flipped over, clawing and biting the stick with sharp teeth. Sean struck it in the head with a heavy stone, and when the rock glanced off, he hurled it a second time. The badger's struggle gradually became feebler. Liam pressed his weight on his spear, pinning the animal to the ground, until it finally lay still. After he withdrew the stick, he drove it in again and again to be certain the badger's wounds were mortal before lifting it onto his shoulder. It was a big one, and as they strode home, they were almost giddy.

But with the passage of a week, Father again started worrying about food. Early one morning as Liam slept in the loft, he was disturbed by arguing. His mother's voice became louder, and she clearly did not care whom she awakened. "The cottage will be empty of every comfort and for what? The Quakers said that the price of maize is so high that our furnishings will bring only a small amount."

"Erin, what good is a table if we have no food to put on it!"

Liam, Sean, Aine and the little girls descended the ladder and stared. Never had they heard their parents in such a heated dispute. Mother followed Father around the room, pleading. "Are you going to give away all that we have saved, all that our parents and grandparents made and created through the years?"

Without answering, Father went to the trunk and looked inside. Mamai's eyes widened in horrified recognition. "No, Seamus, not the dancing dress! My mother wore it, my sisters and I, in turn. My grandmother embroidered the skirt." He placed the blue and green dance dress on the table, undeterred. Liam saw Aine's eyes tear up since this was *her* dress now.

"Erin, we have no choice. We have to try to stay alive, and those considerations aren't important now. I'm sorry you don't agree." With that, he lifted the cradle to carry out to Uncle Paddy's cart in the yard.

"Not our children's cradle!" She rushed over and grabbed the side board. "Generations of Reilly babes have slept here, as will our grandchildren! The dealers know our need is great and give a low price. You can't bargain with them because they don't even speak Irish."

"What is our need for a cradle, over food? I'm only trying to keep *your* babes alive!"

Mother sat limp and dejected on the bench in the wall. She bit her lip and tears welled up, but Father ignored her.

"Lads, help me lift the table and benches onto the cart. I'm leaving the three stools, but wedge in the spinning wheel wherever you can. Aine, get the mirror and hair ribbons." Frozen in place, Aine refused to assist him, but Brighid scrambled up the ladder and returned with the mirror.

Father continued, unfazed. "Also the feather pillows from the loft, but I'll leave the sleeping mats and blankets. Remove the lace curtain from the window."

"The curtain that Grandmother made?" With her question, Aine reminded him that this handiwork was irreplaceable.

"Yes, I'm afraid so." Father went to the mantel, lifted his violin off the hooks, and pausing for a moment, he stroked it lovingly. Then he took a deep breath and handed it to Liam. "Here . . . take it."

Grandda opened the curtain of the side sleeping room and leaned against the door frame for support. "Here. You can have this . . . my coat." He held it out. "Won't need it anymore."

"No, *Atair* / Father. Even when you don't go out, Aine wears it. In this terrible winter, we'll keep the coats as long as we can."

Grandmother stood beside him, holding her shawl. "What about this?"

"No, you won't leave the cottage without it."

Liam was sympathetic with both parents. Father was making a shell of their home, yet the thin figures around him were

wasting away and needed food. Da believed he had no choice, but
was this the answer?

When the cart was finally loaded, Father put on his coat,
and looked sadly at Mamai, but she refused to look at him and hid
her face in her hands. As his daughters surveyed the strange vacant
cottage, they sobbed tearfully. Despite their feelings, Da squared
his shoulders with stubborn determination. He would have to pull
this load himself because soldiers had seized Uncle Paddy's donkey
for the workhouse and would have taken his cart too, had Uncle not
hidden it in the glen.

Sean grabbed his coat. "I'll go with you and help."

"Very well," Father consented. "Liam, you stay here with
the family. They need you." Liam nodded, thinking he had drawn
the harder duty. As they rolled down the lane, he followed them
with his eyes until they disappeared over the gentle, white curve of
the hill.

When he closed the door, his mother and sisters released
their grief with loud groans like a gale building to a crescendo. With
their arms around each other, they huddled together on the bench
carved out of the wall and wept inconsolably. Liam was petrified
that Mother might again slip into the throes of despair as before.

She cried out in agony, "*Go saora Dia sinn* / Good Lord,
deliver us!" Forlorn, they keened in a high tone that rose and fell
like wind, and the shrill cry made him shiver. Liam had heard this
sound of sorrow at Ballinglass and again when Niall had left home
and then when the potatoes turned black. Life worth living was
slipping away, and the angel of death, who stood watching beside
the rotten potato beds in August, was standing in the cottage now.

Grandfather, his face ashen, pulled aside the curtain and
hobbled into the room. He lifted a trembling hand to his weeping
children and opened his mouth to say something of comfort, but

realizing there was nothing to say, he closed it. Tears came to his eyes and with slow steps he turned, held on to the wall, and staggered back to bed. Liam knew that he would pray there, and that was what they needed. Perhaps by venting sorrow with her daughters, Mother would not again withdraw into that dark place. Please, God . . . not again.

Looking out the curtainless window, Liam squinted into the bright sun and searched the lane with his eyes. It was late afternoon when he saw something coming down a hill and knew it was them. He rushed out the door, and when he was close enough, he shouted, "Da, did they have any maize left?" He looked into the cart and saw the answer: only four bags for all the goods he had sold! Surely, they had cheated him somehow. He tried to hide his disappointment, but Da saw it.

Downcast, Father continued pulling the cart with eyes on the road. "I know . . . it's not much . . . not what I hoped for." As head of the family, he had always been confident and proud, but now he seemed weak and defeated.

Sean bristled and came to his defense. "The agent spoke only English and treated all us Irish with scorn and disgust . . . like we could help being poor and that it was a moral failing. Prices were low for the goods and high for the maize. As starving citizens of their British nation, they should *give* us the maize, not sell it at a profit."

When they walked into the cottage, there were no greetings, only gloom. Although the shelf near the hearth still held bowls, spoons, and the Bible, things that gave the look of home were gone, and it was bleak. Father's violin no longer hung above the mantel with its promise of music, and the curtainless window appeared stark and cold. The heavy table and benches had been the center of the room, and now it seemed a space both large and unfriendly. In the emptiness, without spinning wheel or cradle, the three remaining stools looked lonely. His young sisters, weary from crying, had fallen asleep beside the hearth, but Mother and Aine still leaned on each other in the same wall seat.

Sean went over to Mamai and laid the embroidered dancing dress in her lap. "Only Irish appreciate these costumes, and they have no money to buy them," he explained. Drained of emotion, Mamai looked down without responding, but Aine ran her fingers over the beautiful embroidery.

"We still have this, Mamai, and now it will always be ours."

Sean cleared his voice. "Aine, I have something to lift your spirits. We stopped in Partry to look for mail, and there was a letter addressed to both of us: one page from Maire and this from Brian. And they *do* miss us!" Sean took Maire's letter outside to read again in privacy, but Aine began pouring over her page at once.

Her face brightened as she read Brian's words, and turning to Mamai, she shared what was news for them all.

"Brian says, 'The journey over was very difficult in the bottom of the ship. I now realize that we Irish are used as weight at the lowest level of those top-heavy ships so they can stay upright in the waves. The air in steerage was foul with excrement and the vomit of the sick. 'Tis a wonder that we kept our health and many did not. Over sixty Irish were buried at sea and I hear that more died soon after our arrival.

"'Most of us are still looking for work, but Maire is a laundress in a rich household, and it is a fine job since they feed her. I am building train track and tunnels in the city. It's dangerous labor with many accidents, but the pay keeps food on the table. That's what's better here. Not all people eat well, but no one starves. From what I can tell so far, the government is not as oppressive, and even poor people have some rights. Niall was persuaded to join the American army and went with them to Mexico.

"'Despite the opportunity we hope to find here, I long to be back in Ireland with you. It's true, that Irish saying: *An áit a bhfuil do chroí is ann a thabharfas do chosa thú /* Your feet will bring you to where your heart is. If there were not an ocean betwinxt us, I would be back in Mayo with my precious Aine. In my thoughts, I'm there, and I think of you every hour of the day and night.

Devoted as always, . . .Brian Murphy'"

Aine put the folded letter in her pocket, and Liam was sure she would read it until it was frayed.

Mother barely listened to the letter and seemed distant, preoccupied, and angry. With a stoney expression and no light in her eyes, she refused to acknowledge or look at Father. Liam knew that he would leave her alone until this passed, and he left the cottage "for air," or so he claimed. He was gone for over an hour, and when he returned, Liam scrutinized him from across the room and felt uneasy about his flat affect and stiff movements.

The tension in the cottage was eased when Grandmother managed to leave her bed and show an interest in the sharp, hard kernels of maize. "How will you cook it, Erin?" Reluctantly, Mother rose from her seat with movements deliberately labored. She seemed to resent this costly maize and preferred to leave it untouched.

She picked up a handful with disdain and dribbled it back into the bag. "People say this unground maize is so coarse it will cut up your insides unless it is boiled for hours without end. We Irish have never eaten this before and some people call it "Peel's Brimstone" for good reason. It was Mr. Peel who brought it here and it lights a painful fire in your belly."

Grandmamai nodded. "Is this what the Quakers call stirabout? Maybe if we cook it for a long time, it will soften and become more digestible." She scooped out several bowls full and poured them into the pot, stirring them now and then. "If the good Quakers give people this, it won't kill us," she said, giving Mother a hug.

Liam worried about Grandfather who was still in his bed, but Mother said to let him rest until the maize was edible. When at last she began to fill the bowls, she called Liam. "Sit Grandda by the fire and give him a bowl of this."

Liam went into the dark side room and found him in his bed, with his head turned toward the wall. "Grandda, we have some boiled maize! Let me help you get up." There was silence. He was still, so very still, and Liam could see his rosary, lying loosely in his hand. "Grandda? . . . can you hear me?" Liam reached to turn his head and then he saw. His eyes were staring, but not seeing, and his mouth was open. Liam's heart raced. "Da! Mamai! Grandmamai! Come quick!"

Father pushed past Liam and felt Grandda's forehead. Falling to his knees, he held Grandda's boney, limp hand. In a hoarse voice, he confirmed Liam's fear, "He's gone." Tears rolled down Da's cheeks as he gently closed Grandda's eyes and said goodbye. "Dear *Athair* / Father . . . my best friend . . . rest with God."

I 5

An Ghorta Mor

Grandfather's wake was unlike any Liam had ever attended. In normal times the cottage would be overflowing with relatives and friends who wanted to comfort the family and show respect for the gregarious Tomas Liam Reilly. After prayer and condolences, there would have been stories, cherished memories, food, and toasts to celebrate a life well-lived, but now only a few people came.

Many of Grandfather's friends had preceded him to the grave, and others were too weak to leave their dwellings. Having pawned warm clothing, people had become prisoners of winter and dreaded going outside. The typhus epidemic inspired a fear of gatherings since the slightest contact with an infected person brought the horrible affliction to one's door, and now cholera also was striking victims weakened by hunger. Every family was immersed in private sorrow and attended their own frequent burials until they had cried themselves dry and no longer had the energy to weep. The shadow of death was everywhere, and people were giving this terrible time a name: *An Ghorta Mor* / The Great Hunger.

Only close relatives still strong and living nearby came to spend time in the side room and pray beside Grandda's bed. In late afternoon they knelt on the flagstone floor while Cousin Eamon led the gathering in the recitation of the rosary, and then they left the immediate family alone.

In the wee hours of morning Liam went again to the side room. Grandfather lay in his bed nestled in its alcove, and the curtain which usually provided privacy was pulled back and tied. Dressed in a clean white shirt with his silver hair combed neatly to one side, he held rosary beads in his fingers and an intricately carved crucifix rested on his chest. Although he had starved to death, the candle gave a warm glow and softened the gauntness of his face.

Tears blurred Liam's vision as he imagined a future without Grandda. Grandmother sat on a stool nearby, resigned and ready to follow him, not just to the churchyard, but to what lay beyond. When Liam put his arm around her, he felt her protruding shoulder bones and was reminded of how fragile and thin she had become. Her boney hand reached up and patted his with affection. His grandparents had loved them all without conditions or criticism so how does one say thank you? He wiped his cheek with his sleeve.

Tradition dictated that at least one or two family members would remain awake with the deceased until morning when he would be carried away. His little sisters were sleeping in the loft and Mother sat with Aine on her and Da's bed in the opposite alcove. Sean was slumped in Grandda's seat beside the fireplace and seemed lost in memories as he stared mournfully into the flickering flames. But where was Da? Liam wondered how long he had been gone from the cottage but did not ask. Soon Mother directed everyone to the loft for sleep while she and Grandmother stayed awake in the candle-lit room.

The next morning Liam put on his jacket, combed his hair, and shaved his face clean. He lovingly put on Grandda's soft, wool hat which Da had given him yesterday. Uncle Paddy had risen at dawn, dug Grandfather's grave in the Partry churchyard, and had even managed to borrow the church's coffin with a hinged bottom. Surrounded by the family, it now rested on the floor in the center of the room, and it was time to go.

Da stood beside it, solemn, pale, and unshaven. Evidently aware of his own disheveled appearance, he ran his fingers through his tousled hair. When Sean and Uncle Paddy placed Grandfather in the wooden box, softened with a bit of straw, Da was aloof and made no offer to help. Oddly flat and empty of emotion, he gazed straight ahead and avoided looking at Grandda's face.

Removing the rosary, Sean whispered, "Here, Grandmamai."

After closing the lid, Uncle Paddy asked Father to help lift the coffin and carry it into the yard, but as Da stepped over the threshold, he stumbled and startled everyone by almost dropping it. No longer trusting Da's steadiness or coordination, Liam hurried to assist him as they shoved the coffin into the cart.

Tearfully the girls said their final goodbye for without shawls or shoes in this frigid weather, they would remain at the cottage. Mother and Grandmother pulled large, woolen shawls over their heads, wrapped themselves up, and climbed into the cart to ride with the coffin. For added warmth, Liam put Grandda's wool coat around their bare feet.

The small funeral procession began with the cart going first, pulled by Liam and Sean. Liam could feel the eyes of his sisters on them until they rounded the bend and were out of sight. Uncle Paddy and Da took up the rear with Uncle holding Da's arm to steady his mechanical and awkward steps. The grinding wheels on the gravel and the friction of wood planks were the only sounds of their journey – like a dirge.

When they reached the road, they met other funeral groups, coming and going in all directions to various graveyards, carrying the remains of loved ones in sheets, trunks, and whatever could be found. One man being transported on a door had died of typhus or black fever which darkened the skin, and not wanting to get too close, the Reillys stayed back and let them pass. Even in the piercing cold, many men as well as women walked barefoot and coatless with expressionless faces, looking half alive and half dead. One man, who had eaten only maize and not much of that, hobbled on a blackened leg.

When they arrived at the churchyard in Partry, Liam was struck by the change. Because of the blustery, cold weather, he had not been to Mass since before Christmas, but always before, a thick blanket of winter grass had covered the churchyard even in February and made it a lush green. Now with so many dying, there was freshly turned earth everywhere, and it looked like a field tilled for the dead, with only a few patches of grass remaining. Old graves had been reopened and new family members added. The only open grave awaited Grandda, and they pulled the cart beside it.

Father Mullen must have been watching from the chapel and came out in his vestments. "I'm sorry for your troubles," he said to the mothers and shook hands with the men. After they set the coffin down, Father blessed it and opened his Bible to read scripture. "These are they which came out of great tribulation and are made white in the blood of the Lamb. They shall hunger no more, neither thirst any more, neither shall the sun light on them, nor any heat. For the lamb shall feed them, and God shall wipe away all tears from their eyes." Liam felt comforted by the reading and felt that Grandfather was now in the loving hands of God. Together they recited the Our Father.

Sean and Uncle Paddy lowered the coffin into the hole, and when Liam reached under it to release the latch, they heard

Grandfather fall. After Uncle Paddy lifted the box back out, he took two spades from the cart for the burial. Da, however, stood stiffly and stared into space. It seemed to require great concentration for him to stand still and straight, but despite his efforts, he still swayed slightly in the wind. Liam glanced around to see if others noticed his wobbly stance, but evidently they preferred not to show it, if they did. Now was not the time.

Just then, Liam caught sight of a crouching boy, moving through the church yard and carrying something on his back. In a far corner, he stopped, put down his burden, and began digging with his bare hands. Concerned, Liam approached and saw a dead girl of three or four years, skin and bones.

"May I help you?" he asked the boy.

The lad, not more than twelve, stopped and looked up, his eyes in dark hallows. "It's my little sister. I'm the oldest, and my parents are too weak to leave our cabin."

Liam crouched beside him. "This ground is too hard and cold to dig without a spade."

The lad looked down at his hands, which were now bleeding. "I *have* to bury her. I can't let the animals have her."

Liam picked up the small girl with great tenderness. "Follow me and I'll take her over here." The boy walked after him on spindly legs, barefoot, and in a ragged shirt. Liam felt the icy wind through his coat, but the boy was so intent on his purpose that he did not seem to notice the cold.

Sean and Uncle Paddy had shoveled several spadefuls into the grave and were adding more when Father Mullen stopped them. "Wait. Someone is here." He questioned the boy and learned of his mission. "I think we can give Grandfather a small person with whom to rise up on the last day. Lay this little girl beside him in the grave." The Reillys, despite their own grief, felt compassion, and as they looked at the boy, Liam saw their faces soften.

Grandmother began to stir in the cart, and when Mother offered her a steady hand, she got out. "Come here, child!" She took Grandfather's coat and put it around the boy. "So thin, you are! You're a brave brother to carry your sister here all alone. Yes Liam, put that precious sister in beside my Tomas."

Liam nodded, and since that had been his idea all along, he gently laid her down and arranged her reed-like arms across her chest. Smiling, he reassured the boy, "She'll receive no further harm."

Father Mullen sprinkled her with holy water, as he had Grandda. "Let us pray for her also. What is her name, my son?"

"Aileen O'Shea."

"May little Aileen, innocent and pure of heart, rest in our Lord and be welcomed by the angels and saints. May she and Tomas rejoice together in heaven for now and all eternity . . . and pray for us. In the name of the Father, the Son, and the Holy Spirit." Father Mullen concluded with the sign of the cross.

The lad seemed relieved. Then he turned to Grandmother and took off the wool coat. "You better take this back now."

But she waved him away. "No, no. You keep it. I won't be needing it once I'm home." Liam was amazed. To give away Grandfather's frieze jacket? Mother had a shawl, but Aine had nothing. What was she thinking?

But Grandmother patted the boy's shoulder and smiled. "You have sick parents and younger children depending on you, so you need it more."

Liam was both moved by her generosity and bothered. He considered asking the boy to give the coat back, but the expression on Grandmother's face held him in check. Being able to help someone had comforted her and brought a smile to her lips, and his family's faces mirrored her same emotions. Liam's heart also went out to a child with such heavy burdens, but the coat had value. Yet maybe the boy *did* need it more. Yes . . . and after all, the coat was Grandmother's to give, not his.

Grandmother radiated an inner peace. The boy was moved by her concern and when she reached to give him a hug, his lip quivered and tears welled up. Seeing this, Grandmother embraced him and spoke in a soothing voice. "Now . . . now . . . stay strong and go along home. Your family is waiting and needs you . . . and God bless you, dear boy." With that, he nodded and hurriedly ran down the path.

When Grandmother and Mother again climbed into the cart, Liam took off his own coat and put it around their feet. "Just till we get home."

"Thank you, Liam. I know Grandda would be glad that little fella came along at just the right time."

While they were talking with the child, Father had crept to the back of the cemetery and leaned over the fence, retching and sick. Uncle Paddy saw him and called to his brother.

"Seamus, there's room in the cart for you now that the coffin is back in the churchyard. Since your grief has made you ill, you can ride home." Sean and Uncle Paddy hoisted him into the cart, and he sat at the edge with his legs dangling out the side. Pale and nauseated, he held his head in his hands as the cart shifted and jostled down the rough road. Liam guessed that Paddy realized Da was drinking but just wanted to cover for him with the family.

Before leaving Partry, they stopped in the Post Office to see if there were any letters from America, but there was only an issue of the *Mayo Constitution*.

As they passed through the village of Kiltharsechaune – the village of doorsteps, some men at the edge of the stream were excitedly pointing at the water and splashing in the cold current. When they got closer, Liam saw a silver glint in the water.

"It's salmon! They've started their run!" he shouted. Sean whooped, ran ahead, and waded in, but only the quick could catch the slippery fish with their bare hands. He came close but missed again and again before he connected. At last, Sean tossed a big one on the bank where it flipped about with amazing leaps until Liam struck its head with a stone. The villagers cheered Sean's success and kept trying for a catch themselves.

Finally, amid shouts and celebration, a group of men cornered a salmon and then went after more. The noise attracted haggard children who slowly emerged from the cottages and hobbled toward the stream like persons in advanced age. Sadly, Liam realized that these boys and girls would never reach adulthood, even though this salmon run might prolong their short life.

He grabbed the arm of a father and cautioned, "Eat slowly, small portions, or it will surely make you sick." He seized another by the arm and repeated his warning. As they departed, he looked back and wondered if the village of Kiltharsechaune would survive, or would the West of Ireland become a land of ghosts and sheep.

As they entered the yard, Liam could see Caitlin's face against the window pane, and the girls burst out the door as if their family had been gone for days. Since they had taken only a cup of morning milk, they were famished.

"We're sooo hungry." Brighid whined.

"You must be!" Mother put her arm around her. "But we have a big fish!"

"Enough for all of us?" Aine asked quietly.

"Yes, Aine," Liam answered sternly. "Don't be taking less!"

Mother hurried in to prepare the large salmon and, after

rubbing it with butter, she placed it on the griddle over the fire. With rapt attention, the family watched the huge fish cook and listened to the sizzle as it fried. Brighid kept pointing to the salmon and smiling as they breathed the aroma which now filled the room. It was so large that the tail drooped off the edge of the round griddle, and since this thinner part was cooked sooner, Mother cut it off with a knife and divided it among the eager girls. With the table gone, they held their bowls in their laps.

Aine, taking her first taste, noticed that Brighid was almost finished. "It will last longer if you just nibble and take small bites," she instructed. During the tortuous wait, Liam watched the girls chew each morsel and swallowed when they did, eating vicariously.

Mother, thinking the large thick fish would cook more quickly if she turned it over, took tongs and flipped it, but in the process, the fish landed off center, and its weight caused the griddle to tilt. The buttered salmon began to slide. No! There was a collective gasp as the family realized the precious dinner was falling into the flames.

Sean, sitting the closest, sprang forward and caught it just in time. He flipped it back onto the center of the griddle, and then he rushed to the water pail where he submerged his burning hands. There he stayed for a quarter hour, and when he took his hands out of the water, Aine soothed them with a layer of snow.

Mother added more water to a pot of maize and stirred it. "You young ones should not eat much of this because it's too hard to digest."

When Liam began to slice the fish and put it in the bowls, Grandmother protested. "Only a small piece for me."

"No, Grandmamai! You will eat your share!" Liam was almost yelling.

"But I'm really not very hungry. I speak the truth."

"It's just because you've made a habit of eating less."

Liam was too ravenous to continue the argument and attacked his salmon, although he noticed that Grandmother still gave half her portion to Caitlin. At least, Aine ate her share.

After dinner, as they huddled around the fire, shadows flickered on their faces and danced on the walls. Father seemed more himself again and looked up to where his violin once hung above the hearth. Liam knew he longed for it and recalled Da saying that his violin was his first love, before he met Mamai. It brought him such joy, and Liam knew it broke his heart to give it up, but he made the sacrifice without complaint.

Liam whispered to Sean. "We need music. Play your tin whistle."

Sean took it from the mantel and comforted them with an ethereal melody from Ireland's past, and then Mother sang the plaintive song "The Parting Glass," which spoke of the heartache of separation from loved ones who emigrated from Ireland. Liam knew about voids in the heart and yearned for both Niall and Colleen. He could not wish for Grandda who was now removed from his misery.

Unaccustomed to playing solo, Sean put the tin flute back on the mantel. "Da, read to us from the newspaper. Maybe there is good news and help is coming."

"Yes, eating was first, and I almost forgot we have the newspaper." Father smoothed it out and began to read aloud. "In January, the Polish nobleman Count Strzelecki, who heads the charity called the British Association, went to Westport and wrote that no pen can describe the suffering he saw. Now he has purchased food, blankets, and some clothing to distribute to school children in the West of Ireland. Charles Trevelyan has objected, however, and is attempting to block it. He is quoted as saying, 'This will make the children start expecting charity,' and it is unclear at this time how the controversy will come out.

"The Association also wants to give small loans to fishermen in Belmullet in Erris, but Secretary Trevelyan has objected to this also. Once again he has stated that 'The problem is not the famine, but the moral evil of the Irish people. Since the Almighty has willed the famine, the English government would be presumptuous indeed to attempt any rash solution.'"

At that, Sean roared in anger. "He wants *no* solution to the Famine!"

Aine frowned, "Sean, don't interrupt. Read on, Da."

"In a recent speech in the House of Commons, Lord George Bentinck said 'Never before was there a Christian government allowing so many people to perish without interfering.' The members started yells to silence him, but he continued. 'The time will come when we shall know what the amount of mortality has been. The truth will come out, and the world will know what you have done in Ireland.' On February 19th in the House of Commons, it was announced that around 15,000 people die each day in Ireland."

Liam was shocked. "Folks have been saying that it's the destruction of the Irish people they're after! Yes, it's *cinedhíothú!*"

Father looked up. "Bless Lord Bentinck. At least there's one compassionate voice in Parliament. Now hear this! The headline says 'DANIEL O'CONNELL PLEAS FOR MERCY IN LAST SPEECH – HOUSE OF COMMONS. Sick and broken, O'Connell spoke in a hoarse whisper. Though he could barely stand and trembled, he uttered a heartfelt plea: "The Irish are starving by the thousands – no, millions. Ireland is in your hands, in your power. If you do not save her, she cannot save herself. I predict that a quarter of her population will perish unless you come to her relief." The members did not listen or show him respect. Benjamin Disraeli described him as 'a feeble old man muttering before a table.'"

Father tossed the paper on the floor, and his eyes flashed. "Even when O'Connell is near death and goes to beg them for help, the Parliament insults him . . . and us."

Grandmother shook her head sadly. "They were cruel, and I'm glad Tomas can't hear this. He loved O'Connell."

Liam stood, folded the paper, and was about to put it away when the word Castlebar caught his eye. To himself, he read the headline: "Castlebar Workhouse Closed. The workhouse is no longer admitting paupers and it is unknown when it will reopen. On Christmas the inmates waited all day for their maize which came after dark. Such lateness was a regular occurrence. Most inmates buried at the workhouse died of starvation and fever. The few remaining inmates are without benefit of heat or sufficient food and are not expected to survive. Mr. Gibbons, an inspector of the poorhouse, has submitted a report to the Lord-Lieutenant."

Liam's heart stopped. Colleen was gone! He had clung to the hope that being young, she would somehow survive. He dropped the newspaper into Aine's lap and fled to the yard. Fearing that someone would follow him, he hid behind the shed where he broke down. Not Colleen . . . . He shook his head, devastated. Was she one of the first to die or the last? He shuddered as he imagined her final days – trapped, growing weaker, watching people suffer, and finally her own slow death by starvation or illness.

He recalled Father Henry's words that Lord Lucan, with over 60,000 tenants in County Mayo, wanted to close the workhouse. Liam loathed him and the government which set up the workhouses and then used them to keep the destitute cornered and out of sight until they died.

Why? He tried to make sense of it all. What was it that Trevelyan said – that the *Irish* were immoral – while he, a man of power, wills millions to die? He clinched his teeth and looked out over the frozen hills, blue-gray in the moonlight. Outraged in the face of such great injustice, he felt hot even in the cold night air.

Then he heard someone's feet crunching through snow and frozen weeds. Liam decided to stay hidden because he did not want company, and whoever it was would not remain outside long in this cold evening air. But the feet kept coming, and someone was entering the shed. The door of brush and thatch creaked open, and Liam heard the cow softly low as if to question the intrusion. Hearing rustling inside, Liam peeked through a crack and saw Da in the corner on his knees, digging under straw. At last, with a satisfied sigh, he sat down with a large jug of poteen between his legs.

Alarms went off inside Liam's head as his emotions boiled over. Following his first impulse, he rushed into the shed and kicked the heavy, clay jug hard, tipping it onto its side. Shocked, Da watched with wide-eyed horror as the clear liquid gurgled out onto the straw. Grabbing the jug, he drained the last dregs into his mouth, and when it was empty, he flung it aside. Panicked, he crouched on his knees and gathered wet straw, futilely trying to recapture what was spilled. He looked pitiful in his desperate need and realizing it was hopeless, he slumped over.

Then he turned burning eyes on Liam. "You had no right to do that! That was *mine* and I *needed* it!"

Liam gripped his hands into fists. "No! That only clouds your mind! We need you to be strong . . . to be a *father*, not a weakling!"

Da broke down and began to weep. "But I *am* weak . . . no use to anyone. Can't keep the family alive . . . can't do anything." He put his face in his arms which were propped on his knees and sobbed.

Liam had never seen his father cry, and it touched him to the core. He felt cruel. "Oh Da, I'm sorry. You're a good father, *really* you are . . . always kind and strong before this!" Liam sat down and draping his arm around his shoulders, he felt him trembling.

Father stared ahead with bulging eyes. "I'm . . . I'm scared. The hunger . . . it's . . . it's coming on us closer every day . . . it's gonna take us down! And I'm helpless . . . can't stop it."

Liam looked into his face intently. "What's happening to us . . . it's not your fault, you know. Don't blame yourself. We'll survive, despite them, and get the family through this, somehow. The salmon are running now, and Sean and I can help!"

Father kept wagging his head and started to shake. "It's coming . . . that hunger." He put his face in his hands, as if to blot out the scenes in his mind. "We won't be spared."

Liam tried to steady him, putting a firm hand on his back. "I understand your fear, and I have fears too. I've been terrified that Mamai would relapse into the melancholy . . . but she hasn't. Some way, with our prayers she's gotten stronger. Sometimes our fears don't happen." Liam paused and became grave as he contemplated his own words. Then he looked away into space. "But sometimes they *do* happen. I was afraid that Colleen would die in the workhouse, and now she has."

Father raised his brows "Colleen?"

"Yes, the girl from Ballinglass, Colleen O'Neill. She took my heart, and I haven't been able to get her out of my mind. I always dreamed of saving her or finding her someday . . . but now all the inmates are dead or dying."

Da nodded sympathetically and put his arm around his son. "I never knew how you felt. You never told me. She and her family went to Castlebar, didn't they? I'm so sorry."

Liam shrugged. "There's nothing I can do now but live each day and try to keep us all alive. But we need you, Da. And that poteen . . . it only makes things worse."

Father had started to listen. "I know. I've got to do what I can. The jug's empty now, and I don't have more. I'm thinking that is better."

Together they went into the cottage, and long after everyone else was in bed, they were still sitting by the fire, talking. When Liam finally climbed to the loft, he still feared that one day Da would again succumb to the poteen, despite his promise to leave it alone.

16
Day by Day

After the emotional upheaval of the night and the news of Colleen's death, Liam's sleep was tortured. Her willowy figure floated in and out of his mind. In the middle of the night, he opened his eyes, and above him in the dark rafters, he could almost see her face . . . touch her hand. The loss cut deep into his soul, and nothing could ease the ache. He felt hopeless, incomplete, and broken somehow. Without real prospects for happiness, he only aimed at survival.

Fitful and tossing, he finally dozed off again, but in his nightmare, poteen flowed from the mouth of a tilted jug, and no matter how many times he kicked it, the stream was never-ending. When the jug seemed empty, it would mysteriously refill. Repeatedly he tried to break it with stones and a club, but the jug was stronger than he. At dawn he awoke, weary from the baffling struggle.

Last night he had promised his father that he and Sean would catch fish and keep the family alive . . . out of the "pathway to the dead." He had to keep that pledge, and as a ray of light seeped under the thatch, he crawled over and shook his brother.

"*Dúisigh!* / Wake up! Salmon are running. We can't waste time sleeping."

Sean growled, but sat up. "Where now? How about Lough Carra or Lough Mask?"

Liam pulled on his shirt. "Maybe. Let's take the net and a pail, but first, a bowl of stirabout."

"Ugh! I can't digest that stuff."

When they descended the ladder, Father, already awake, had laid a brick on the fire and was stoking it. Hearing them, he twisted around and nodded at Liam reassuringly. "The cow is looking poorly, and she's down in weight. So today I'll take her up the hills and feed her by hand what grass I can find."

Liam pulled a stool towards the fire. "That would be good. Sean and I will go to the lakes for salmon."

Even though he had no tobacco, Father massaged his pipe and clutched it in his teeth. "Stay away from the landlords' fishing grounds. I hear some have set man-traps that clamp shut with metal teeth on a foot or leg, inflicting great injury. A young lad from Ballintubber was caught in one at Lough Carra; his torn leg turned black and he died. When they don't have enough watchmen, some landlords rig up spring-loaded guns."

Liam held his hands up to the blaze. "Da, you've warned us so *many* times! You must think we have no memory."

Mother scooped out boiled maize into the bowls and handed one to each. "I'm concerned about how much of this we have consumed. Perhaps I should reduce the amounts."

Frustrated, Father sighed. "We're eight mouths, don't ya know, and your servings have not been too generous. I just have to find a way to get more food. Erin . . . I know we've talked about this before . . . but now we are poor enough to qualify for work relief, so I should try to get on the rolls. I could make six-pence a day, and while it's not much, 'tis better than nothing."

Mother frowned. "Seamus, what can you be thinking? The pay is not enough to keep two people alive, much less eight! The Anglos running the programs are paid well, but not the Irish workers whom they're supposed to be helping. Worst of all, many is the time that they don't pay wages at all. You read that in the newspaper yesterday."

Father looked beaten down. "But I ask you now, what else can I do?"

She wiped her hands on her apron. "You can plant a crop. We still have the seed oats, and next month we can plough the soil."

Now Father, too, was frowning and Liam could see an argument brewing. Exasperated, Da threw up his hands. "And how do we live till then? Without potatoes, we can't feed ourselves. Even if we plant oats and survive to harvest them, Sligo will just come and take it all for his own profit, giving us nothing for our labor but the privilege of living here in a cottage our family built! Just like every year."

Mother put her hands on her hips. "But that's something." Her eyes were wide. "We *have* to keep our cottage. Eviction is doom!"

Father's brow furrowed. "Paying rent does not make us secure. If a landlord decides to convert to ranches, we farmers are in the way, and they will evict us, even if rent has been paid. Sligo has been slower than some to evict, but he's changing. I've heard of whole villages where he's giving notices to quit, so we can't count on him."

Mother became more tense and her voice shrill. "But Seamus, breaking stones will take your strength, and you're not eating enough for such hard labor. You'd have to walk five . . . ten miles to the work site in freezing weather."

Father shrugged. "I'm more able than most who do it. Some I see are so weak that they can barely stand. They stagger down the roads with their spade, and I wonder if they'll make it to the works before they collapse. I'm much stronger than they, and I still have a coat."

Mother continued, undaunted. "The work isn't even worthwhile. The English passed that law saying the projects must be useless and of no benefit to Ireland. People break stones to build a road to nowhere and a bridge where there is no stream! What will people a hundred years from now think when they find roads that start and end in the wilderness and a bridge over dry land?"

Father nodded. "I know. The work kills many with its severity, but I would survive it."

Mother stood before him, her eyes pleading. "Are you forgetting the clause that Lord William Gregory just put into the law? To receive relief of any sort, we must agree to give up farming all land more than a quarter acre. It's a trick to get farmers off the land, and you said so yourself."

At the mention of Gregory, Father's face flushed with anger. "Yes! You're right! For that quarter-acre clause, Gregory's name will be despised in Ireland for all time, and may he burn in hell! But the choice they are giving us is to die or get out. We have no money to leave, and I'm not ready to lie down and die!"

"But Seamus, what if Trevelyan stops the relief work? Then we would have given up our lease for nothing, so think of that."

With hands clasped, Father slumped over and stared at the floor. "Well, the hunger is coming harder and faster on us every day!" Liam knew this thought terrified him and that he would think of nothing else, but he was trying. He had no answers to her arguments, but their need for food could not be postponed for long.

Aine had descended the ladder and, having heard much of the debate, she looked strained and worried. Then she cleared her throat and held up two pieces of paper. "Brothers, I have two letters for you to mail in Partry – one to Niall and the other to Brian and Maura. Sean, add a note to Maura on this end of the paper."

Sean snatched it from her and retreated to the wall seat.

Liam was surprised at the request. "And tell me, where do we get the money for stamps?"

"When Brian wrote me, he enclosed a bit for stamps so I could write him back."

Mother sank to a stool. "And what have you written to our Niall?"

Aine's voice dropped to a whisper. "About Grandfather . . . how he starved himself for us and how I fear Grandmamai is not far behind . . . how we've sold almost everything. And, of course, that we love and miss him."

Mother reached for the letter, a precious link to her son. "May I add something?"

"Of course, Mamai. Do you want me to write for you?"

"Yes. Tell him to be strong and hold his temper when they're hard on Irish . . . and to go to church and pray for us . . . if they'll let him."

With the letters in their coats, the brothers started out for the lakes. At the roadsides, the living lay with the dead in the same ditch, too weak to move. Liam could see that many, having endured long and sustained hunger, had famine dropsy which swelled their bodies until the skin split. Liam averted his eyes at the horror and stared at the gravel, but even when he was not looking, the images floated before his eyes. Would he ever be able to purge them from his mind? Somehow, he doubted it.

When they passed through a small village of about fifteen cottages, he was dismayed to see weeping families, tearing down their own houses. The roofs were stubborn to dislodge, and the work was back-breaking. Shivering in rags and crying, the children watched their parents in confusion and fear.

Curious, Liam stopped. "Why are you demolishing your own cottages? If they evicted you, don't do work for them!"

"They told us that if we ripped them down ourselves, they would pay us something. A few shillings or so."

One woman was in the latter stages of pregnancy and, except for her protruding stomach, she was dangerously thin. It was rare now to see a woman with child, and Liam feared for both the baby and mother. Soon they would take to the road without even "the Savior's horse," as a donkey was often called, and the parallel touched his heart.

Hearing galloping horses in the distance, they gazed toward the sound and saw a large party of soldiers on the hill, riding down on them.

One man murmured, "It's some of the Fifth Dragoon Guards. I wish to God the government would spend money for food, instead of more soldiers!" As the mounted men trotted into the ruined village, the leader eyed with suspicion the people in tatters. The men stopped working and stood, while the women and children, with tear stained faces, glared back with hurt and hate.

The officer scowled at Liam and Sean. "Are you part of this village? If not, move on!" He shoved his crop into Liam's shoulder, in case Liam could not understand English. "Move, I say!"

Liam wanted to grab it and pull the soldier off the horse, but managed to restrain himself. Yet when he saw Sean's eyes blazing with defiance, he feared that his impulsive brother might react so he gave him a push himself.

They sauntered away to the main road where a food convoy was passing. Sean clinched his jaw. "In the newspaper it said that since the famine, the English are eating more Irish cheese, bacon, grain, butter, lambs, and hams than ever before."

Liam snorted. "When Queen Victoria swore to protect her subjects, it is clear that she meant to leave us Irish out."

Sean looked thoughtful. "I'm glad that Maire did not stay here and marry me, but now she wants us to marry in America and she's waiting."

Liam answered without hesitation. "Then you should go as soon as possible. If Niall only sends enough money for some of us, you leave first and send passage back to me when you can." Sean nodded gratefully. They were brothers and did not need to say more.

After the convoy passed, they walked on to the lakes. The clear, still loughs reflected the hills and blue sky and provided a needed escape, however brief, from scenes of suffering. The weather hinted that spring was scarcely more than a month away, and snow only remained in small patches where shade was dense. In the rocks and crevices near the shore, Liam glimpsed shimmering pearl scales as the salmon returned to lay eggs in the places of their birth. It was so tempting to fish here, but it was posted: private fishing grounds.

Much of the shoreline around lakes was off limits and reserved for the landlords so places where Irish were permitted to fish were crowded. The brothers were forced to join other men in a stream near the road where all scrambled and lunged at the silver-scaled fish, trying to trap them with nets, pails, and even their bare hands. All this activity drove the fish away to calmer waters and convinced Liam and Sean that they should also move on. As they emerged from the cold water, they shivered and their wet pants clung to their legs. On the shore, they put on their wool jackets, grateful to have them.

"Liam, I heard accents from further south. The salmon run may be shorter this year with so many people coming to Mayo's lakes."

Liam frowned. "Don't be thinking so much."

As they continued walking, the road went close to the northern bank of the serene Lough Mask where large boats were anchored in the center. Laughter floated across the water as nobles dressed in heavy coats, scarves, and fine hats delighted in the harvest taken from numerous fishing lines and large nets.

Sean grimaced. "To them, it's just sport, not survival. Maybe we can come back late, after dark."

While they stood watching, a rotund fellow in a high hat standing near the bow leaned way over to lift his line, and his voice echoed across the quiet lake. "The devil! That sneaky fish stole my worm! More bait!" he bellowed to servants in nearby rowboats. Because his large belly obstructed his view, he lost his balance as he turned to sit and his arms circled and flapped like a fat bird coming in for a landing. Finally, he tumbled face first into the cold water with an enormous splash that sprayed the frowning and disgruntled aristocrats. When he bobbed back up, blubbering and shaking his bald head, his wig and hat were floating away. On shore Sean and Liam roared with laughter and did an imitation, waving their arms in circles.

The boat full of gentry turned and glared at them, and a plump man took off his hat and leered with his chin jutting out. "Get those impudent rascals!" he yelled to servants in the small boats. With the brothers still laughing and doubled over, the boatmen rowed furiously and made for the shore.

"They're not coming for us, are they now?" Sean asked.

Liam, sobered by the thought, stared as paddles stirred and splashed. "That they are! Time to get going!"

The chase was on as the brothers sprinted across the lane, leaping a ditch and dashing through fields of last year's stubble. The servants were on land and now in full run. The Reillys raced through a grove of trees, down a hill, and on to the Partry road. When they rounded a curve in the lane, they were briefly out of the sight of their pursuers.

"The cemetery!" Liam panted and hurdled over the surrounding stone wall. Spying the hinged coffin in disuse beside the chapel, he ran for it and jumped in. Sean dived on top of him and pulled the lid down, but with the two of them, it lacked an inch from shutting.

They heard voices from the road and the squeaking of the metal gate as someone swung it open and entered the church yard. Liam held his breath, praying that they would not notice the slight opening in the lid and decide to investigate. The voices speaking Irish came closer to their hiding place.

"Where did they go? Did we lose them?"

"They may beat us if we return without them!"

"When we catch those lads and take them back, they'll whip them with a heavy cane until their own family won't recognize their bloody faces."

Someone groaned. "I'd hate being forced to watch that."

"Well, they aren't here . . . must have gone a different way."

"Almost laughed myself at their antics," another chuckled.

"'Tis a good thing you didn't!"

As the voices became softer and more distant, Liam wondered if they had left. "Sean, can you see through the crack?" he whispered.

Sean chuckled. "Can't see them. I sure never thought of a coffin as a refuge!"

"Fortunately, neither did they! Crawl out but stay low to the ground," Liam directed. As Sean rolled over the side, he let the lid clap shut, and Liam cringed. "Keep it quiet!"

Sean sneezed. "They're gone."

"With the noise you're making, I certainly hope so." Peeking over the side in all directions, Liam lifted the lid and crept out. "We'll be on our way then. Stay alert in case they didn't give up so easily, but it sounded like those Irish boys had mixed feelings about finding us."

In Partry they went to the postal agent, but before Liam sealed Niall's letter, he wrote on the back an earnest plea: "Brother, I don't know if we can hold out much longer. Is there any way you can send us passage money soon? Otherwise, we may not need it." After Liam purchased the stamps and dropped the letters into the mail bag, he murmured a prayer that the American army would deliver it into Niall's hands . . . please, God.

On the other side of town where a small bridge crossed a swollen stream, the muddy bank was thick with men and boys. Cheers rose with each catch, and groans followed a salmon's escape. It was a game of life and death – both for the men and the salmon.

Sean took off his coat. "Every place free to us is crowded so we might as well try here." He grabbed the net, waded to a rock, and climbed on. The men on the bank, in their eagerness for a catch, churned the water and ended up driving the salmon toward Sean. Liam threw off his coat and joined him on the rock just as a large one glided nearby. Sean, with net in hand, crouched and anticipated its speed and direction. At just the right moment, he scooped it up and lifted it out, but the salmon, too big for the net, thrashed about with great energy.

Liam, fearing that he would jump free, grabbed his slippery tail just long enough to strike his head with a stone. "He's ours!" They had chosen a good spot for this day. Sean's skillful timing snared two more salmon, and before they slithered out of the net, Liam finished them off with a blow from his rock.

Sean grinned. "We're a good team, don't ya know." With

teeth chattering, they waded back to the bank, but before they started for home, they found a piece of vine and pierced the mouths of the heavy fish to carry them.

They had not gone far when they met a scattering of people from the evicted hamlet. The men limped along, looking miserable and broken, with their wives and children trailing. The pregnant woman was at the rear, looking pained with each step.

Liam called out. "I hope they paid you something!"

Their look of humiliation and defeat said it all. "We waited hours for them to return. When they finally came back, we reminded them of their promise, but they just laughed. Scorn was all we got."

Sean's eyes narrowed. "Hell isn't hot enough for the likes of them."

Liam held up the salmon. "At least you might eat tonight. I wish we could spare you one of these, but at that bridge ahead, there's more fish tails than water. You'll see."

At home Father was bringing in the cow from the hills, and she already seemed more alert since the feeding of good grass. They stood in the yard outside the shed, examining her when they heard a horse whinny. Liam glanced back and was startled to see soldiers riding into the yard and dismounting.

"Mr. Riley, we've come to collect a new levy for the workhouse. What have you? Your cow, I presume." The color drained from Father's face.

Liam cringed. If only Da had come home a little later.

The officer pointed to the cow with his crop. "Take it," he said to his second in command. "Let's look inside."

Liam scrambled to get ahead of them and pounded on the door. "Open, Mamai. It's soldiers from her Majesty's army."

There was a wait before the door opened a crack, and Brighid's face peered out. "Who is it? We're getting dressed."

The officer frowned and became gruff. "What is she saying? We have no time for this!"

Liam smiled and explained in English. "It won't be long, sir. They were bathing."

The horse jangled the bridle as the officer tied the reins to a rose bush, and when a thorn pierced his glove, he shook his hand and cursed in English. Impatient, he kept hitting his thigh with his crop. "Here, here! We're going in."

When Aine opened the door and motioned for them to enter, Liam was surprised to see the cottage looking much emptier than before. There were no clothes on the hooks, no bowls on the shelves and only two stools in the floor, rather than three.

"We'll take these stools. Where are your clothes? No dishes? Bedding?" the soldier asked.

"You can check in the side room where my grandmother has the typhus. She's in the bed." Aine pulled aside the curtain hanging in the doorway.

The officer barked an order to the soldier on his right. "Look in there."

He cautiously peeked in, keeping some distance between him and Grandmother. "Someone's in the bed."

"Well, let's get out of here! These stools and the cow will do for now." The soldiers scurried out to others waiting in the yard and heaped the stools on top of the confiscated goods in the military wagon. After they tied the cow to the back, they mounted and left.

Liam turned to Aine. "Where did you hide the bowls and clothes?"

"In the loft. Those soldiers are all alike and run at the mention of typhus."

Father looked more ashen than before as he sank into the wall seat beside the hearth. "Damn . . . we *needed* that cow. We've *always* had milk. They keep taking more and more." He cleared his throat. "Well . . . now it's decided. I've been thinking about it a long time, and tomorrow I'll go and see if I can get on the work relief rolls." Liam worried that the tavern in Ballinrobe might entice him in his present state of mind and offered to accompany him.

"No need to waste your energy when I can go alone. You and Sean need to catch salmon since that is what's keeping us alive."

The next day Father went to Ballinrobe but came home, troubled. "I ran into Captain Lawrence in the street and with his help, I got on the rolls while almost everyone else was turned away. But they made me forego all claim to this land, except for a quarter acre . . . land our family has leased and farmed for generations. I wonder. Was I a fool to do it?"

Liam sat on the last remaining stool. "They leave us no choice."

Mother was quiet. Then, almost whispering, she asked, "Will they evict us now?"

Father leaned over and put his head in his hands. "I'm not sure, Erin."

When he had an opportunity to talk privately to Liam, he confessed his temptation. "Captain Lawrence offered to buy me a Guinness in the tavern and I was sorely tempted, I can tell you that! It took all the strength I could muster to say no . . . but I was afraid I wouldn't be able to stop once I started."

Liam hugged him around his slumped shoulders. "Thank you for being strong."

The next morning he heard his mother pleading with Father. "Seamus, take this pail of stirabout to eat at mid-day. You'll need it."

"No, I'm an adult, and the children need it more. We have to keep *them* fed." The door opened and a cold wind rushed into the room with a howl. Then he was gone. In the loft Liam lay on his mat, bothered by a nagging feeling that no good would come of this relief work, despite the few pence a day he would earn.

Every day Father walked to the work site, ten miles there and ten miles back. It was dark when he left and dark when he returned. After just weeks, he had grown thinner with swarthy skin circling red eyes and had developed a rasping cough that awakened the whole cottage at night. As Liam listened to Father's continuous hacking, he stared up at the rafters, worried and uneasy.

Another concern was Grandmother who had been staying in her bed more and more. Liam knew what this meant but had no answer because even when they were able to catch a good fish, she would barely eat and could not be forced. On the day she died, Father had already left. Near the end, she was wandering in her head. "I'm so hungry," she would mutter, and yet, when they tried to put a spoonful of maize on her tongue, she turned her head away and closed her mouth tightly. Then she would repeat in a sing- song voice, "I'm so hungry," and the ritual would begin again. But just before she died, she seemed to know that her final breaths were coming.

Mamai called out. "Come quickly, children!" and they gathered at her bedside.

Brighid's small voice spoke for them all: "Grandmamai, we're here."

Her eyes fluttered open, and looking around for her grandchildren, she acknowledged them, one by one. With a faint smile she weakly raised her hand and touched each precious and beloved face. Then her eyes rolled back in her head, and she gasped her last. The family wept for their own loss, not hers.

Fewer people came to her wake that night than had come to Grandda's. Cousin Eamon again led the rosary, and the prayers were finished before a bedraggled, exhausted Father finally stumbled across the threshold.

The next day Sean and Liam took her to the cemetery. Grandmother was so light that Liam could have carried her to the churchyard alone and almost did. The cold and blustery weather kept his shoeless and coatless sisters inside while Mother took to her bed where Liam heard her sobbing. Father had to work, and only Uncle Paddy, thin and more stooped than ever, followed his mother's body to the grave. Since the soldiers had confiscated Uncle's cart for the workhouse and the hinged coffin was already borrowed, Liam and Sean carried Grandmamai in a sheet tied at both ends. The only grave available now was the common grave left open for several days at a time, and after Father Mullen concluded the prayers, they threw lime and sawdust over her. Liam sent Sean home with the precious sheet while he stayed on guard all night to make sure no animals came near. The next morning, men closed this pit, but with so many dying, they dug another nearby.

As Liam walked home, he recalled a report he had read in the Mayo newspaper. The London *Times* had belittled the Irish and accused them of being uncivilized because they did not give "decent burials." While this burial was not what they preferred, at least he still had enough strength to deliver Grandmother to the earth, while many poor Irish did not.

A week later, he and Sean set out for the glen to look again for salmon. Near the trees, they heard a girl crying like her heart was breaking. Concerned, Liam and Sean glanced at each other and loped down the incline. In the shadows, a young girl lay over a boulder next to the stream, her head buried in her arms, a basket on the ground. As they got closer, they saw to their surprise that the girl was one of their own.

"Aine! What's wrong, little sis?" Liam asked gently. He leaned over and put his hand on her head. Startled, she sat up and stared at them, her eyes glistening and her face wet.

"It's nothing, really. I . . . I just came . . . with the basket, for nuts and things." Reluctant to say more and embarrassed at being found in this state, she cast her eyes down and sniffed.

Sean sat next to her on the boulder. "Hey, we're your own brothers, and you can't keep your sorrows from the likes of us!"

"'Tis the truth, Aine. You might as well be tellin' us what's happened," Liam added.

With eyes still lowered, she shook her head in an emphatic no. "It's nothing . . . truly."

Sean kept pressing. "Sis, you can't leave us wondering."

Finally, she sighed. "It is foolish, I am . . . and us with so many troubles far greater than mine."

Liam gently patted her knee. "We'll understand, I can promise you that."

Aine looked tentatively at him and then glanced at a nearby pool with water still enough to reflect branches and sky. "Well, I was thirsty . . . came here . . . and when I leaned over, I saw myself." Remembering the sight again made tears trickle down her cheeks. She touched her straw-like hair, no longer shiny and wavy. "I couldn't believe it was me. My hair . . . my face . . . all changed. I'm ugly now!" She put her face in her hands and began sobbing again.

"Ah, Aine," Liam murmured. "You'll be back to your old self as soon as *an droch shaol* / the bad times have passed. Then you'll be as good as ever!"

Sean's eyes were sympathetic and sad. "I understand your feelings. The hunger has taken a terrible toll on all of us, but for a beautiful girl like you, it must hurt even more. Though you're thin, you have the same pretty eyes."

Aine looked at her brothers sheepishly. "We are *all* suffering and sickly, but seeing how I really looked was . . . terrible! I know

I'm being prideful and just thinking of myself, but I can't help it!" She hung her head and touched her face. "The bones protrude and my cheeks are sunken and hallow."

"You're too hard on yourself," Liam said. "You're Mamai's right hand . . . a second mother to our little sisters. If you have a fault, it's being too unselfish. You still need to care about yourself, too."

She looked up quizzically. "If Brian were here, do you think he'd turn away without giving me a second look?"

Sean shook his head. "Brian knows a good lass when he's found one! Remember the Irish proverb – "Absence makes the heart grow fond." And you'll always have us brothers at your back, as long as God spares us."

Liam stood up. "Yes, you can count on us. We need to fish for salmon now, but let us walk you back to our lane before we go."

"You'll not be telling anyone about this, will you now? Me . . . caring about my looks when we're slowly starving?" Aine asked.

Sean put his finger to his lips. "Not a word . . . but it's a good thing you shared your feelings and didn't lock them up like Mamai did when the melancholy almost consumed her." The brothers stood watching as Aine walked home, and when she turned and waved, they felt they had comforted her somehow. Having no time to ponder, they resumed the urgent search for salmon.

Sean suggested they sneak into the private fishing grounds at Lough Mask, but Liam had doubts since another lad, this time from Ballyhean, had bled to death when he tripped a spring-loaded gun. "But that's the purpose of the traps," Sean pointed out. "We can't let them scare us and lose our nerve. We just have to watch out and be careful . . . *very* careful."

Liam was not much for taking such risks, but he wasn't sure it could be avoided. They had to have food and the streams to which they could legally go were over-fished, so he let Sean persuade him to trespass. He only hoped that the huge tracts forbidden to Irish would be difficult for the landlords to guard due to their great size.

Watching for man-traps hidden in the underbrush, he probed the tall grass with a long stick and avoided swinging it lest he trigger a spring-loaded gun. At the bank, Liam was the look-out while Sean waded into the water with his net and waited. Not even a bird song broke the silence. Liam nervously searched the rolling green hills with his eyes for what seemed like an eternity. Finally Sean netted a salmon of good size, and Liam urged him to accept this and move out of danger.

But encouraged by success, he insisted, "One more. We should be allowed to fish here anyway, and the cautious will starve!" he complained in a voice too loud. Time dragged and Liam broke into a clammy sweat, despite the cold air. After a second fish was snared, Liam demanded they leave. When they got back to the road, he crossed himself and thanked God for they had risked their lives and won.

Sean strung the salmon on vine and held them up. "Nice size, and we'll give Aine an extra share."

For the next three weeks, Father continued going to the work site, but it got harder for him to rise in the darkness. Liam could see that he was pulling strength from deep inside, strength he did not have. He fretted about Da, but kept it to himself. At the end of each week the English paymaster in handsome clothes rode up in a fine carriage to tell them that money was short and their pay would be made up the following week. But when the next week came, the story was the same.

As Father sat hunched over in the seat next to the fire, he worried about those whose need was greater than his. "The paymaster said we should be patient. But there are widow women with babes tied to their backs who come to break stones each day, and they have no sons old enough to fish for salmon as I do. They return home to hungry children who wait in the darkness in hopes that they will bring food, and they'll die being patient!"

The next day while fishing near Partry, Liam and Sean passed the postmaster's station and checked for mail. The only piece was the *Mayo Constitution,* with a notice that the subscription was lapsing soon. Reading aloud as he walked, Liam learned what he had feared most. "Trevelyan has announced that the government is terminating all relief work! Instead, soup kitchens will be set up, but it will be months before they are organized. Every member of the family, even the sick, will have to walk to the distribution place, carrying a bowl, and be named on an approved list, or they will be turned away. And to be eligible for soup, you must give up all but a quarter acre of the land you work."

Liam looked up. "Knowing Trevelyan's attitude, he'll be in no hurry to start the soup lines, and people on the work rolls will never make it that long." He continued reading: "Trevelyan's plan is only to provide soup for five months because, he says, by then the potatoes will be harvested." Liam lowered the paper and bellowed, "Who has potatoes to plant! He *must* know that they've all been eaten or taken by landlords. Sean, don't you see? He's already making an excuse to shut down the soup lines as soon as he can . . . even before they are opened."

Sean looked grim. "Mamai said this would happen. We've lost the lease for nothing."

"Don't say that. Da is trying to keep us alive, and he's doing his best."

When Father returned that night, they were waiting for him with the newspaper, but he already knew. "Today they told us that this week will be the last. On Friday they will finally pay us with maize, so I've got to make it till then. 'Tis better than nothing."

That night when Father woke him with his incessant coughing, Liam wondered if indeed he could make it. After all these weeks, he understood Father wanting to hang on till paid, but it was clear that he was quite ill, and if not for the maize, he might give up. Liam wished he could go in his place, but he was not designated on the rolls as the provider.

On Friday they waited and watched the moonlit lane for his return. They had caught a small salmon and saved a portion for him. The girls went to bed early, and they urged Mother to do the same.

Sean sat in Da's seat by the fire. "Mamai, we'll wait up and make sure he eats. *Ná bíodh imní ort* / don't worry."

But Liam *was* worried and tried to keep it from showing on his face. Restive, he kept going to the window. Please bring him home, Lord. Da was no longer strong, and Liam wondered if he would be able to carry the maize bags on his back. The hour grew late – later than he had ever been before. What had happened?

Finally, Liam could no longer contain his anxiety, and despite the curfew and possible arrest, he decided they had to risk it. "Sean, get your coat. Something's wrong. We have to go find him."

They walked with an urgent stride, while their eyes searched the bodies lying at the roadsides. Liam peered ahead, trying to see into the distance, but fog was settling. Out of the smoky haze a stooped figure stumbled toward them, looking straight ahead like a spirit in trance. Was it Da? Liam's heart pounded, but as the man got closer, he saw it was not. The dampness made the cold seep into their bones.

They quickened their pace. A mile farther, they saw a crumpled figure lying in the middle of the road, and they started running. Somehow, they knew! Da did not move, but Liam squatted down, raised him to a sitting position, and cradled him against his chest. He felt hot and feverish. If only they had brought water. "Da, we're here. What happened?"

Father roused and opened his eyes briefly before he closed them again. "They never came. I waited and waited . . . in the dark . . . afraid to leave. No pay . . . no maize . . . and the lease for the land is gone." With that, he slumped back against Liam, unable to say more. Together Sean and Liam draped his arms over their shoulders and managed to support him on his feet. They had to get him home.

I 7

Darkness Descends

The family crept around the cottage with cat-like feet, and one by one they peered into the side room through the half-closed curtain. Father's breathing was ragged, his face flushed as he thrashed about in his bed and raved in feverish delirium. "No! Don't . . . ." Then his words became a jumble.

Mother sat by him and kept replacing the cloth on his forehead. Again and again she sent Aine to the yard to refill her bowl with remaining snow, protected by the shade of the stone wall. Mother folded it into her cloth, but since Da's high fever quickly melted it, water rolled off his forehead and puddled on the flagstone. She spooned bits of snow onto his parched tongue, and he swallowed without opening his eyes. Aine was Mother's extra hand and anticipated her needs before she asked.

Liam noticed that his little sisters rarely whined, even though he knew they missed their milk and were hungry. Still, he worried about them, especially Caitlin who was normally so spirited and impish, but these days she was quiet and slept a lot, with hair thin and wispy. Most troubling was the way she rubbed her eyes incessantly.

"Caitlin, come here." Liam cupped her small face in his hands. "Open your eyes wide." Frowning, he examined her and saw small, raised spots on the whites of her eyes. "Don't rub your eyes so much because it looks like you're making little sores on them. Sit on your hands, if you must." Saddened by his stern scolding, she scampered to a dim corner and sat on her hands. Father's moaning from the next room distracted Liam from Cait and reminded him that he had to get some food and soon. The salmon caught yesterday was gone, as was all the maize Father had purchased so dearly with the furnishings. Liam motioned to Sean and Aine.

"We might as well eat the seed oats we've been saving for a possible crop since now we are not allowed to cultivate more than a quarter acre."

Sean nodded. "No use to keep them."

Aine brightened. "Where are they stored? I'll cook oats now."

Liam pointed to the seat in the wall. "They're in the cavity under the boards."

The brothers got their coats and reached for the hats, long worn by Father and Grandfather. Before Liam and Sean left, they crept into the side room, stood by Da, and said a silent prayer. When he finished, Liam whispered to Mamai, "Sean and I are leaving now to fish, but is there anything we can fetch before we go?"

"Yes. Please fill the water pail and bring in more peat. Be careful now. We'll be listening for your footsteps and awaiting your return."

After getting water and taking a long drink from the ladle, they opened the door. Thunder rumbled and gray clouds churned in the sky. When the wind ripped off Father's hat, Sean ran to retrieve it and pulled it on low.

Joining other men at a small lake near the road, they watched as the wind pushed choppy waves across to the other side. The lack of sun made the water murky, and since there were no bubbles, it seemed like the fish had retreated to the depths. Due to overfishing, fewer salmon were making it inland from the coast. With his net, Sean crawled out on a log and passed hours in silent watching. When pricks of rain drops started peppering the surface of the water, most of the men went for shelter.

Sean glanced back. "Should we go home?"

"No . . . shush." Liam had seen something. Then when it splashed, he yanked the line out and grabbed the twisting, slippery trout. "Ah. A good one too!"

Sean eyed it hungrily. "Let's take it home and cook it right now."

As they retraced their steps in the pelting rain, Liam shivered and thought how good it would feel to get to a dry place. They had eaten nothing all day, and when they opened the door, Aine welcomed them with steaming bowls of cooked oats.

Liam was ravenous, but while eating, he pointed with his head to the side room. "Any change?"

"He sleeps longer and doesn't talk." Aine looked puzzled. "Is that a good sign . . . or not?"

Liam shrugged his shoulders. "Who knows? In County Mayo doctors are rare and we've no way to pay them."

Sean set his empty bowl on the floor. "The best thing we can do is get back out and hunt. Da is counting on us." The coats were too damp, so they spread them near the fire to dry and just wore the hats. It was late afternoon and the rain had stopped. Admiring the rainbow which arched over the horizon, Sean's expression brightened. "Maybe it will bring us luck." As they walked the road toward Castlebar, looking for badger or rabbit holes, Liam carried his sharpened stick, over an inch in diameter, and Sean, his sling shot.

When they found nothing, Liam started fretting. "About now, I'd chase a fat rat if we saw one! What if we don't find anything? It's almost dusk, and we'll have to go back soon."

Sean's jaw tensed. "Not empty-handed! The family is depending on us, and we *have* to kill something!"

Just then, a rabbit lolloped across the road, but ducked under the iron fence of a landlord's hunting preserve. Sean would not be deterred. "Let's go over. No one will catch us, and the rabbit won't go far!"

Liam felt conflicted. "I don't know. Da always warns us."

"We have to." With that, Sean hoisted himself over the high fence and fell to the ground on the other side. Liam followed, not wanting to let him go in alone.

Hearing them, the rabbit froze in his tracks, and Liam crept closer with his spear poised. Then the hare changed his strategy and hopped away, disappearing down his hole. The brothers took a position up wind and waited.

A dove's coo made Liam jumpy and anxious, and he scanned the hills for watchmen. "I don't see anyone."

Reassured, they focused on the hole, and at last, whiskers and head emerged, then the body. The rabbit stopped and looked, wiggling his nose. Sean's quick hands grabbed him and twisted the hare's neck until he was limp.

"Ah . . . he's done," Sean said with satisfaction, "and he'll make a fine dinner . . . maybe two!"

Liam lifted him onto his shoulder. "He must be ten pounds!"

Suddenly a shot shattered the stillness! Sean groaned and doubled over as maroon blood oozed from a jagged hole in his side.

Liam stared in shock, frozen and unable to move. "Oh my God!"

Sean fell back and put a hand over his gaping flesh as blood spread and puddled in the grass. "Run! Take the rabbit and run! You can't help me."

Still, Liam hovered over him, unwilling to leave, torn between his heart and his head. He looked up, and on the hill a bearded man was reloading.

"Go, damn it! Go!" Sean's voice was raspy, his face pleading and desperate.

A second shot vibrated in Liam's ears, whizzing close to his head, and his instincts took over. Crouching low, he headed for the fence, hurled the hare across, and clamored over the top. He kept running, but he could still hear his brother's voice, begging him to leave.

Sean! No! . . . not Sean! Tears filled his eyes and made everything a blur. He choked up. No . . . no . . . it *can't* be! He reached the road and cut across a field. Knowing they would pursue him, he ran blindly like a crazed man, but all he could see was his brother, lying on the bloody grass.

When he reached the cottage, it was dusk. Crushed by the enormity of what he had to tell, he slumped on the stone fence and buried his face in his hands. No . . . this could *not* have happened. *How* could this have happened? He felt rigid, unaware of time, not wanting to move ever again. Night fell and finally the door opened.

Aine's silhouette's stood in the doorway. "Liam? . . . Sean? . . . Are you there? We've been waiting and worried . . . . Why are you out there?" Liam could not answer. Aine came out, closed the door, and admired the rabbit lying on the wall. "What a fine rabbit! You need to skin him." She hoisted herself up, sat beside him, and looked about the yard. "Where's Sean?" Liam remained hunched over, still covering his face. How could he have *let* this tragedy occur? If only he had been shot, instead of Sean.

Aine studied Liam and could see that he was devastated.

"What has happened? What is it?" Gripped by profound sorrow, he could not reply and choked back a throat of tears.

"What's wrong, I say?" She looked quizzically at the rabbit, at Liam, and at the empty yard where Sean should be. She sat, staring ahead into the darkness, trying to imagine what could have made Liam so hopeless. Then she shuddered and gave a low groan. "Oh no . . . not that." All Father's warnings must have sounded in her head, and somehow she knew! Her shoulders shook as she abandoned herself to grief, stifling the sound of her cries in her apron. Liam could not bear to look at her, and tears rolled down his cheeks. Such a cruel and sudden loss. If only he had stopped Sean . . . not let him go in there.

Exhausted finally, Aine heaved long sighs. Then she leaned over and whispered. "Where is he now? Do you think he might still be alive?"

Liam shook his head. "It was bad . . . the guard had a gun."

Aine wiped her eyes with her apron and put her arms around him. "Oh, Liam." He saw her eyes soften. "I hope you don't blame yourself."

With his elbows on his knees, Liam's hands hung loosely, and he stared at the ground. "I didn't want to leave him, but . . . he wanted that rabbit brought home."

Aine moved closer. "And for you . . . not to be killed too."

"T'would have been better."

She stroked his down turned head. "No! You must not think that way. Losing one brother is bad enough. Not two! Don't add the burden of guilt to your sorrow. God spared you to get us through this. Don't you see that? It's what Sean would want you to do."

But Liam felt drained of the will to go on and did not want a morrow.

Aine sighed. "The girls and Da are asleep so we won't tell

them until morning, but I must go in and tell Mamai. She's awake and worried about her boys . . . how can I tell her this?" She was limp as she slid off the wall and slowly opened the door.

Liam sat in the darkness, numb. He knew Aine was right. Sean would want him to help them survive, but could he find a way or the strength when he just wanted to die himself?

After a time, Mother came out in the yard and draped his dry jacket around his back. Her eyes were red from crying and her face, tortured and furrowed. "Liam, thank God you were not also taken." She put her arms around him and leaned her head on his shoulder. Aine soon joined them, and the three – Aine, Mamai, and Liam – sat on the wall and wept bitterly in the gloomy darkness, letting sorrow flow like a river into the night.

Finally, Mother held her head up and looked skyward. "I must go back to your Father, but he's still sleeping so I won't tell him yet. Come in soon, Liam." Aine followed her, and Liam was again alone.

He could not bear to climb the loft and see Sean's empty mat. No . . . he would stay here all night. He sank to the ground and slouched in the corner of the wall. Looking up at the stars, he asked, "What now? . . . God, help me."

He waited for morning on the damp grass. Even when the first rays of sunlight peeped over the cottage, he could not bring himself to go inside. When he heard his little sisters' wailing, he knew they had been told about Sean. Liam could not go in . . . not yet . . . not ever.

Then he heard the clop of donkey hooves and looked over the wall. "Liam, my boy." Father Mullen's voice was sympathetic, and his eyes teared as he embraced him. "Let's go in to your parents and sisters." Liam realized that somehow he knew what had happened.

When they opened the door, Mother rushed to him and

collapsed. "Oh Father, we have great need of you!"

"I know. That's why I'm here." After hugging them, one by one, he sat down. "I've just come from the sheriff's station by a circuitous route to prevent them from following me here. They summoned me to identify the body of a young man who was killed on Lord Lucan's preserve. It was Sean. Of course, I did not admit to knowing him . . . nor did any others brought in from the street. The constables claimed they just wanted to return his body to his family, but we all knew better. They said there were *two* lads, and we figured they wanted to arrest the other one. I presume that is you, Liam, and hopefully the reward will not lure an informant. I blessed Sean's body before they took him to a common grave." Father Mullen looked around with questioning eyes. "Where's Seamus?"

Mother twisted her apron. "He fell ill from the works and is in the side room. I'm afraid to tell him this terrible news."

Father raised his brows. "Those works killed more than they saved. Do you want *me* to tell him, Erin?"

"Would you Father, and give him a blessing?"

Father stood up. "Yes. Since I came from a dying man at the house before this, I have the host of communion." He went to the side room and parted the curtain wide so all could hear and see. Mamai and Aine stood with him in the arched alcove beside the bed.

Liam could hear the prayers of the last rites and saw the anointing with oil. Father Mullen's hand lifted the sacred host and laid it on Da's tongue. After communion, Da laid back his head and moaned. When Mother caught her breath and made a high cry, Liam knew his father had died. With the priest supporting her, she stumbled to Da's seat beside the fireplace where she confirmed to her children with sad resignation, "Your father is gone." Caitlin and Brighid ran into her upraised arms, whimpering.

The priest spoke in a mellow voice. "You can take comfort that his last act on earth was receiving the Lord." The priest smiled gently. "Won't he be surprised to see Sean in heaven since we never told him of his death, but now they are together and beyond all suffering. I'll go and tell Paddy." He embraced them all again and opened the door. "Before I leave, I'll skin this rabbit on the stone wall and put it over your fire to roast. Sean would want that."

They went to the side room to prepare for the wake. Everything was soon white: the bed sheet hung around the alcove, Da's shirt, and the white in his hair which had changed since the coming of *An Ghorta Mor/* The Great Hunger. After they set out their last candle, Liam placed the crucifix in his father's limp hands. With a heavy heart, he remembered all Da had done, trying to keep them alive, and regretted ever calling him a weakling. In his mind, he could hear the sweet, mellow tone of Da's fiddle as he drew his bow across the strings. Da was a gentle man, kind and honest . . . one whose spirit was sure to be "up and off and on his way to God" on this the last day of his life. To the family, Liam began quoting from memory the "Blessing of Light," which was Da's favorite and his.

Their grieving was interrupted by a knock at the door, and Aine went to open it. When Liam emerged from the dimly lit room, he saw Captain Lawrence standing in the doorway, with his tall, erect form silhouetted in the bright light of the day.

"Aine, is that you?" Lawrence looked shocked at her appearance. Liam now saw his sister through Lawrence's eyes. Her hollow cheeks and sallow complexion were a far cry from the radiant beauty of eight months ago with ivory skin and glowing health. Gone was the shapely form which was now so thin she seemed older than her years. But what did he expect?

The captain took off his hat. "I have brought you oats. May I come in?"

Aine stepped aside. "Yes, please. Come in."

He set a large bag of oats by the hearth, and without asking, he took Da's seat in the wall. His shiny, black boots and coat with gold buttons seemed from another world. He looked around, surprised to see the cottage so empty without table and furnishings.

"Where's Cait?" he asked as he reached inside his coat. She stepped forward. "Is this little Caitlin? The girl who skips for candy?" He pulled a bag of taffy from his inside pocket. "This is for you and Brighid. Hold out your hand."

With little change of expression, she extended a frail hand to receive it. "What is it?" she asked.

Lawrence paled at the sight of her. "It's taffy! Remember how you like taffy?"

Brighid now stood beside her, and while both children murmured a thank you, gone was the childish joy of last summer. Their reactions were flat.

Lawrence cleared his throat and blinked his eyes. "Well. Things are worse than I imagined." He cleared his throat again. "I've just come from the sheriff's office where I viewed Sean's body, but out of consideration for you, I did not identify him, knowing that police were still investigating the trespass into Lord Lucan's preserve. However, I did ask if I might have his Irish wool hat as a souvenir, and as a British officer, they obliged me. I thought you might want it." He pulled out Da's hat which Sean had been wearing.

The sight of it took Mother's breath away, and she clutched it to her chest like a treasure. "Thank you, Captain. This means more than you know." Her voice cracked. "My husband's hat . . . he also died . . . this morning." Aine repeated her words in English.

Lawrence's eyes widened. "Indeed! Your husband also? So young! May I ask, what caused his death?"

Liam felt a rising indignation and replied in English.

"He died of hunger, overwork from breaking stones, and British indifference."

Aine looked startled. "He means you no disrespect, sir."

Lawrence cleared his throat again. "I can't say that I blame Liam. I admire his courage to speak up and perhaps what he says is true . . . I suppose it is, actually. There are some soldiers in my company who are seeking a transfer out of Ireland because they dislike the mass evictions and the suffering from hunger. I'm one of them." He repositioned himself in his seat. "Say now, is there anything I can do? I could possibly borrow an army wagon to carry his coffin to the churchyard, if that would be of any help."

Liam felt a surge of pride. "To tell the truth, my father would prefer to go to his final resting place in a bed sheet, rather than a British army wagon . . . maybe the same wagon which took away our grain, our cow, our donkey, our cart, our sheep, and even my cousin, Tomas . . . with all due respect."

"But thank you for the oats, Captain," Aine added. "You can scarcely imagine how much we *need* them."

Lawrence's mouth had a nervous twitch. "Well, now . . . I should be going." As he went out the door, he turned and stared at Aine in disbelief. Liam knew that while the memory of her former beauty had drawn him here, he would not return.

Only a few relatives and neighbors came to say the rosary with the family. Mr. Burke had borrowed the hinged coffin for his daughter, so Liam's description of Father being taken in a bed sheet, sewn shut, proved true. Uncle Paddy, more stooped and older each time he came, helped Liam carry Da's rail thin body. Mamai wrapped herself in her shawl and followed, but spared her daughters the memory of the open burial pit.

Before Uncle Paddy left for home, he shared some news. "Remember years ago when our neighbor's son, Cian Connolly, was transported to Australia for violating curfew? Well, he wrote a letter home saying he saw Tomas in a column of chained prisoners, building a road." Tears filled Uncle's pale, blue eyes. "But at least he's still alive!" Looking down, he sniffed.

Liam put his hand on Paddy's shoulder. "You know, I'm now remembering something Sean said as we watched them carry Tomas away in irons. He said – 'He may be the fortunate one, rather than us.'" As Paddy pondered Sean's prophetic remark, he nodded, growing solemn and sad.

The next day as Liam sat next to the fireplace, his feelings were blunted. No one in the family had the inclination to move or talk, and they lay about almost dozing as a way to deal with their overpowering melancholy. There was such stillness that the sound of a bumble bee as it buzzed across the room seemed loud. Liam watched it, and when it eventually found a way to escape over the half door, he was envious for he, himself, felt trapped in a world of death. It was up to him now to keep the rest of the family alive, but he felt so tired and disheartened, he wondered if he could.

18

With Time Running Out

A month passed and April brought warmer weather, leaves to trees, and buds to the primrose. Wild berries, charlocks, and nettles reappeared, and ice blue gentians and yellow gorse competed for space between the road and the wall. Although the land welcomed spring, the suffering of Eire was imposed by man, not nature, and it continued, unabated. Ireland was an armed camp, and in no other place in the world had a nation concentrated so many soldiers in such a small area.

Lonely and depressed, Liam wandered down the Partry road with only the wind for a companion. Sean had always been at his side, and it was hard to believe he was gone. It reminded him of the proverb: *Giorraíonn beirt bother* / Two shorten the road, for without his brother, the road seemed endless.

Liam went to Partry every day looking for a letter. It was their only hope. Having no pigs to pay the May rent, they faced certain eviction, a catastrophe his mother and sisters could not survive. When Liam came to the post office, there was still no mail, but the clerk handed him the final issue of the *Mayo Constitution* which at least was something.

Walking home, he read how people were calling this year Black '47, and deaths were expected to exceed one million. The newspaper praised landlords, like George Henry Moore who had ordered his agents to give a milk cow to every widow on his property, but more typical were the wholesale evictions of Sir Roger Palmer of County Mayo, who owned 90,000 acres.

In County Cork on December 15, 1846, a British magistrate had visited Skibbereen and found the entire village dying or dead. Two English clergymen then traveled to London, and on bended knees they begged Trevelyan to send food to the area, but he refused. Records have now revealed that in 1846 tenants of Cork, Skibbereen's county, had paid 50,000 pounds sterling in rent to only twelve landlords, all British lords and knights and one Anglican clergyman.

Another headline read: "Government Soup Lines Delayed While London Leaders Debate Recipe." It's another tactic to postpone the soup lines while starving people die, Liam guessed.

An editorial named three men -- Sir Charles Wood, Sir George Grey, and Charles Trevelyan -- as people who sit on the Prime Minister's cabinet and staunchly resist efforts to commit any treasury money for aid to Ireland. A critic of this committee is the Irish Archbishop, John MacHale, who has written a letter to Prime Minister Lord John Russell. He pointed out that the government paid twenty million pounds in compensation to English landlords in the West Indies when they were forced to free their slaves. So why spend so little to save Irish lives? he had asked. The editorial claimed that the government could have purchased Ireland's grain, stored it, and fed the people who grew it, if they had wanted to. Liam thought to himself – they still could.

By the time he got home, Liam's temper was hot and his pulse throbbed. He was in a fighting mood and tossed the newspaper to Aine and Mother. "Read this! My blood is a boil. Some powerful men in London don't *want* to save us and are deliberately starving us! It's an unforgivable thing they do!"

Mother raised her brows. "Unforgivable, you say? Nothing can be that because we have a Christian duty to forgive our enemies."

Dumbfounded, Liam shook his head. "After all that has happened, how can you talk of forgiveness! I can't understand you! We need to use this anger to change things. The English can't be trusted to govern us! Not now. Not ever again!"

Mother slumped onto the stool. "Then maybe we should forgive them and *still* change things."

Aine came between them with a bowl of oatmeal. "Here, Liam. There's not much left of Captain Lawrence's oats. It's a good thing that British horses are fed from large bags or it would be gone." It was Liam's only food of the day, and he ate with gusto, clacking and scraping the bowl with his spoon for the last bit. Then he laid the bowl on the floor.

Walking past him, Caitlin stepped on the earthen dish and shattered it. "Oh, no" she cried, without looking down.

"Caitlin!" Liam yelled. "Watch out! Don't be so clumsy. You're always bumping into things. That bowl was older than you and now it's broken to bits!"

Sobbing, Caitlin went to a corner, crouched against the wall, and hid her face in folded arms. Liam felt remorse, but in his angry state of mind, he said no word of comfort. Aine gave him a sharp look and motioned for him to follow her outside. After closing the door behind them, she heaved a long sigh and climbed onto the wall.

"Liam, don't you know?"

"Know what?"

Aine looked up with tears brimming in her eyes. "I thought we *all* knew. Caitlin is going blind."

Liam's heart stopped. "What! How do you know!"

"I take care of the girls so I would notice. Since Cait remembers where things are in our cottage, she can find her way around, and it's not always obvious that she can't see. It is happening gradually and at first, only night was the problem. She would grope in the dark, unable to find her mat until I took her hand and led her. It worried me, but I wasn't sure what it meant."

Liam could not bear hearing more and tried to will away the horror with his lamenting. "Not blind! Not Caitlin! *Not our little Caitlin!*" He leaned against the wall, limp and weak, and felt his legs buckling. He recalled the rough spots he had noticed in her eyes months ago and how he had scolded her for rubbing them. "This can't be true!" He shook his head in denial.

But Aine persisted. "Her eyes are often swollen. She sees shadows, but bright light bothers her, and she shades her eyes and squints. Haven't you noticed? With so many people in Ireland now losing their sight, the hunger has to be the cause. This never used to happen. Never! Mother thinks her sight will return, if we can get good food later."

"Is that true?" Liam jumped at the ray of hope. "I'll get her more food!"

Aine looked down. "I doubt it will change. Father Mullin says the blindness from starvation is permanent, but don't tell Mamai."

"Oh God! Not this." Liam breathed deeply to stifle the flood of sorrow that welled up inside. "We've *got* to find a way to help her." He grabbed his lance-like pole, hidden under the lilac bush. "I've got to get some food, and I'm going hunting." He had to get away, to be alone, to escape, *to do* something.

As he jogged to the glen, everything was a blur as tears filled his eyes. Caitlin can't be blind. It was too cruel . . . an innocent child

. . . so many children. The starvation was now robbing them of their sight, if not their life. As he sat by the stream, he listened to the sound of water and gazed up at bare branches, starting to leaf, but nothing relieved the deep, penetrating grief that gripped his insides. Where was hope? He felt overwhelmed and wanted to give up . . . weary of the struggle . . . tired of being strong. Please God, help little Cait because I don't know how.

And Sean, gone so young . . . bleeding in the grass . . . pleading "Run! Take the rabbit and run!" I left my little brother to die alone among strange, cruel men. All for a rabbit. They killed Sean for a rabbit.

Weary and heart-broken, he rose to walk north on the Castlebar road. If only he could bring home meat for Cait. He had gone several miles when he found himself beside the bank of earth topped by the tall fence of Lord Lucan's game preserve.

He rambled up the embankment and looked through the cast iron bars to the field beyond. Somewhere in the distance was the rabbit's hole where Sean had died, and Liam felt inexplicably drawn to it. It was like his brother was still there alone, waiting for him to come back, yet he never had. Would Sean's blood be in the grass, on the ground? He wondered. He had to get in there, to touch the place where Sean once lay. He had to. Without thinking, he climbed over, dropped to the other side, and loped over the soft earth. Would rain have washed away all traces? He ran faster.

Locating the rabbit's hole, he knelt in the grass and went through it with his fingers. Yes! Blood had collected amid gravel and around the base of weeds. A pebble encrusted with Sean's blood was all he had left of his brother, and he slipped it into his pocket. Liam's face felt hot, and tears welled up. Now maybe he could say goodbye. "Rest in peace, little brother," he whispered.

Suddenly the crack of a gun echoed in the air, and a bullet

whizzed by, close to his ear. On the hill he spotted him – the bearded man who had killed Sean was reloading. Liam considered for a split second. Could he reach the trees in time? No.

Filled with rage, he grabbed a rock, charged up the hill, and threw it hard. The rock struck the guard's forehead, and he stumbled backwards, dropping his ramrod. As he scrambled to retrieve it, Liam kept running. As the guard shoved the rod into the barrel, a trickle of blood was making its way into his eye. He was ready to fire again, but Liam was on him and hit the gun barrel, turning it aside as it went off. The guard's eyes bugged out as he stared at Liam's sharpened pole and, realizing what it could do, he gave a grunt and raised the gun's butt to strike a blow.

With all his strength, Liam rammed the pole through his chest, and there was a crunching sound of bones breaking. From the guard's mouth, red foam bubbled and his eyes rolled back. His knees buckled, and he sprawled on the grass. With pent-up fury unleashed, Liam jabbed the pole through the guard's neck, and blood gurgled from the second wound.

Breathless, Liam stood, sucking in air. He knew the gun shots would alert other guards, and he had to flee, but a silver watch on a chain in the grass caught his eye. He scooped it off the ground and dropped it inside his shirt before he turned and ran. When he reached the fence, he pitched his pole over and followed it.

To avoid the road, he cut through fields, jumping one fence after another. Still running and hunched over, he followed the stream to the glen where he would hide until dark. He was breathing hard when he crawled into the charred remains of the tumbled-in scalp.

In his head he could see the guard's clenched teeth and protruding eyes. Never having taken a human life before, he hoped this would be the last, but the guard had fired no warning shot and intended to kill him, just as he had Sean. Yet, Liam could not deny that slaying the man who had killed his brother had brought him satisfaction.

As he slouched on the damp earth, a rustling noise told him he was not alone. From under a scrap of thatch, an enormous rat rambled out, and Liam instinctively lunged with his spear and pinned it to the earth. How could rats be so fat when people were so thin? With horror, he suddenly understood. Well, this time it was man who would eat the rat, not the other way around. For the sake of his family, he would skin it here and claim it was a small badger. He ripped the rat's gut with the spear point, killing one who preyed on Eire.

He decided to clean both his blood-spattered shirt and spear in the stream, and afterwards he shuffled leaves and other plant debris over the wet ground. Crawling through the tangle of fallen poles and thatch to the back of the scalp, he hung his shirt on a protruding root sticking out of the earth embankment. No sooner had he twisted through to the rear than he heard something on the road, and crouching in his dark corner, he froze.

Riders, galloping down the slope, slowed to a trot and then walked their steeds. They were so close that Liam could hear a horse snort, shake his bridle, and the friction of leather saddles as men dismounted. Then a horse lapped water. More splashing . . . the riders must be taking a drink, he decided. His pole . . . where was it? His eyes darted about the hiding place, but it was not there. Did he leave it by the stream?

Someone coughed. "The road to Castlebar . . . I bet they went that way. George's group will bring them in."

Another voice. "Never know . . . may still be ahead. What did the other guard say? . . . a pocket watch taken?"

"Yeh . . . hope they try to sell it. Authorities will notify the pawn shops around."

Again, Liam heard a saddle squeak and a horse shake his

metal bridle and whinny. Then silence. As another mounted, there was again the friction of man on leather. "Let's go." Spurs jangled, and horses galloped up the slope.

Liam waited as long as he could before he wiggled from behind the fallen thatch. Searching for his lance near the stream, he found it partially hidden by fern. That slip could have been his undoing, and he exhaled in relief. As he looked back at the scalp with its fallen roof and jumble of posts, Liam realized that to search it, a soldier would have to crawl through on his knees and soil his fancy uniform. Fortunately they chose to avoid the inconvenience.

When darkness fell, Liam put on his shirt, slipped the watch and chain inside, and crept out. The skinned rat could explain the blood on his trousers, but the lance and stolen watch would condemn him. Careful to keep a low profile, he ran in a crouched posture through fields, away from the road. A full moon helped him watch for patrols and hurdle the maze of stone fences. When Liam opened the cottage door, he found Mamai and Aine pacing the floor, distraught. Even in the shadowy light of the fireplace, he could see Mamai's eyes, full of worry and alarm.

"Where have you been! I've been out of my wits!" Liam knew the tone. Worried mothers always turn angry, once you're home. It would never heal . . . her loss of Sean . . . and she feared losing another.

"I got this badger around dusk, so I waited till dark." He held up the skinned rat and with the sight of meat, both forgave him.

Aine shoved a cold bowl of oats into his hand. "The last of Lawrence's oats. At least, we have meat for tomorrow!" She turned to Mother. "Now that we know he's safe, let's go to bed."

The next day, Uncle Paddy hobbled in and flopped onto a stool. "Did you hear the news? In the village they say a guard was killed yesterday . . . stabbed. Police are looking for suspects."

Aine held out a cup to catch dripping fat. "Where did it happen?"

"Over on Lord Lucan's hunting preserve, close to where . . . over at Lord Lucan's." Mamai looked at Liam and blanched, but he quickly averted his eyes. Uncle Paddy saw her face too, and his mouth dropped open. "Maybe not. Maybe it was a different place." He tried to change the subject. "Aine, what are you cooking?"

"A small badger . . . I *think* it is." Aine gave Liam a knowing smile.

Paddy shrugged. "Be glad for whatever. We've eaten things we never touched before. Anything to keep soul and body together. Say now! The Quakers came and gave me some seed potatoes to plant! God bless those people."

Aine's face brightened. "That's wonderful. There surely won't be blight again this year. And how are Aunt Una and the girls?"

"My Una is looking poorly. She gives most of her food to our daughters, as all parents are doing. Well, I'll visit again in a few days."

As he left, he whispered to Liam. "I'd keep that spear thing hidden for a while." Then he shuffled out the door.

Mamai still had not spoken and seemed stunned. "Liam, did you go there yesterday, to Lord Lucan's?"

"Yes."

"What about the trouble over there? It could lead an informant to name you!"

Liam looked at her squarely. "I was drawn to the place where he died, and the guard came around and tried to shoot me. I could not have run faster than his bullets, so I charged at him while he was reloading." Liam reached over and put another brick under the dripping rat. "Years from now, it would have been hard for me to live, knowing that the bearded guard was out there somewhere, hearty, well fed and not sorry."

Then he took the pebble encrusted with Sean's blood from his pocket. Having carefully protected it on his journey, he handed it to his mother. "Here. It's all we have left."

Upon realizing what it was, she gasped. "Oh, my Lord!" Holding it in both hands with great reverence, she gazed at it for a long time, and Liam decided she was praying. Finally, she made a request. "I'll sew a special little pouch with a draw string for this pebble, and whenever I die, bury it with me." Then she looked into Liam's eyes with earnestness. "Son, tonight when you are alone, you need to talk with God. You *killed* a man."

The next afternoon, Liam was sitting in Da's seat next to the fire. The fields were ready for tilling, if only there were seeds to plant or people to plant them. Since the Reillys had given up their lease and eaten the seed oats, Liam was idle. Lacking energy, he had grown dead to his feelings, passive in the face of catastrophe. He had seen this numbness in others and now recognized it in himself.

Over the half-door, Father Mullen's face appeared. "Liam, my boy. Can I come in?"

"Yes, Father. Rest yourself." Listless, Liam did not stir from his seat, and even lacked curiosity about the priest's mission.

Father Mullen pulled up a stool. "Where's your family?"

"My little sisters are asleep in the loft, and Mother and Aine have gone to search for charlock and nettles."

Ignoring the lack of a welcome, Father Mullen conversed in a friendly manner. "Yesterday I went to Castlebar . . . had not been there in weeks. I stopped to see Father Henry. Remember him? We took tea at his cottage. He was on the Board of Guardians of the workhouse and told us how Lord Lucan did not properly support it and would close the doors, if he could. Do you remember? Well, he has done it . . . at least for now."

Liam nodded grimly but looked away, uncomfortable with the conversation. Despite Liam's disinterest, Mullen continued with his news. "Father Henry feels responsible, and although he protested and did all he could for the poor inmates, he thinks he failed God and man. Almost everyone in the workhouse was starved out or died of fever." Father leaned forward. "But as more and more died, the little food they had went farther.

"One of the English caretakers in the workhouse took pity on a young girl who caught typhus. For days she wavered between life and death, and when she managed to recover, the caretaker was inspired to secret her out of that dark, cold place. Before dawn, she led this young woman through the deserted halls to a back door and unlocked it. After making sure no one was around, she gave her a paper with Father Henry's address and left her alone to flee unseen.

"Father Henry heard a knock on the window and opened his door. He believes to this day that God sent that frail angel to him for deliverance so he could, at least, save one, if not the others. Father Henry's brother in Brooklyn, New York, had sent passage money from a family who needed a servant, so after the girl regained strength, he bought her a ticket. The girl was Colleen ONeill from Ballinglass."

At first, Liam could not believe what he was hearing. Then his heart leaped. "Colleen alive! Are you sure?" Astounded, he sat up straight.

"Yes. From Father Henry's own mouth, I heard this story. Before the girl left, she asked for paper to write a note and told him to give it to me for you." The priest laid the letter in his lap and patted his shoulder. "I'll see myself out, son." He put on his hat and left.

In a daze, Liam stared at the letter like it had been delivered by an angel from on high. Then with trembling hands, he managed to open it.

"My dear Liam,

I saw you below the window at the workhouse and knew you wanted to help. My heart ached, and I cried till all tears were gone. My family is buried in the workhouse mass grave. But God seems to have another plan for me. I've been given passage money to New York by a kind priest who knows a family that needs a servant. I'm leaving Ireland in a few days, but I wanted to say goodbye and that I'll never forget you. Take care of yourself.

With love, Colleen"

Liam felt a surge of hope in a sea of despair. Somewhere across the ocean was his precious girl, and because she had managed to survive, he could believe in miracles again. He folded the note, put it in his pocket . . . and smiled.

I 9
Like Links in a Chain

Once when Liam went to check for mail, he carried Caitlin on his back, hoping the outing might lift her spirits, but the effort had exhausted them both and thereafter, he went alone. Even now, the farther he traveled down the road, the slower his pace became. Overhead, dark clouds threatened a chilling rain, and Liam tried to shake a sense of doom. In less than two weeks, Sligo's agents would demand the rent.

As he approached the postal station, his stomach churned. He tried to steel himself against having false hope, but . . . maybe today would be the day. His frequent inquiries for mail made the clerk aware of his desperation, and now as he gazed at Liam over his spectacles, he wagged his head and said in English "nothing" even before Liam asked. He turned to leave, wondering if their letter sent half way around the world had ever reached Niall.

Back in the countryside, he was so drowsy that he wanted to lie down beside the road but resisted. To save food for the family, Liam had been shorting himself, but he had to keep going . . . one foot and then another. "When he entered the lane toward home, Liam saw his young sisters sitting on the wall and heard Brighid prompt Caitlin.

"Liam is coming so wave your hand." Although Cait could only see shadows, she kept up the pretense and waved vigorously.

"Do you have food?" Caitlin asked. She sat up straight and listened, but Liam could not answer the truth – no food, no mail, no hope.

He lifted Cait off the wall to carry her in. "A good drink of water will make you feel better till we can eat." Liam looked around. "Where are Mamai and Aine?"

Brighid opened the door. "They have gone to Ballinrobe because today the Quakers give the stirabout and rice. I hope they get there before it's all gone and walk back fast."

Liam hoped the same since the salmon were now scarce. He bobbed Caitlin on his knee, and though she was a bit old for this, he'd do anything to encourage her smile.

Brighid watched. "Liam's a donkey, Cait, so don't fall off!"

At last the door opened, and fresh air from a soft misting flowed in. Mamai held the half-door ajar as Aine struggled to the hearth with a heavy pail of mush, almost tipping it. She released the handle and shook her palm in pain. "That's heavy and should feed us for several days. They filled it to the top, and it's still warm enough to eat. The Quakers let you take food home to your family, but when the government starts their soup lines, you will have to be on a list or they'll turn you away, even if death is in your face. Every member of the family will have to walk long distances and present a cup, even the sick. That's what people say."

"What happens if you don't have a cup?" Brighid asked.

"Then they'll turn you away," Aine replied.

Liam scooped up a bowl for Cait and put a spoon in her hand. "Here. You eat first."

Mamai moved around and whispered in Liam's ear: "Any

mail?" When he shook his head, her face fell. Wooden spoons clacked against clay bowls as they frantically scraped up the mush of corn and rice.

Too soon Cait's bowl was empty, and she asked, "Did I miss any?"

Brighid peered over. "No, you got all they gave you."

"I'd give you more, Cait, but we have to stretch it and make it last," Aine said. As she began washing bowls, she entertained with news. "In Ballinrobe some people are hiding in the fields at night and cutting the traces of horses that draw food carts to Westport. It does no good, but I guess it's a way to protest the food convoys."

Brighid's eyes grew wide. "But if they catch them, they'll do bad things to them, won't they!"

"Yes, but they do bad things to poor people anyway. Everyone in Ballinrobe was talking about what happened at Delphi and that lake . . . *Doo Lough* / Dark Lake. A relief officer told over 600 starving people in Louisburgh that in order to be admitted to a workhouse or receive any kind of aid, they had to present themselves for inspection to an official by the next morning! But unfortunately this official was not there and had gone to Delphi, Lord Sligo's fancy hunting lodge, for a meeting of the Guardians of the Workhouse.

"So the desperate people decided to make the rugged twelve-mile walk through mountains and streams to Delphi. That night families with women and children slept outside in cold weather. The next day they arrived before noon and asked to be inspected, but servants reported the guardians were enjoying a long lunch and did not want to be disturbed. They waited for hours in a mixture of freezing rain and snow until finally two Guardians came out, refused to inspect them, and demanded they leave.

"So in despair, the starving families began the long walk back, barefooted and dressed in rags. Exhausted and in a weakened condition, having received no food, they faced terrible wind and endless rain with sleet. Wading through swollen rivers, their rags were soaked anew and froze to their legs like stiff iron, making it difficult to climb the steep goat trails through the mountains. When they came to the place called *Strappa bui* / cliff path, many lost their footing and fell into Doo Lough and the surrounding valley. Soon others succumbed to exposure and starvation until emaciated bodies littered the trail all the way to the southern bank of the Glankeen River. At least four hundred never reached their homes and died that night. The next day government authorities, unable to bury so many bodies in the rocky ground, threw some of them into a mountain slough."

Liam's eyes narrowed. "Our people will never forget the callous cruelty of those well fed guardians who feasted inside Sligo's mansion while starving families stood in the cold outside. I believe that hundreds of years from now, people will still remember the tragedy of Doo Lough and might even walk in their footsteps along the trail in memory of their deaths!"

A soft rapping turned their heads, and there was Father Mullen, leaning over the half-door. "May I come in?"

"Of course, Father." Liam offered his fireside seat under the arch.

Father Mullin pulled Caitlin onto his lap and gave her an affectionate hug. "How is this bright, little lass? I see you've been to the good Quakers," he said as he eyed the pail of stir-a-bout. When Aine relayed the news from Ballinrobe, the priest seemed preoccupied and gazed into the fire, solemn and searching. Then, clearing his throat, he began to share what was on his mind.

"Hear me now for I have important things to tell. As you know, those who have money are leaving Ireland. They board unsound ships and are put in the deepest hole without proper water or food, packed in so closely they share disease. People say that if a cross could be placed on the ocean for every Irish buried at sea, there would be a path many miles wide all the way to Americay!" His voice became incensed and strained. "But this all suits the government just *fine*! The London *Times* has written with glee that soon the Irish will be as rare in Ireland as Indians in Manhattan! Charles Trevelyan calls the famine a 'blessing from God,' and Sir Charles Wood hopes to replace us with Protestants! It's clear they want us to die or flee and will continue to evict us for many years to come.

"Everyday I hear of Mayo people who have died on ship. So it is with sorrow and trepidation that I see any undertake the journey. But what are our Irish people to do?" His voice became hoarse, and tears brimmed in his eyes. He sat Caitlin down on the floor, took out his handkerchief, and blew his nose. Trying to regain his composure, he swallowed hard.

Finally he put his handkerchief back in his pocket, and with resignation he sighed deeply. Reaching into his coat, he pulled out a package wrapped in brown paper. "So what I have here should make you happy. Niall has sent bank issues for you to go to New York and mailed them to me because he thought my mail would be more secure. As much as it pains me for you to leave Ireland . . . " His voice cracked. "As much as it pains me, much as I'll miss you, I advise you to go."

Liam could hardly contain his joy. "At last! Passage!" He rose and looked over Father's shoulder to study the bank notes, and new energy flowed through him.

Caitlin looked straight ahead. "What's he saying? Is he sending us to Australia with Tomas or to Niall in Americay?"

Brighid sat up on her legs. "I don't want to die on one of those crosses in the ocean!"

Father Mullen patted Brighid's head. "You'll see Niall again, and won't that be good?"

"Yes, it will!" Caitlin called out. "He forgot my birthday, but he'll have a present waiting, I think."

Father Mullen looked in the package. "Shall I read his letter aloud?" They nodded.

"Dear Family,

When I got your letter, I sent all my savings to the Murphys in New York where the Irish Emigrant Society helps people on this side get bank notes that can be cashed in Ireland. Some of you can come now and the rest later as we earn more money. Like links in a chain, we'll eventually bring over the whole family. When this war is over, the army will discharge me in New York City, but until that time, the Murphys will take care of you. Brian and Maire are eager to see Aine and Sean, for whom they still profess great love, and will meet every ship from Westport in the months ahead.

Your loving son and brother, Niall Seamus Reilly"

Mamai put her hands together and looked up to heaven. "Glory be to God! I've been praying for this all my waking moments."

Father Mullen folded the letter. "Take whatever food you can. I've checked on the ships leaving Westport for New York, and one will depart within a week." He rose from his stool. "You should leave tomorrow, so I'll give you a blessing now."

As they knelt on the flagstone, Father touched each head and traced a cross on each forehead. "May the Lord bless you as you go over the deep place. O God of patience, take them by the hand in case of a blow from a strong wave and hold them in your palm till their last day. Amen."

"Amen!" said Caitlin, a bit too loudly. They rose and embraced the dear priest who was also their teacher, advisor, and friend, who had baptized them and given them their first Holy

Communion. Liam had long awaited this money, but now he felt conflicting emotions. It was hard to leave the land and people he loved, and Father Mullen was right: the journey was full of danger.

The priest put his arm around Liam's shoulders and steered him into the yard. "Take good care of your Mamai and sisters." But when they were away from the door, Father Mullen looked back, lowered his voice, and his face grew earnest. "Liam, I'm doubting that Niall sent enough money. Children are half-fare so they count as one, but as I figure it, you're still one ticket short. Your mother could stay behind with your Uncle Paddy."

Liam was stunned. "No! If anyone stays, it'll be me."

Father Mullen shook his head. "But you're young so you should go because you can give the girls more protection and strength."

Liam grabbed the priest's arm. "Tell no one of this shortfall!"

"I understand. It's up to you." With that, Father Mullen put on his hat and left the yard.

Liam knew that if he stayed in Ireland, he would have to slip away at the last moment before his mother realized his intention. He hated the thought of tricking her and leaving them alone, but for now, he had to get them to Westport and buy what tickets he could.

The priest had scarcely left before Uncle Paddy appeared over the half-door. "What's this I'm hearing from Father Mullen? You're leaving Uncle Paddy and going to that parish across the big water?"

Liam smiled. "You make New York seem close, and I wish it were."

Uncle handed him a flake of white stucco he had chipped off as he came in. "A reminder of home. Don't let the word out this close to Gale Day that you're leaving, or the agents might come and, claiming that you owe them, take your sleeping mats and anything that remains. When the Quakers gave me seed potatoes, I got them in the ground fast before the agents knew I had them, or they would have taken them, like they did with the Trainors. Now they'll have to wait till harvest and hopefully they'll accept a crop of potatoes as rent. Well . . . we'll be back in the morning to tell you goodbye, all of us." As he coughed and turned away, Liam shared his uncle's feelings.

Trying to choose what to take was difficult. The family surveyed the cottage carefully, for without a cart, the burdens had to be light. "What clothing we have should be worn in layers to avoid carrying it," Liam instructed. "We'll roll two sleeping mats together and tie them with vines. Aine and I will cach carry two on our backs so we'll have four."

But despite Liam's advice to travel light, Mother unhooked the picture of the Holy Family and took the Bible off the mantel. "We've always had these." She put the flake of stucco from the cottage in the cloth bag with the encrusted pebble and tucked it in her bodice as things near and dear to the heart. When Aine folded the embroidered dancing dress and put it inside two blankets, Liam could not object, knowing that to her it was precious.

Aine laid the wool shawls of Mother and Grandmother beside the picture. "In the morning, I'll wrap these around the girls, and Mamai and I will wear the wool jackets of Da and Sean. We best get to sleep now because we have a long journey."

As they climbed the ladder for their last night in the cottage, Liam felt pensive. He remembered all the joys of family life around the old oak table and even recalled the morning that he rushed down the ladder to see the newborn Caitlin with red fuzzy hair and a button nose as she lay in the cradle. He could almost hear the sounds of childish games and pillow fights with his brothers in the loft and the stern warnings of his parents . . . "Get to sleep now!" He sighed deeply, and looked up into the familiar beams and breathed in the earthy scent of sod and thatch he loved.

Aine must have heard him and peeked around the quilt. "I think I know what you're feeling. This cottage is part of us, and despite burdens, these walls rang with music and merry times, and before it was all taken away, it sheltered family and friends with a real closeness."

Liam nodded. "'Tis true, but Ireland is *still* under the British heel, with no rights. Like Father Mullen said, they want us to die here or flee, and we're lucky to have passage money."

Her eyes brightened. "And Brian and Niall are in Americay." And Colleen, Liam thought to himself.

"Liam, I've been intending to ask. How much did Niall send us?"

Liam was wary of answering. "I haven't counted it yet, but don't you worry. Come closer so I can show you something." He reached into a torn seam in his mat and pulled out the pocket watch and chain which glimmered even in the dim light.

Aine breathed in sharply. "Liam! Where did you get that?"

"Lord Lucan's guard. It fell out of his pocket. I regret it's engraved with a "W" on the back, but I hope to pawn it in Americay, where no one will question how a poor Irish lad like me happens to have such a fine watch . . . and with a W."

Aine was nervous, just looking at it. "Put it away. Quick!" She hurried back to her mat as though the oak beams had ears and might talk.

Early the next morning, Aunt Una, their girl cousins, and Uncle Paddy came to say goodbye. Auntie presented a small trout they had smoked all night. "I wish I had oat cakes for you," She said in a raspy voice.

Liam was shocked at her gaunt appearance and guessed she would not live long. "This is more than you can spare, as it is, Aunt Una."

Mother tied the wooden spoons and clay bowls in the curtain that had separated the rooms and gave them to Brighid.

Liam carried the iron cooking pot with the pail of Quaker stirabout inside, but covered the top with a folded blanket. He and Aine tied the sleeping mats with vine and put them on their backs.

Caitlin realized that she was being spared. "Is Brighid carrying something? I want to help too."

Mother smiled. "Take this picture of the Holy Family then and the Bible and hold them well."

Cait wrapped her arms around them tightly. "You can count on me."

Then Mother turned to Una. "The rest is yours, so pawn whatever you can . . . this stool . . . the extra mats . . . this heavy quilt from the loft and the trunk." Una nodded gratefully.

As the moment of departure inched closer, Liam gave each cousin a gentle hug. More memories flooded over him – all the Christmases, Tomas and card games, music by the hearth, thatching and turf cutting as a community, all gone. He bit down hard on the inside of his cheeks to hold his feelings in check.

Uncle Paddy wiped his eyes on his sleeve. "Remember the fine Feast of Departure we had for Niall? Sorry there's no time for people to tell you goodbye, but we're keeping it a secret until you're gone and Sligo can't interfere."

Tears rolled down the cheeks of the women and stood in the eyes of the men. Words were trapped behind a swell of emotion, and no one could say much.

Mother gently ran her hand across the mantel and touched Da's violin hook. She moved the crane at the fireplace and glanced back at the ladder and loft, once crowded with offspring. Then she pursed her lips, stood tall, and opened the half door. Her children followed.

The rose bush in the yard offered pink blooms in farewell, and Liam picked one for his mother. As he looked back into the dark room and slowly closed the door, his heart was full. This cottage had sheltered Reillys for generations, and now it seemed like Da, Sean, and his grandparents were still there . . . in the shadows . . . saying goodbye.

With his family, he trudged down the lane, torn between a need to leave and a reluctance to break ties with all he knew . . . a home he had never left . . . people he loved. Every time he looked back, Uncle Paddy, Aunt Una, and the cousins were waving. As they topped a rise, he heard Paddy bellow, "Pray for Ireland!" and that was the final glimpse.

Liam took a deep breath. "Mamai, if fortune should favor me and I return someday to these sacred shores, I'll put up stones in the graveyard to remember the family we leave there. In Americay, I can send money back because I'll be beyond the reach of police and landlords."

Mother, looking down at the path, lost control and began to sob. Liam reached for her hand. "It's the natural thing to cry, Mamai, and maybe we *have* to look back before we can look forward." Despite the fear of staying, bittersweet tugs made hearts heavy, and they walked for miles in tearful silence, not saying a single word. But, somehow, there was solace in remembering.

By mid-day they reached the torched village with a well where Liam had stopped before when going to Westport. But now the place was no longer deserted, and several homeless families hid behind the remaining walls and peered out at them – leery and suspicious, fearful of roving land agents. Liam smiled and spoke to reassure them, but only the children responded. The adults seemed scarred and traumatized by ruthless evictions. They made him uneasy, and he kept his coat over the iron pot to hide the pail of mush. After taking water from the well and resting, he was anxious to move on.

Walking along the road, the little girls chattered about the big boat and whether they would get wet, but then the chatter turned to fretful pleading.

Cait drooped down on the road. "Can't we have some stirabout? I'm so hungry I could eat a spider!"

Brighid leaned on the wall. "At home we got more than *this.*"

Liam turned around. "No. We have to make this last as long as possible."

Mamai sat on a rock, as wilted as the rose she carried. "Liam, what about giving each of us three spoonfuls every two hours or so."

Liam could see that they would not rise from their rock perches without food and laid down the pot. He dipped the spoon into the pail and moved from one open mouth to the other and back again three times around.

Aine giggled. "Liam, a father bird, you are . . . feeding your chicks!"

He covered the pail again and smiled. "Whatever it takes, but now it's time to fly." Like old people, they rose with great effort, and their steps were so slow that Liam feared the journey might take three days, instead of one and a half.

Then a distant noise distracted them from their weariness. What was it? The countryside had been so peaceful. Far away but coming closer, they could hear the yowls of dogs . . . packs of barking hounds. A shrill trumpet pierced the air as they appeared atop the hill, and behind the hounds came the thunder of galloping hooves. The Reillys gawked at the spectacle as a frightened fox ran for his life in their direction. The snarling dogs raced forward, gaining ground on the frantic fox that was slowing from exhaustion. When the dogs caught up with it, the fox cried out in high pitched agony as they ripped it apart.

The riders pulled their horses to a quick halt, after what must have been a strenuous ride, and one horseman joked while his white steed foamed at the mouth. Ignoring the Reillys, the aristocrats gathered to celebrate the kill and allowed their horses to tromp through a sprouting field. Dressed for their sport in black, felt hats, red coats, silk scarves at their throats, and handsome riding boots, they reached into their jackets and pulled out small, silver glasses and flasks for toasting. Then they turned and rode away with revelry and hounds yapping.

A somber Aine contemplated the bloody ground. "Like the fox, we are . . . ."

The family had walked several miles farther, when Brighid stopped again. "Please let us have three more bites!" They stood unified in their demand, and Liam realized resistance was useless. He dipped the spoon into the thick meal and handed the first bite to Cait. Brighid, like an animal about to seize game, intently followed the spoon's journey from pail to her sister's mouth.

Aine, fixated on the next full spoon, swallowed when Brighid did. "Remember to chew a long time to make it last," she warned. The eating ceremony dragged out to ten spoonfuls for each until finally, despite their protests, Liam put the pail away. When they rose to walk, the little girls stumbled and were so drowsy that Cait dropped the Bible.

"You didn't hurt it, but let me carry the picture, too," Aine suggested.

"No! I'll be better." But her eyes were heavy, and she leaned like she might topple over. Mamai appeared stooped and fragile with large elbows on arms as slender as reeds. In this one year, she had aged ten. Even though it was not quite dusk, Liam decided to stop. Off the road and up the hill, the ruins of destroyed cottages stood silhouetted against the sky, and Liam pointed them out to

Aine. "Let's climb up there for the night. The walls will block the wind and hide us from soldiers."

Caitlin sighed. "I can't take another step." She dropped to the grass and curled up like a kitten.

Liam looked down at her. "Stay here, Cait. I'll carry this pot up and come back for you."

Brighid lay down beside her. "Me too."

After ascending the hill in stages, the family settled in. Liam and Aine spread out the mats and carried water to mother and the girls who drank without pause. "More, Liam," Brighid demanded, but when he returned with a second bowl, all were asleep so he spread blankets over them.

As night fell, Liam stood alone amid the ruins and sensed it all – the village life that had been and the death that lurked here now, shrouded by darkness. Meandering past fields of stubble, he watched clouds move across the moon and felt sorrow seeping from the rocky ground. A mist crept in from the sea and cried the tears of mothers whose children lay in nearby mounds. Restless spirits blew through the weeds and rubble, out the doorways, and down the worn paths where their feet once trod. With the wind as their voice, tortured souls murmured their story of eviction and starvation. They moaned the truth about how Ireland had died and they whispered a mournful plea. Tell them . . . tell them . . . tell the world how government officials across the Irish Sea welcomed the angel of death, refused to stay her hand, and applauded her great harvest as a blessing. Not until the wee hours did the voices hush and hide in secret places, and Ireland again fell silent.

2 0
Please God . . . No!

Over the jagged remains of a stone wall, the sun shone into Liam's eyes, and although his weary body begged for rest, he shook himself awake. Father Mullen's warning that they were a ticket short was weighing him down, and he needed to get to Westport. He carried water up from the spring while Aine scraped the last bit of stirabout into the bowls. But as soon as Brighid's spoon scraped the bottom, she began to beg for more.

"Can't we eat Aunt Una's fish?"

Liam rolled the mats and tied them with vine. "We'll eat it tonight."

Brighid was glum. "It's not a very big fish."

"It's more than many have this day, so don't complain." Liam hoisted one of the mats onto his back, eager to leave.

Aine returned from the stream with the pail washed clean, while Mother led Cait up the hill with face and hands well scrubbed. Liam gave each person a load to carry and prodded them back to the road.

Ahead, dust clouds hovered in the air, a sign that a convoy was passing. They caught up with it and stood aside as the column stretched down the road as far as an eye could see, turning and twisting over the hills like an enormous sea serpent. As Liam leaned against the wall and squinted into the sun, he pondered the tragic destruction of his country. Foot soldiers with fixed bayonets dared anyone to interfere with the enormous exports of food. If even some food were allowed to remain, there would be no starvation. But why land clearance and eviction?

Frowning, he turned to Aine. "You know, Father Mullen is right. Eviction will continue for many, many years to come." He crossed his arms. "The British want our land, but without the Irish people. That's why they're trying to bring more English and Scots into Mayo."

Aine looked puzzled. "And why do they hate us . . . just because we're Catholic?" Liam shrugged, unable to explain what he did not understand.

From a passing cart, grain trickled out unnoticed from an inch-long split in a bag. "Look Liam, oats!" Aine whispered. "When this convoy has passed and is out of sight, we'll follow that trail of grain and scoop some from the road." After a half-hour of stooping, they had collected a full pail.

As they came closer to Westport, they saw emaciated families collapsed along the roadside. Memories of the town flooded back and haunted Liam . . . the soldier who bayoneted the starving man . . . the thousands of frail, barefoot farmers marching as one . . . Maureen McGuinness, so changed they did not know her. He prayed that after he was in America, God would show him a way to tell the world the truth about Ireland's starvation.

Aine shaded her eyes with her arm. "Are we coming to Westport?"

"No, it's the Irish settlement on the outskirts. Long ago, the Penal Laws segregated Irish and English, forcing Irish to live five miles outside of corporate towns. This village is worse since last August when I passed through . . . more weeds and cottages in ruins." Orphaned children, some as young as four years, besieged them, and it distressed Liam to ignore their pleas and turn his back on them.

"Don't we have oats to give?" Cait asked.

Liam's temper flared. "Sh! We've none to spare. Walk faster!" Even though he felt selfish, he kept the oats hidden under a blanket and avoided their eyes.

At last they entered Westport. Crowds filled the streets, jostling for a position on the walkways. Mounted soldiers in dapper uniforms patrolled in groups of four, sitting tall on well-groomed horses that whisked their tails at biting flies. Mamai, Aine, and Brighid gawked in amazement at buildings three and four stories high. Caitlin could only see shadows but listened intently to the cacophony of sounds: the clopping of iron horse shoes on cobblestone, a bellowing donkey, squeaking cart wheels, shouting venders, squawking sea gulls, and crying children. The smell of smoking fish tantalized them all and made their mouths water.

Boney beggars, barely clinging to life, swarmed them with outstretched palms. In a stupor with dull half-closed eyes, their hoarse voices chanted, "A crust for our children . . . have mercy." Mother and his sisters became tearful and anguished, but Liam stayed focused on his mission and by walking briskly, he forced his family to chase him.

"The National Bank of Ireland . . . where is it?" he asked a passerby.

"Right there in front of you," the old man answered. Liam looked up at the bank's ornate carvings and gold lettering on a jet black sign and handed Aine the iron pot.

"Guard this and wait for me here." He smoothed his hair,

tugged on his shirt, and entered. Unfamiliar with banks, he did not know what to do. The interior with its high ceilings and massive, dark furniture made him feel small. People were lined up before three windows framed with brass, so he took a place. When it was his turn, he spoke in Irish, but when he tried to switch to English, he stuttered. Since the drafts from the American bank were written in English, he decided to let them speak for themselves and stuffed them through the opening.

The teller, dressed in a suit with a silk tie at the throat, read them and made calculations on a pad. When he reached into his drawer and took out English bills, Liam lost track of the count and had to trust him. "Thank you." He had not spoken the *Sasanach* language in a while, but it was coming back. Outside on the boardwalk, he put the money in his shirt and asked a clerk leaving the bank for directions to the shipping office.

"Down a block and across the street," he answered.

"This way," Liam motioned to his flock. Carts loaded with trunks and cooking pots creaked past as men pushed them toward the harbor. The driver of a fine carriage lashed his whip as he pressed the horses forward and shouted to pedestrians, "Give way! Gentleman passing!" Inside Liam could see the sheen of a passenger's satin coat.

Since Aine was carrying bundles and mats on her back, Caitlin gripped her skirt for a lead. But not realizing that Aine had stopped for the carriage, she stepped into the street. "Stop Cait!" Mother yelled and jerked her back, just in time. She hugged Caitlin and crossed herself, without even noticing the scrape on her own arm made by the horse harness and buckles as they passed.

"Mamai, you're hurt!" Aine dabbed the blood.

"It's nothing." Mother grabbed Caitlin's hand in a firm grip.

An angry Liam glared, "I can't be watching these children,

so *you* must!"

Aine snapped back. "Keep your harsh tone to yourself! It's our best, we're doing."

When a break came in the traffic, they scurried across the street to the shipping office and waited outside while Liam went in alone. As he stood in the line, he practiced his English, and after the man in front stepped away, he blurted it out. "Tickets to Americay, to New York town."

The agent answered without looking up from his schedule. "A ship leaves tomorrow afternoon. How many persons?"

"Tomorrow?" Father Mullen's information had been off four days, and Liam was surprised. "Three adults and two children." He withdrew the money from his shirt and laid it on the counter. The ticket agent counted, paused, and started over.

Then he looked at Liam over his spectacles. "You only have money for three adults. Children are half fare, so you could take both of them for one adult ticket. Is that what you want?"

Liam's heart sank. "Passage for two adults and two children, then." Aine would have to be their shepherd.

"What names should be on these?"

Liam listed his sisters and mother, spelling several times "R-e-i-l-l-y."

The clerk folded the tickets in brown paper and handed them to Liam. "The passenger roster is filling up, so if you want to purchase another ticket, do it soon."

Outside, Liam tried to remain calm and hide his worry. "The ship leaves tomorrow. Mamai, we'll leave you with the sleep mats and the girls on this corner while Aine and I go sell some things." The pawn shops were only a few doors away, and Liam guessed that the need for passage money caused them to cluster near the shipping office. He now had to devise a strategy.

Liam reached in his pant's pocket and touched the cool, silver watch and chain. He had planned to pawn it in New York where the initial engraved on its back would not lead police to Lord Lucan's watchman, but now things had changed.

"Aine, I think we'll get better prices of we divide our goods. I'll walk in after you with more to sell, and we won't let on that we know each other."

"How much do we need?" she asked.

"A great deal, I'm afraid. The truth is . . . we didn't have enough money for my ticket, and I may have to stay behind."

"No!" Her eyes widened and her voice got shrill. "We can't leave you. We won't!"

Liam answered calmly. "You may have to. You are strong and can handle it, and I'll try to come later."

Her voice quivered. "How long have you known this?"

"Father Mullen alerted me, but don't tell Mamai."

"Liam, it would break her heart to leave you. You *have* to go with us! I can't do this alone."

"Well, our only hope is to sell the guard's watch for a good price. It's the most valuable thing we have, but we still must bargain hard. You will seem more innocent than I, and if you are questioned about it, you speak better English. Remember it has a "W" on the back so make up an explanation. Can you do it?" Aine nodded. Liam looked around furtively as he pulled out the watch which had been hidden since the day he killed its owner.

"Give it to me! Quick!" Aine said. She clutched it in the folds of her skirt and pushed through the doors. Liam waited outside, looking through the window, and by the time he entered, she was pleading to the dealer. "This is all I have, kind sir. It was the gift of our dying priest, Father Walsh, to get me to Americay."

The dealer seemed bored with her story, and Liam reasoned

that he met desperate people all day and was accustomed to having them at his mercy. "That's all I'll give," he said.

Aine's face flushed. "But that will scarcely buy a night's lodging!"

He shrugged his shoulders. "It's enough to get you to Liverpool." He put the money on the counter and the watch beneath the glass.

"No! Before I'll sell our blessed priest's gift so cheaply, I'll donate it to the church. Give it back."

The dealer looked surprised, then irritated, and his eyes narrowed. "What a fine watch this is for an Irish priest to have!" Perturbed, he handed it over. Aine grabbed the watch and ran from the store. Liam's heart was racing, but he knew he must distract the man from this idea so he stepped forward quickly.

"What about this, sir . . . a heavy, frieze jacket? Lots of wool . . . no wind gets through." The dealer lifted it to check its weight, and although it was heavy, his face was full of disdain. Liam looked him in the eye. "It will sell in London, I dare say."

The dealer reached into his drawer and slapped a few bills on the table. "Well, here you are. Take it or leave it."

Liam counted the money and pondered his move. The price was low, but he needed to satisfy the dealer so he would forget about the valuable watch. "Very well. The coat is yours."

A tearful Aine waited between the buildings. "I failed you, Liam. He didn't even mind not getting the watch! We'll never get enough money for a ticket!"

Liam shook her by the shoulders. "Listen Aine! He wanted it very much. He recognized its value and was angry when you took it back. Be strong. Think about what's at stake here. A low price won't help us." As they walked to the pawn shop next door, Liam noticed that the sun was lower in the sky and realized that time was running out.

Aine took a deep breath. "Give me Grandmother's shawl in case I need something more." She draped it around herself, tossed her hair over it, and squared her shoulders as she entered the store. When Liam opened the door minutes later, she was arguing with great emotion.

"Can't you give me more than that for such a fine watch? I'm an orphan and have lost my family to the typhus. Our dying priest, Father Walsh, gave it to me in hopes it would buy passage to my brother in Americay." With that, Aine burst into tears, hid her face in her hands, and swayed back and forth.

The dealer, who had seemed skeptical, started to waver. Aine bent over the counter and laid her head on her arm, crying harder. When she raised her face, Liam was amazed to see that her cheeks were wet with red, puffy eyes. The man twitched his moustache and rubbed the watch, turning it over and polishing it with his handkerchief till it glistened. He wound it, put it to his ear, and listened. Then he frowned again. "Do you have anything you can add to this?"

She wrapped the soft wool around her more snugly. "You're not thinking of taking Grandmamai's shawl, are you? Without a wrap, I'll die at sea of coughing. 'Tis a warm wool from our own sheep."

The man cocked his head. "Yes, give the shawl and it will be enough for your passage. Make up your mind. There's another customer waiting." He nodded toward Liam.

Aine removed the shawl. "It's all I have left of my family, but you give me no choice." She heaved a sigh and wiped her face on her skirt.

The dealer smirked, put them both behind his counter, and turned to Liam. "What have you?"

Aine cleared her throat. "Sir, my passage money?"

Again he raised his brows. "Oh! Yes." He counted it out and pushed it across. "This should get a ticket." Aine tucked it in her blouse and left.

Liam unfolded the bundle and laid down five earthen bowls with wooden spoons. He did not haggle because he needed to get tickets before the shipping office was closed. He found Aine next door, waiting in front of the ticket office, and with eyes sparkling, she reached up and hugged his neck.

"We got your passage money!" She gave a sideways jump, as in step dancing.

"Aine, you got far more for that watch than I could! . . . a good price! What an actress you are!"

"'Twas no act. The thought of leaving you on shore terrified me . . . made me cry." She gave him a shove. "Now, get that ticket!"

The agent recognized Liam. "One adult?" This time he had no trouble with the spelling and finished the "y" with a flourish. "Here you are."

Liam looked down at the black ink and, with relief, read it again. "Liam Reilly."

The agent closed the register's wooden cover with a clap. "That's the last place in steerage. Your ship, *The Venture*, will sail at two o'clock tomorrow afternoon, but I suggest that you be there an hour before."

On the corner where they had left them, they found Mamai looking abandoned with her little daughters huddled close and peering out from her skirt. "What took you so long? These girls are weary," she complained.

Cheered by getting the extra ticket, Liam chuckled. "Did you think we made off with the money and were leaving without you?" he teased as he steered them down the street. "First we need to buy extra food for the journey and then find a place to stay the night."

They passed Tom Moran's Hardware, but entered the shop of M. Malloy, Ironmonger and Grocer. Seeing displays of chamber pots reminded Liam of how the vendors in Westport had shouted warning to all maidens: the ships lack sanitary facilities. Yes, he would buy one and counted out the sum for his first purchase. Next, Mother asked for dried meat, and although it looked none too new, she said to buy it. Liam moved the coins across the counter, one by one.

His eyes searched the shelves. "Do you have cheese?" The grocer produced a moldy piece that was far inferior to Da's. "Is this your best?"

The grocer nodded. "Good cheese gets a higher price in England, and the landlords export it."

Mamai stood at Liam's shoulder and whispered, "I'll scrape it well."

Liam put the strips of dried meat and cheese into the iron pot and paid the grocer. "Might you know of a cheap place we can pass the night?"

The grocer wiped his hands on his apron. "P. McCarthy lets out space above his pub. It's just around the corner, close to the docks." As he talked, his head tilted in that direction.

"Thank you." Since Liam's arms were full with the iron pot and food purchases, Mother carried the chamber pot and blankets. Aine now carried the two sleeping mats in her arms and peeped around them while she led Caitlin by the arm. This left Brighid to carry the bag with bowls and to hold the doors open.

Colorful, hand painted signs on the store fronts entertained them. A shoe cobbler warned that it was "Better to have one good sole than two good uppers." McCarthy's pub, a pale yellow, stucco building with green paint peeling off the wood trim, had a sign in the window that enjoined all to "Come drink to the health of your enemy's enemies."

Outside its double doors, wives and children waited with worried eyes for men to come out, but the Reillys pushed through and entered. Due to smoke and few windows, the interior of the pub was dark, and the air was strong with the musty smell of dust and sweat. This pub, unlike ones in Partry and Ballinglass, had no card playing or music, no jovial stories. Oppression and hardship had made the somber clients vulnerable to the lure of strong drink. Gripped by fear, they had too many bad memories they wanted to drown.

The man behind the bar anticipated Liam's question before he asked. "Two bits for the lot of ya and out by noon." He continued drying glasses. "You'll share the room with others. 'Tis no hotel!"

"We'll take it." Liam laid the money on the bar. "Where's the stair?"

"Off the hall, near the back door. There's a creek behind us for water."

Liam nodded, impatient to be out of this smoky depressing room, and as he climbed the creaky, narrow stairs, he was glad they sailed tomorrow. Soon there would be no more people near death, no orphans to shoo away, or landlords to appease. He was ready to get his family out of Ireland, and he'd deal later with the guilt of leaving so many of his countrymen behind.

The room at the top of the stairs was empty. They spread out the four sleeping mats and made a pile of their belongings in the corner with the chamber pot handy. Very weary, no one complained when Liam pulled out the smoked fish that Uncle Paddy had given them and divided it with a knife.

Mamai's pale blue eyes had a new glow. "I thought I'd never

see Niall again! I've lost so much . . . your father, Sean, and your grandparents . . . but at least, I'll regain a son."

"For sure, Mamai." Aine rubbed her back. "Things will be better. We'll see Niall and the Murphys. Maire and Brian will meet us at the docks!" Her own eyes brightened at the thought and then clouded. "Poor Maire! Full of joy, she'll come to find Sean and be heartbroken to learn he was killed."

Mamai's eyes saddened. "And won't Niall be shocked to learn how many of us are gone."

A knocking interrupted conversation. The door opened slowly, and there stood a group of five. "The bartender says we're to share this room with you," said the young man, holding two pouches and three blankets.

Liam stood up and welcomed with a smile. "Of course! You paid the same as we so find a place."

The man, handsome with auburn, wavy hair, put down his bundles. "I'm Cian Burke and this is my sister Ailis and my wife Marta."

"That's my name, too!" Brighid said. "Brighid Marta Reilly."

The wife smiled. "'Tis a good name, you have."

The little daughters were shy and tried to hide behind their mother, but the young father pushed them forward proudly. "These are the small ones . . . Miriam and Molly." The children, like their parents, were shrunk and pinched from want, with sunken eyes and coarse hair, but Liam realized that they, themselves, appeared much the same.

Aine whispered to the children, "We are glad you're here."

"We're from Ballyhaunis," Cian said. "And you?"

"Near Partry." Liam replied. "Are you here to take a ship?"

"Yes, we're trying to go to Liverpool and find work. I hope to earn enough to get us to Americay someday. And you?"

Caitlin sat up on her legs and blurted out. "My brother Niall is already there! He sent us the money to go to New York on a big boat!" She turned toward Liam's voice. "This brother has the tickets, don't ya!"

Cian covered his toddler with a blanket. "That's very lucky to have a brother in Americay with money. When do you leave, tomorrow?"

"Yes," Liam answered. "Two o'clock."

Cian's eyes hardened with anger. "Our landlord gave us notice to quit our cottage even though I had planted a field. I had pawned everything to buy that seed, and the seedlings were up for all to see. Still they drove us out!"

The door creaked open again, and three wild looking men with long hair and beards stood in the hall. "We're supposed to share this floor."

Cian motioned him in. "Find a place and put yourselves down. We've all walked miles across Mayo today and are about to sleep. Where are you from?"

The men acted like they might not answer. Then one drawled out "Louisburgh . . . not too far."

"Where are you heading?" Cian asked.

"England." The man lay down and stared up at the ceiling. Impassive, they refused conversation and forced a grim silence. To Liam's relief, the men soon closed their eyes and began to breathe heavily and snore. He trusted the Burkes, but sharing a room with these rough men made him uneasy.

The journeys had drained the strength from everyone. The Burke children were already asleep, and Brighid and Caitlin were dozing off. The room had grown dark, and the snoring of the Louisburgh men made a rhythmic monotonous sound that drowned out noise from the pub and street. Liam, overcome by fatigue, closed his eyes and drifted into a deep slumber.

Suddenly something roused him. Opening his eyes, he listened. Except for the snoring, it seemed quiet. He surmised that the hour must be late because the pub below was closed and the darkness was inky black with no light even from the street. His eyes adjusted, and he looked over at his family, but all seemed well. He lay wondering what had awakened him.

Remembering the tickets, he checked his shirt where they had been tucked away, but it was smooth and flat! There was nothing. He sat up, patted his chest, and thrust his hand inside his clothes. It was true. They were gone! Shock and horror filled him as he realized what had happened. "Please God . . . no."

He stumbled to his feet. The men from Louisburgh still lay on their side of the room. In the dark he blinked at the place where the Burke family had slept, but it was now bare floor . . . empty. Then he knew. They had stolen the tickets and fled. In his mind he could hear Caitlin's voice telling about Niall, the tickets, and sailing in the morrow. Of course! They could use the tickets because their family was so similar – the same number with two women, one man, and two female children. He had trusted the wrong people.

Liam's heart pounded. Rage boiled up, and he wanted to tear Burke apart with his bare hands. He opened and closed his fists. He looked down at his sleeping sisters and mother. Should he awaken them with this terrible news? No. He could not bear to tell them the tickets were gone and that the boat might sail without them! Panic surged through him. He had to find Burke and get the tickets back. He *had* to! He opened the door and hurried down the creaking stairs into the night.

21

The Search

As Liam bolted from the back of McCarthy's pub, the door slammed behind him, and a rat scurried from under the wooden step. Below him he could hear the stream gurgling over rocks and somewhere a loose shutter creaked in the wind. Standing in the moonlight, he took deep breaths of the clammy air and surveyed the row of buildings backing up to this alley.

With so little of the night remaining, the Burkes would not pay for another floor and would hide till morning beneath a building or wharf. Because the ground sloped toward the stream, large wooden piers supported the rear of the buildings and created a cave-like expanse of damp earth beneath them. Under each structure was an area large enough to conceal several families, and he would have to search them all.

Liam crouched under the flooring of the first building and bumped his head on a support beam as he tried to navigate through the darkness. As the ground rose to street level, the space became narrower and blacker. Small glowing eyes stared at him, and when his vision adjusted, he realized that his wanderings had disturbed rats as large as small dogs. Some retreated to the far corners, while others looked back at him with a boldness that was unnerving.

Somewhere a man coughed. Could it be Burke? Liam wished he had brought the knife, but in his haste, he had left it in the room. Half-way in, he saw a form sprawled out, and as he looked him in the face, the man raised his head. When Liam saw it was a stranger, he returned to the alley, and the man lay back again.

There was no need to search the main streets since the homeless were forbidden to sleep in the public part of the town. This alley hid them – the living, the dead, and the living-dead – and during the night, police wagons collected bodies. A man tottered past Liam like a phantom, and no longer caring when death came, he begged nothing. His body had even consumed the flesh of his lips, and dry skin hung in folds.

When Liam leaned his head under the next building, the terrible stench of typhus repelled him for even before death, rotting limbs reeked. Gagging, he lifted his arm across his nose and backed away, knowing that such a smell and the contagion would also drive Burke elsewhere.

He hurried down the row and crept under another floor where a young woman with long, wavy hair like Marta Burke rocked and crooned to her small child. Had her husband left her alone in order to hide more easily? He crept closer and saw to his horror that the strange woman's baby was already dead.

Farther back, he could hear the voices of young children, and so he hunched over and moved in their direction. Two small children whimpered and draped themselves over a man lying on his back with eyes closed. "Are you warmer now, Da? . . . Mamai, why is he so cold?"

Liam moved on quickly but the man's wife followed him, wild-eyed. "Wait! Don't run! We're sailing tomorrow! Aren't you coming with us?"

Confused, he looked into her face. Her flush and odd smile told him that she was either delirious with fever or had lost her mind. "I can't, dear woman. Go back to your husband now. Go!"

Leaving her in the alley, Liam pushed on to the wharves where the docks or beach would provide a good place for the Burkes to sleep till dawn. An avalanche of food awaited shipment across the Irish Sea, and in crowded pens, livestock made a den of animal noise. Soldiers, guarding the produce of County Mayo, marched to and fro with their gun barrels gleaming in the moonlight. Liam hastened across the boardwalks that connected to the harbor.

"Halt! Stay where you are! No ships leave tonight," a hoarse voice bellowed. The soldiers glared at him, threatening to shoot if he continued. It would be too risky for Burke to bring his family here so Liam turned around.

In the east on the horizon, a tinge of pink light surprised him with the hint of morning. With day, the streets would be full of people, and he would never find Burke. His pulse quickened and he hurriedly backtracked along the stream.

But the dead and dying who littered the path slowed his pace. Coming round the corner, a police wagon, piled with thin and blackened corpses, blocked his way. Three men walked beside it and did the grisly work of collection by seizing an arm and a leg and hurling bodies on to the top. On the ground near him, a lad groaned, in a semi-conscious state, but the men, like mindless brutes, heaved his body up. The lad slid to one side and wedged against the rail, his arm dangling between the slats. Although Liam realized that the man was now destined to be buried alive, he was helpless to save him.

Feeling trapped in a nightmare, a holocaust, Liam was frantic to get away. He plunged into the creek, splashed through the water, and emerged behind the body gatherers and their wagon. He had no time . . . no time! He started to jog and beads of perspiration formed on his forehead.

He *must* have passed Burke . . . or had Burke gone the opposite direction, away from the harbor? Now he was back at McCarthy's rear door where he started, and he felt panicky as he realized how many streets and buildings still lay ahead. He turned southwest, running faster, crouching as he looked under floors here, then there, beneath one, then another. Breathless, he searched between buildings, behind barrels, and under a tall stairway that led to a second floor.

Wait . . . in the shadows . . . there under the stairs. Blankets hid the faces of several people sleeping. A man was slouched over a small child cradled in his lap, and though his face was buried in the blanket's folds, his thick auburn mane looked familiar.

Liam's muscles tensed as he reached in and pulled him out by his hair. "Give me those tickets, you bastard!" He shook him hard, whipping Burke's head around.

Burke looked dazed. "Let me go!"

Liam drew back an arm and slugged him in the jaw. "Where are my tickets!"

Burke stumbled, his face defiant. "They're *mine* now!"

Liam drove his knuckles into his cheek bone. "You scum!"

Under the stairs, the women cowered and started a high keen, while the children cried and clung to their mother. The wife shouted, "No! No! Don't!"

Burke looked desperate and was struggling. He pulled a knife from his pocket and with new confidence, he inched forward, eyes bulging.

Liam retreated. He had to get that knife. In the dim light, he could see Burke's fist clinching the shiny blade's handle, and like a coiled snake, Burke's arm was ready to deliver the sharp point into his head, his chest, to slow him and kill him. Liam kept backing until suddenly he was against the brick wall . . . cornered.

Wham! Liam jerked aside, just as Burke drove the knife into the window frame next to his head, and in passing, the blade cut Liam's cheek. With the knife buried in wood, Liam sprang away from the wall, but Burke yanked out the knife and pursued. Liam lunged, grabbed Burke's hand and twisted it, forcing him to rotate his body. He pounded Burke's wrist against the stairway repeatedly and heard bones crack. The knife fell to the ground, and Liam kicked it away. Then Liam grabbed him by the shoulders and hammered his head against the brick wall again and again. He could not stop.

His wife screamed. "No! Let him be!"

Liam's hands were slippery with blood, as Burke's body went limp and heavy. When Liam released him, Burke slumped to the ground and appeared unconscious. As he lay in the mud, Liam searched him, and inside Burke's shirt, he found the tickets, still wrapped in brown paper.

"You've killed him!" his wife Marta shrieked. "You've killed him! You devil from hell! You bloody son of Satan. May the light go out from your eyes!" In hysterical crying, she ran and laid her head on her husband's chest. Liam studied Burke. He could see discolored bruising and one eye was already swollen shut, but was he dead?

Not wanting to know, Liam turned and fled. It was still early morning, but he knew his family was waiting and fearful. From McCarthy's back entrance, he dashed up the stairs, two at a time, and pulled open the door. There in the empty room his worried family sat alone, slouched on their bundles.

Mother raised her arms. "Oh, Liam! Praise God! We're half crazy with worry!"

Caitlin frowned. "You're bad, Liam, to leave us."

Aine jumped up. "Where did you go? You're cut! . . . oh, your hands!"

Liam held up the package of tickets. "In the middle of the night, Burke stole these, but I got them back. He looks worse than I do."

Mamai's mouth fell open. "That nice man, Burke?"

Liam shook his head. "Surprised me, too."

He reached for the sleeping mats already tied up in vine. "Let's get out of here. Who knows? They might return to continue a fight we don't need." Liam felt uneasy and could still hear the wife, screaming: "You've killed him! You've killed him!" If he had, it would bring the police, and besides, he did not wish Burke dead.

Anglican church bells tolled the coming of day, and the streets were stirring. From a tavern door, an owner tossed out scraps of yesterday's food, and children and adults swarmed, stuffing dust-covered garbage into their mouths. Liam could see that with the starvation, civilization was slipping away.

At the docks, workers paced to and fro, busily loading the ferry to Liverpool with livestock, cheese, grains, butter, eggs, and hams – all while the hungry gaped longingly at the produce of their own land. It was a sight Liam would never forget or forgive.

Police and soldiers moved among the crowd at the harbor and kept a watchful eye, making Liam uncomfortable. He gazed down below the docks to a sandy strip along the shore where some travelers encircled a peat fire. There his family might mix in and not stand out. If Burke's people wanted to make trouble for him, he should make himself hard to find. "Hey, Aine! Let's wait down there until time to sail."

She looked below. "Yes, that would be good . . . and you should wash your cuts in the salt water." He glanced down at his bloody shirt and wanted to get rid of the evidence.

Liam led his family to a group sitting around the blaze, sharing each other's company. Pots were positioned for cooking and whiffs of boiling barley and oats circled in the sea breeze. Liam ran his fingers back through his hair and cleared his throat. "May we join you?"

A young man looked up, revealing a hideous face contorted by scar tissue, a broken nose, and a socket with a missing eye. It jarred Liam, but he tried to mask his revulsion. The man nodded and gave a smile which was made crooked by a ridge of raised flesh. "Yes. Sit. My name's Neil Gallagher, and here is my brother Ciaran." He gestured to his other side. "This is Peter Flynn and Donal Wallace from our village." Each smiled and extended his hand. "Yes, cook whatever you have, and we'll share water we got upstream," Wallace generously offered.

"Thank you." Liam set their pot on the fire. "Aine, let's cook some of the oats we gathered."

Mamai sat a safe distance from the flames and took Cait on her lap. A woman with a leathery face peered from under her shawl and began to make friends with Mamai. "Where you people from?" she called from the other side of the fire.

A wistful look crossed Mamai's face. "Near Partry and the lakes. A pretty place."

"Turlough for us. All the rest are gone . . . my daughters, everyone." She seemed to wilt and grow smaller with the telling.

Mamai wrapped her shawl around a dozing Cait. "The same with us."

Aine sifted oats into the pot from the pail and concentrated on vigorous stirring in order to avoid glancing at the man's mutilated face.

A hungry Brighid peered over her arms. "I could eat all that by myself." Then for the first time Brighid saw the man's red, raised scars and empty eye socket. Speechless, she stared with a terrible awe.

Liam tried to break the spell. "Brighid, come with me to the ocean. I'll clean my face, and you can wash my shirt." But she seemed frozen and did not move. Liam put the tickets in the waist of his trousers and pulled off the blood-spattered shirt.

Neil eyed the shirt with interest. "Got in a fight there, did you?"

"Yes, a fellow stole my tickets to Americay, but I got them back."

"Ah . . . worth a fight, those are," Neil said.

Brighid found her tongue. "Did *you* get into a fight?"

"I was caned by my landlord, while his agents held me down . . . if you call that a fight. It's certainly not a *fair* one."

Brighid's eyes grew sad. "Would nobody help you?"

"No one was allowed to. When I demanded to know why he was evicting us, the landlord vowed to teach me a lesson . . . some *respect,* he said. If any person had raised a voice or hand in my defense, they would have gotten the same treatment. The law was on the landlord's side, not mine."

Liam's eyes narrowed. "No law should give him the right to do that to you."

Neil frowned. "There was a time when the Ribbonmen might have intimidated the landlord, but now they're starved out."

Liam got on one knee and leaned close. "Were you a Ribbonman?"

Neil replied in hushed tones. "The membership is secret, don't ya know. But I never joined because our priests opposed the group. But look at me now!" He pointed to his grotesque face. "I wish I had."

Neil looked around to check for unfriendly ears. "Since I'm sailing soon, I guess I can talk freely." Yet, he continued to whisper.

"To my way of thinking, the secret groups were the only way we Irish could stand up for ourselves. The Ribbonmen always nailed a warning note to the door first. If a landlord or his agent didn't pay heed and went ahead with a heartless action, then he might find his field afire or his horse's throat cut. But never without a *big* reason.

But what other way can we poor Irish defend ourselves? The law makes the landlord all-powerful, and he can do to us whatever he wants. Yet, it gives us no rights at all. We're not allowed to have guns, while the landlords are stocking up on weapons to use against us . . . while they starve and evict us. Most of the time the blood suckers live in England and out of our reach! Now since this great hunger, we're under the landlord's heel, as never before . . . at their mercy!"

"Mercy?" Liam stood up, his voice hoarse. "What mercy? They have none."

Still shaking his head, Liam tugged Brighid away and crossed the sand in long strides to the water's edge. He gave his little sister his shirt, and she imitated all the washing motions of Mamai and Grandmamai, whipping it on the waves and rocks with a vengeance. He winced as he splashed salt water into his cuts and rubbed his face and hands clean of blood.

Liam studied the action of the waves as they retreated into the Atlantic, sweeping sand and shells back to itself. No sooner had the tide drawn away than it pushed up the sand again, wetting his feet. Over miles of deep water across this ocean was a special girl somewhere in Brooklyn. He touched her letter, folded in his pocket, but there was no need to read it since long ago he had memorized the words and every stroke of her quill on the paper.

As he watched a sea gull soar, arc, and float on a current of air in perfect balance, he yearned for such freedom. Then it dipped toward the waves and hovered there, searching for unseen fish. Soon I, too, will be free – free to find her, to earn my way, to profit from my labor, and to have rights. Liberty is so close now, but I have to be careful.

He glanced up at the docks and saw a policeman, observing the shore people from above. Was he looking for him? No, not yet. Maybe never. Probably a routine inspection, but it still made him nervous. He wished he knew if Burke were alive or dead, for if he was alive, there was nothing to fear.

Aine came up behind them. "Here! Bowls of oats for the both of you." Brighid gave a squeal, threw down the shirt, and sat on the sand to eat. Aine lifted the shirt and inspected the stain.

"Did the blood wash out?" Liam asked.

"No, not all of it." She looked back. "Does that worry you?"

There was a long silence. Then Liam took her arm and steered her down the beach.

Aine was scrutinizing him. "Tell me!"

"I'm not sure but . . . I may have . . . killed him." He kept looking at his feet as he walked.

Aine stopped, closed her eyes, and let out her breath. "Oh, no. Did you have to?"

"He wouldn't give the tickets back, and I had to fight him. I hit his head against a wall." Liam folded his arms. "I don't know if he was unconscious or dead. It was hard to tell."

Aine's eyes sparked with a new urgency. "You've got to stay out of sight as long as you can! They may be hunting for you."

"That's what we're doing."

Aine moved closer. "Don't tell Mamai. She'd be scared, and she'd show it."

Liam nodded. "Let's go back to the group. We've got to be natural and talk without showing fear. I can't act like a wanted man."

Brighid was chasing after them down the beach, holding a bowl of oats in outstretched arms. "Liam, you forgot to eat!"

"Thank you, Brig. I'll take it now."

Back at the fire, men were talking. "At least we're not heading for British Canada. I would walk hundreds of miles to cross into the United States and avoid British rule."

Neil laughed. "Should the ship make a wrong turn, I'll go with you. I'm sure we'd have lots of company. I hear people walk clear to the border." The heads around the fire bobbed in agreement and enjoyed the thought of escape. If you go to Quebec, the fare is half as much as going to New York but any Irish will pay the difference, if he can.

Neil pointed to the bay. "See that sand bar? The government should have improved this harbor long ago and carved it out, but they never spend money on Ireland! They tax here and spend it over there." He leaned his head to the east toward England.

Liam looked out and could see it easily. "How does that bar affect us?"

"When my brother went to Americay two years ago, he was three days waiting. The tide was too low to float the ship over that bar and on out. Makes it tough."

Liam felt his heart stop. "When will we know?"

Neil tossed a bit of sand in the air and studied the ocean. "In a couple of hours. If the tide comes in deep enough, the bar will disappear." He leaned back on his elbows. "Sure glad me brother went to New York when he did! He's the one that sent us money for tickets! To bring us over, he saved half of the little he made for two years, digging sewers. Families can't go without help from someone."

"My brother Niall helped us." Liam laid down his bowl. "Are you going on the *Venture* too?"

"Yes, if she sails today."

Liam looked out at the Atlantic. "How long will it take to get to New York, do you think?"

Neil scratched his head. "Hard to say. You need good wind, no storms, and a smart captain to make it in less than five weeks, but it can take more, a lot more. This ship, *Venture,* does not have much sail, so it will be slow. My brother's ship took so long that they cut back on water to a cup a day per passenger, and it was torture. To make more profit, ship owners take just enough food and water for a short trip."

Too late Liam remembered Father Mullen's warning to Niall: sail on American ships, not British, because they try harder to enforce laws for the protection of passengers. Which was this ship – American or British? He did not want to know since it was too late to change.

Brighid scampered through the sand. "Liam and Aine! Caitlin's awake now so let's take her to the water and play."

Neil stood up. "I'll go with you since it's our last chance to enjoy a beach in Ireland."

The Reillys trooped to the water's edge with their new friend. With Aine holding Caitlin's hand, she waded out, but when the waves lapped around her ankles, she became stiff and balked at taking another step.

"Is this a nice ocean? It won't grab you, like that other one, will it?" she fretted.

Mamai gave Liam a curious look. "What is Cait talking about?"

Liam shrugged. "A bad dream maybe."

While the children played and Neil dozed, Liam worried and watched the tide. They had to get on that boat *today* because the longer they stayed in port, the more danger he faced. Hours passed as he noted the tide's advance, inch by inch. Gradually, the surf crept higher and forced them to retreat up the sandy slope until finally the bar disappeared.

Liam decided to shake Neil awake. "If you sleep much longer, you'll get soaked. Look. Will we sail today?"

Neil sat up and squinted his one eye. "That's a high tide, for sure!" He brushed sand off his damp pants and scanned the dock. "People are gathering so we better get up there." He slogged through the sand to rouse his mother and brother, and although Liam dreaded going dock side and into the crowd, he prepared to do the same.

Once on the boardwalk, Brighid gazed up at the tall masts. "Caitlin, the ship almost touches the sky!"

Caitlin turned toward her voice. "Can you tell where we will sleep at night?"

Liam surveyed the crowd and recalled that on Niall's ship each passenger had to pass inspection by the ship's captain and be judged fit for the journey. Eyeing other travelers who appeared weak and sick, he guessed that escape for some was coming too late. He wondered if Cait's blindness would bar her from the voyage. She could see shadows and only stumbled now and then, but if she raised her eyes, they would see the grey spots.

The docks were chaotic. Wheelbarrows loaded with water casks clattered up the gang plank, and vendors, shouting the virtues of their wares, convinced trusting travelers to give their last coin. As boarding time grew near, emotions stretched thin, and in the space of a quarter hour, families expressed love and devotion to carry through a lifetime. Composure dissolved into tears and cries, moans and whimpering. One lad choked up and, after giving his brother a weak hug, disappeared into the crowd to grieve alone. Liam remembered feeling the same.

To Liam the wait seemed endless, and he tried to be inconspicuous by lowering his head and looking down into the pot he carried. Aine, standing at his elbow, suddenly gasped in surprise and grabbed his arm.

"Liam! I see Cian Burke! Thank God! He's alive!"

Relieved by the news, Liam looked up and saw Burke across the dock with his family. But when he realized two policemen accompanied them, a clammy dread crept through him. Burke had not yet seen them so Liam hunched over and tried to avert his eyes, but they still locked on the man.

As Burke climbed atop a wooden chest and scanned the crowd, he spied Liam and began talking excitedly. Pointing him out to the police, he leaped off the chest and started pushing through the crowd. Liam was terrified. Yes! He was coming his way!

22
Slán / Goodbye

Liam froze as he watched Burke stride confidently through the crowd, leading two constables and his family straight to them. His cheek bones were discolored and his left eye swollen shut as he faced Liam, glaring. "Officer, here he is. The man who attacked me and stole our tickets!"

"What! That's a lie!" Liam yelled. "*Our* names are on these tickets." Liam reached in his shirt and pulled them out, and with trembling hands, he fumbled with the brown package. Finding his ticket, he held it up. "Here it is . . . Liam Reilly. That's me!" He shuffled it aside and read the names listed on the other. "Aine Reilly, Brighid, Caitlin, and my mother, Erin." When he read her name, Mother stepped forward, curtseyed, and forced a smile.

The officer's stony countenance remained unchanged. "That's what you say now because it suits your purpose." He placed his hand on Burke's shoulder. "*This* is Liam Reilly, and the names you read are those of *his* family. You surprised him in the alley, knocked him unconscious, and stole his tickets. I can still see blood stains on your shirt."

Liam shouted, "Officer, hear me. My brother Niall in America sent me a bank draft for the tickets! I bought them yesterday, and the ticket agent would remember me!"

The constable shook his head. "The ship is ready to sail, and there's no time for an investigation." Burke's audacity astonished Liam, and he could not believe what was happening. Burke must have gained the policemen's sympathy with his bruised face and crusty wounds and may even have claimed to be a Protestant.

Desperate, Liam began to plead and beg. "Sir, please! I'm telling the truth. It was *he* who stole *our* tickets!"

Burke's wife Marta looked Liam in the eye and smiled smugly. "You thought you were going to get away with this, didn't you? Now you're getting what you deserve." She slipped her arm around her husband. "Let's get on board."

The two constables grabbed Liam, one on each arm. "You're under arrest."

Mamai was white and trembling. "No . . . this is wrong!"

Aine stomped her foot and screamed at the wife. "You she-devil! How can you stand before your children and lie. Now they know you for what you are!"

Burke's sister Ailis stepped between them and slapped Aine in the face. Aine screamed and in the tussle, she dropped her bundles and pushed Ailis with such force that she fell into Marta. Then Marta pulled Aine's hair and spit on her. As they shouted accusations, a noisy crowd surrounded them, cheering for their favorites.

"Don't let her pull your hair! Hit her back!"

Another shouted, "Who beat up your husband?"

"Kick her in the chins!" a woman urged Aine, who promptly did as commanded.

Suddenly the crowd hushed as the large shadow of

three soldiers on horseback loomed over them, and one soldier dismounted. "What's going on here?" he demanded.

Though frantic, Liam tried to speak English calmly. "This man is trying to claim my tickets by saying that he's me. But I . . . . "

The soldier interrupted Liam and turned to the constables. "Do you have things under control here? Any need of us?"

They shook their heads. "We can handle it." He put his hand on Liam's shoulder. "This man is going to the jail."

After the soldier mounted again and nudged his horse forward, he called back, "If you need us, we'll be nearby." Perspiration beaded on Liam's brow and his heart thumped in his chest as he realized they were on the verge of losing everything.

One constable advised Burke. "You best go ahead and board. The ship is about to sail."

Frowning, Burke extended his hand. "But he still has my tickets! Give them to me."

As the second policeman reached for the brown paper pouch, Liam felt the man's grip on his arm loosen. Yanking his arm away, Liam bolted into the throng and dodged around people, shouting in Irish. "Make way! Make way!" The people, milling about the dock, moved aside for Liam, but seeing the police in pursuit, they closed ranks and shuffled into their path, feigning distractions.

Behind him, Liam could hear the whack of police batons and their angry shouts. "Move aside! Now! You Irish sons of apes! Out of the way."

Liam scanned over the crowd and saw four soldiers on horseback at the far edge of the dock. From a distance and in uniform, they all looked alike, but he had to take a chance and he started waving and yelling. "Captain Lawrence! Captain Lawrence!" One of the soldiers, upon hearing the shouts, abruptly shifted in his saddle and searched with his eyes. Taking hope, Liam kept waving.

"It's me!" He maneuvered around people and cut in front of others in a desperate effort to reach the soldiers.

A surprised Captain Lawrence dismounted. "Liam, you're here in Westport!"

Breathless, Liam blurted out, "Please! Help us! We're in trouble."

The constables, wielding their batons, forced their way through and when they caught up with Liam, they jerked him by the neck and pulled him off balance. "We're arresting this man! He stole tickets!"

Liam held up the brown pouch with his free hand. "Here, Captain! Read these and tell them we are the Reillys! They don't believe me!"

Lawrence leaned his head toward Liam. "I know this man." Removing his glove, he took the pouch and read the names. "Yes, the names on these tickets belong to his family." He looked around. "Where are they?"

Showing deference to the captain's rank, the policemen bowed and became meek. "At the ship, sir."

"Take me to them." Lawrence led his horse, and Liam walked alongside.

On seeing the constables and the soldier returning with Liam, Burke turned pale, his swagger vanished, and his cowering family peered around him.

Lawrence angrily looked Burke up and down. "Is this the man who says he's Liam Reilly? Well, I can assure you he's an imposter." He smiled at Aine, Mother, and the little girls, huddled together, exhausted from fright and stress.

"Greetings. I'm glad I was able to help! You best board this ship quickly because its departure is nigh." A seaman struck a large bell, and another untied a heavy rope that secured the gangplank.

Liam shouted above the noise. "Captain, we're lucky your circuit had you in Westport today and not in Ballinrobe! *Slán / Goodbye.*"

Lawrence looked startled when Mother reached out and hugged him. "Captain Lawrence, *slán! Go dte tu an cead /* Goodbye! Long life to you!"

Liam lifted his iron pot and hustled his family up the gangplank. Aine clutched her bundles and followed, but halfway up, she stopped and ran back to Lawrence, who was now astride his horse.

She reached for his hand and smiled. "Fare thee well, Captain Lawrence! I'll never forget how you saved us this day!" Then she scurried away and caught up with the family.

No sooner had they stepped onto the ship's deck than the planks behind them were removed. The roll call was beginning, and as the first name was read, a small lad skipped to the front and stuck out his tongue.

Liam lifted Caitlin and whispered. "Put your head on my shoulder and pretend to sleep. If they tell you to stand, cling to me and act drowsy, but *don't* turn your eyes upward." Liam could feel his heart beating against hers.

Caitlin's name was called next and Liam stepped forward. "This is Caitlin. We've walked quite far today and the child is tired."

"And *your* name?"

"Liam Reilly, her brother."

The first mate with quill pen in hand scoured the list, and not finding his name, started going through it more slowly a second time. After long and anxious moments, the mate at last confirmed, "Here it is . . . Liam Reilly . . . at the bottom," and Liam exhaled.

From the platform, the plump captain looked down. "Open your mouth, Reilly." Liam complied. "Dismissed!" Liam marched back with Cait's head still on his shoulder as they called for Aine, Erin, and Brighid Reilly in sequence and quickly judged them as healthy.

As soon as they were excused, Aine could hardly contain herself and hurried to Liam. "Brother, when did you get the idea of trying to find Captain Lawrence?"

Liam grinned. "When you started that commotion and caused the soldiers to ride up. I had this feeling he might be here somewhere since half his time is spent in Westport."

Still reliving the near disaster, Aine rolled her eyes. "And he *was* here, thanks be to God."

As the crew prepared the sails and called to each other in the language of ships, Liam squinted up and tried to guess their meaning. Men climbed rope ladders to high perches and swung like squirrels from pillar to post. They seemed to defy gravity and even laughed on occasion.

"Liam, what keeps them from falling? Aren't they afraid?" Brighid asked.

Before he could answer, sailors who had gone to check for stowaways reported to the captain, "All clear, sir."

The first mate bellowed, "You may go below." A crush of bodies crowded down the narrow ladder to steerage. People jostled and pushed aside any who could not hold their own, and Liam carried Cait to protect her from the trample of their feet. Liam wanted to be close to the hatch, but not being the first down, he had to creep farther into the tunnels. Because the ceiling was lower than five feet, he was forced to stoop to avoid hitting his head, but Caitlin, still in his arms, could not see to duck.

"Ouch! That hurt," she whimpered as she bumped her head.

So this was steerage. Liam surveyed the area, sold to the poorest, and decided they had paid too much. The aisles between the berths were so narrow that one person could scarcely pass another. Crammed into the hull, these passageways angled in different directions and created a maze. The two tiers of pinewood shelves for sleeping were two feet apart and about eighteen inches wide, forcing many occupants to sleep on their sides. They were packing in more people than the ship should carry, and Liam likened the narrow bunks to being wedged into a coffin alive.

Since there were no windows or openings, the air was stuffy and dank. The only light or air which filtered in came from the open hatch, and Liam hoped the hatch was not well fitted. He had heard that in storms or whenever it suited them, the crew would force steerage passengers below and close it, risking inadequate air or even suffocation.

Caitlin grimaced and covered her nose. "What's that bad smell!"

Liam, too, stifled a gag. The greater the distance from the opening, the more foul the air became. Evidently, the chamber pot he'd purchased was not common equipment, and the ship "made no provision," just as the vendors had said. Passengers were forced to relieve themselves between boards at the far ends of steerage. The revolting putrid odor told him that the ship was not cleaned between sailings.

Liam now realized they were facing a new horror. A long journey in this dungeon, deep in the ship's belly, would change his family forever, and although they could escape from steerage to a better life in six to eight weeks, would they still be sane? No one would knowingly accept such conditions unless they faced the workhouse or a mass grave in Ireland. In the chaos, children cried, the sick moaned, and people shouted the names of relatives from whom they had been separated in the confusion.

"Liam . . . Cait! Where are you?" It was Aine's voice. Moving toward the sound, he slid sideways down a narrow aisle and wiggled past families who were wedged in the passageways.

"We're coming!" he yelled above the den. He found them, claiming four berths: two on top and two on bottom.

Aine looked grim and, in order to breathe, she put her apron over her nose. "We have much to endure."

Even in this wretched pit, Mamai tried to be motherly. "Liam, hold these bundles while I spread out the sleeping mats."

A wrinkled woman stuck her head out of the next berth. "The first time waves wash down, you'll be pitching those out. The hard wood is better than wet feathers." Mamai looked dismayed.

Liam patted the mat. "Well, until that happens, it will offer some comfort. Perhaps we are too far from the hatch."

The darkness of steerage was even blacker for Cait. "I can't even see shadows here!"

Aine took her hand and ran it across the familiar mat. "You'll sleep here on the same feathers as you did at home."

Mother glanced around at the humanity packed in like stacked wood. "Do we cook on deck?"

Liam was not sure. "Maybe . . . when they let us go up. Let's hope they do . . . let us go up." Liam felt his hopeful spirits draining away and feared the answers to questions Mamai had yet to ask. Neil and his family must be somewhere in this labyrinth and maybe they knew the truth.

Suddenly the ship shuddered with a deep grating noise like something scraping the hull, and this caused a hush to come over steerage. "That's the anchor. We're getting underway," said the man across the aisle, and his announcement was quickly passed along. There was a rush for the hatch as people shoved one another in a struggle to get topside. Liam grabbed Cait, and they were pushed by the river of humanity to the open deck.

These conditions were unfit for humans, and Liam seethed with indignation. Whoever owns this ship must only care about making the highest profit, he decided. He noticed two sailors speaking Irish with an Ulster accent and approached them. "Is steerage always this crowded?"

One of them laughed. "Oh, the farther out we get, the more room you'll have." A chill went down Liam's spine. He understood what the sailor had implied, but he could not let his mind go there ... not there. His family had to make it – *all* the ones he had left.

He found Mamai, Brighid, and Aine at the rail facing the shore, and he and Cait squeezed in beside them. On the dock, he could see Burke and his family, weeping, and oddly he felt pity. Burke was a victim too.

Mother retreated into her shawl, and like a shell, it covered her curved back and drooping head. Her pale eyes mirrored his own confusion, and when she touched his arm, she spoke so softly that he had to lean close to hear.

"Liam, is God punishing us for sins, like the English say? Why is He scattering us all over the earth, destitute and crushed in spirit? Father Mullen said that suffering makes one compassionate, so is that why God sends us Irish so much of it?"

"No, Mamai. Don't blame God. It's the policies of the government that have caused this." He put his arm around her thin shoulders and tried to comfort her. "But maybe the Almighty will bring something good out of it ... someday ... someway ... for Ireland and for us."

Caitlin gripped the rail. "Aine, tell me what you are seeing."

Aine crouched next to her. "Over our heads, the sails have unfurled and are puffing out with wind. Can you hear them? We are sliding away from the land, and people are waving and praying for our safe journey. Now the town of Westport is getting smaller and smaller."

Caitlin frowned. "I hear sniffling. Are people crying?"

"Yes . . . they love Eire and will never see it or their family again. So it's hard."

Liam understood those feelings. He could see the perfect cone of Croagh Patrick and the white path curling upward to the little stone church at its summit. Before them were the thousand islands of Clew Bay, jutting out of the shimmering sea.

As the ship sailed down the western coast, no one left the rail for fear of missing their last memory of Eire. In reverence, people only whispered as they glided past the hills of Mayo and Galway with their dramatic ridges of gray rocks. Liam looked up at the Irish sky with sun-kissed clouds tumbling, churning, and floating above them and pushing inland with energy and grace. Once over land, the clouds split the sun's light into bright rays that radiated down as if someone had left heaven's door cracked open. Majestic, black cliffs endured the assault of powerful ocean swells which slammed into them before falling back in spray and white foam.

The magnificent shoreline filled Liam with pride, and he leaned to Mamai, "Aye – it's true what people say: 'Ireland is the boundary between heaven and earth.'"

Liam was being torn from the homeland he never wanted to leave . . . from everything he had known of kinship. No more the sweet smell of a peat fire or lilting music by the family hearth or soft shamrocks underfoot in the glen. As the wind blew their ship south, he remembered Tomas and wondered if they would sail near Spike Island where he had been imprisoned before being taken to Australia.

Hours passed and from somewhere on deck, a tin whistle began a slow, plaintive song in a minor key. As the ship floated past the counties of Kerry and Cork with their many bays and narrow inlets, the fingers of land seemed to reach out into the ocean and beckon them back home . . . begging them not to desert Ireland while she was still in bondage. As the late afternoon sun sank to the edge of the horizon and began to slip into the sea, the tin whistle subsided and all realized the end of the island was near. The tip of land became smaller and more distant until it was shrouded in misty darkness . . . then gone. Pressing against the rail, staring into emptiness, the people stood motionless and mute. They knew Ireland was falling silent.

23

A Meeting At 10 Downing Street
Spring 1849
and
The Historical Aftermath

Under the inn's portico, the horses shook water from their manes and jangled their bridles. The footman opened the dripping carriage door, and Nassau Senior slid onto the tufted, leather seat. As the carriage jerked forward, rain pelted the windows, and the horses' hooves clopped loudly on the wet cobblestones of London's streets.

Despite the dreary weather, Senior looked forward to an interesting day and enjoyed this time away from Oxford. Being a member of the small group which set the nation's policy for Ireland raised his status at the university, and he proudly basked in his importance as the economist who advised high government officials.

When the carriage pulled up before the plain facade of 10 Downing Street, the doorman rushed forward with an umbrella to ward off the downpour. Senior crouched beneath it and quickly spanned the few steps to the shiny, black door below the fan window.

As he stepped inside, a grandfather clock started its mellow gong and confirmed that he was exactly on time. A servant escorted him up the stairs which wound around the entry and down the hall to the reception room where Trevelyan was waiting.

As the door opened, he looked straight into the face of the unsmiling Assistant Secretary of the Treasury, Charles Trevelyan, who acknowledged Senior with a stern nod. His hair was combed to the side and oiled flat, and his small, narrowly spaced eyes peered out like an alert fox. Though Senior agreed with his politics toward Ireland, he resented the man's arrogance.

More to his liking was Sir Charles Wood who, as Chancellor of the Exchequer, outranked Trevelyan politically and socially but still greeted Senior with a genteel smile. His narrow nose separated expressive blue eyes, and he compensated for a receding hairline by growing full sideburns to the jaw.

Standing with his back to the glowing, marble fireplace, Wood warmed himself. "How is our economist . . . and Oxford?"

"Well, on both counts," Senior replied.

Sir George Grey crossed his legs as a servant presented tea on a silver tray. "Good morning, Nassau. Join us for a cup . . . a new brew from India."

"Indeed. I'll try it." The waiter filled a cup from the samovar nearby and presented it to Senior with all the deference demanded of servants – bowing his head and averting his superior's eyes.

Trevelyan, who had been shuffling papers at his desk, looked up. "Gentlemen, we have a full agenda and should begin." He cleared his throat, and like a strict schoolmaster, he waited until all were attentive and Sir Charles had taken a seat.

"We are finally seeing what can be accomplished in Ireland when we stop interfering with the famine! I'm happy to report that we have halted all our government relief programs. Because we British were being criticized by other nations for not doing more to help the Irish, our government opened its own soup kitchens in May 1847. But only five months later in September, I announced that the famine was over and closed them, even though we still had money allotted which we had not spent.[1] Although the Quakers still distribute food, they are discouraged, and I predict that by this June, they also will stop. The British Relief Association ran out of money last year in July.[2]

"To keep order in Ireland, we added another 10,000 troops in 1848 to the regiments already there.[3] Also policing the island are the militia, the armed Protestant yeomanry, the constables, and warships surrounding the coast."

Senior lit his pipe. "That should be enough military force to quell any revolt, should they be tempted to start one. But what about the death rate? Only when the population is *greatly* reduced can I analyze the economic results of this experiment. In 1848, they said the famine would not kill more than a million people, and I think that will scarcely be enough to do much good."[4]

Trevelyan held up a bound report. "Despite the fact that in a grand gesture, our Parliament outlawed evictions on Christmas Day and Good Friday,[5] this report says that evictions are increasing by the thousands, and new laws have made it easier for landlords to evict tenants. Not until this year did we keep records on the number of evictions, but in the next three years, it looks like a quarter of a million people or more will be evicted, and the trend will continue thereafter.[6] Eviction results in death usually and sometimes emigration – hopefully not here to England. We have sent some Irish who fled here back to Ireland and. . . ."

A knock at the door interrupted him, and Trevelyan looked irritated. "You may enter."

The servant stood erect, looking straight ahead, more like a statue than a man. "The Earl of Clarendon, Lord Lieutenant of Ireland, has arrived and awaits an audience."

Trevelyan glanced at the mantel clock. "Lord Clarendon insisted on presenting his case in person today, and though he is early, we'll see him now." He turned to the servant. "You may escort the Viceroy in."

When the distinguished Lord Clarendon entered the room, Senior rose to greet him and received a firm handshake. Wood also stood. "How are you, Lord George? . . . and your family? I trust the trip across the Irish Sea was smooth."

Clarendon smiled warmly and extended his hand to him and to Sir George Grey for he seemed to know these men well, but to Trevelyan, he gave only a frosty nod. After the exchange of pleasantries, Lord Clarendon opened his pouch and began. Seeing grave concern and worry in his face, Senior became alert and sat forward.

"Gentlemen, I come here in person because extensive correspondence with Prime Minister Russell and you, Sir Charles, has been to no avail, and I've been unable to receive a civil answer.[7] I dread some wholesale calamity![8] I am at my wit's end, and I cannot imagine how we are to get through the next six months, particularly in the South and West.[9] In addition to epidemics of typhus, dysentery, and blindness, cholera is now occurring. Potatoes which tenants planted at great sacrifice in 1848, were destroyed again by blight. The workhouses are bursting at the seams with many times their proper number and are bankrupt. It is enough to drive one mad. Day after day, I read horrifying reports and appeals, yet I must answer them all with a negative."[10]

Clarendon paused and looked at each of the four. "*Surely* this is a state of things that justifies your asking the House of Commons for an advance of money! For I don't think there is another legislature in Europe that would disregard such suffering as now exists in Ireland or would coldly persist in a policy of extermination."[11]

Trevelyan's eyes narrowed. "Come, come! You must know that the people conceal their advantages, exaggerate their difficulties, and relax their efforts in order to try to get relief.[12] It is my opinion that too much has been done for the Irish, and we need to leave them to natural causes. I admit the matter is serious, but we must await the result."[13]

Clarendon's face reddened and his nostrils flared. "What result? By the 'operation of natural causes,' you mean wholesale deaths from starvation and disease! The numbers of deaths are increasing and will be so great that our government will be blamed and shamed for the lack of aid."[14]

Trevelyan glowered. "It is not the function of our government to provide food, but to protect the merchant and landlord agriculturist.[15] God grant that we not do anything that would turn into a curse what was intended for a blessing."[16]

Sir Charles Wood sipped his tea. "I'm sure there's exaggeration here! The state of Ireland is not as frightful as you describe."[17]

Sir Grey frowned. "It may be that *if* numerous deaths should occur, the government will be blamed. But there is such a resistance to spending more money on Ireland that the Government will be severely blamed if they advance money to pay debts."[18]

Clarendon held up a bundle of envelopes tied with a cord. "Here are letters from resident landlords who say the best of their farmers are fleeing. More than five thousand a week are leaving Ireland.[19] Large tracts of land in the West and South are deserted, and shops in Dublin are shuttered and closed."[20]

Wood gestured with his lace handkerchief. "I am not at all appalled that the tenantry is going because that seems to me a necessary part of the process.[21] As I've told you in letters, only through a purgatory of misery and starvation can Ireland emerge into a state of quiet and prosperity?[22] We need a clearance and large scale eviction that replaces the Irish with loyal and Protestant

British and Scottish yeoman. It's happening already, and Scots are now managing large grazing farms being created in Mayo and Galway."[23]

Trevelyan leaned back on the chair cushions. "Yes, and as I have said many times, by acting to keep Irish at home, we would be defeating our own object. We must not complain of what we really want to obtain."[24] He gave Clarendon a mocking smile. "The English people don't want to be taxed for Irish bog trotters, and the last Queen's letter requesting donations for Irish relief received little response.[25] I've worked diligently to keep money in our treasury from going to help the Irish. It's not with the physical evil of the famine that we are contending, but with the moral evil of the selfish, perverse, and turbulent people."[26]

Lord Clarendon flushed. "In February 1848, a Catholic priest, Father James Maher, asked me: Can the people be saved? Then he pointed out that if the French threatened our possessions in the Mediterranean or the Americans approached the frontiers of British Canada or property was endangered, would the millions be provided to protect them?"[27]

Clarendon did not answer the question, but silently gazed around the room. Senior realized that his point was well made. No one could help but say yes in his mind and without a doubt, the money would be given.

The Lord continued, now pleading. "Please allow me to speak again for the emigration plan on which the Prime Minister and I have collaborated. I understand that you want to consolidate farms in Western Ireland in order to rear and feed livestock. To do this, we still need to get rid of some 400,000 people in a clean sweep.[28] But what are we to do with them? It seems the best option is still to help them emigrate to the colonies where their cheap labor is needed. As you know, on February 8th Lord Russell brought our emigration idea before the cabinet. At that time you strongly opposed the proposal, and it was defeated.[29] Now all aid for Ireland has dried up, so in the face of this crisis, won't you reconsider our plan?"

Trevelyan gave the Viceroy a cool stare. "No public money should be spent for that purpose. Many Irish are already emigrating without government help."[30]

Wood spoke slowly and deliberately with his large eyes bulging. "Let matters take their course, *regardless* of the social consequences."[31]

Grey squirmed in the brocade chair and frowned. "It is our opinion that the Irish need to be taught a lesson by the all wise Providence . . . not be rescued by an emigration scheme."[32]

Clarendon bristled and clinched his jaws. "Then you are abandoning the population to suffering that will equal or exceed the deaths of Black '47.[33] Edward Twistleton, the Chief Commissioner of the poor laws in Ireland, has resigned. Why? . . . Because, as a man of honor and humanity, he cannot be an agent of a policy that he said must be *extermination*.[34] So is there nothing I can say to shake you from this doctrinaire policy of doing *nothing* for Ireland?" He looked coldly at Trevelyan. "You seem to have their full support."[35]

Sir George Grey raised his hand. "Before you go . . . As Home Secretary, I am receiving complaints from the governors of the penal settlements in Australia that they are being overwhelmed by vast numbers of prisoners sent from Ireland. They say that most are too young and of such general good conduct that they are unfit for the treatment and work to which they will be subjected. Some as young as twelve years old! It is an embarrassment!"[36]

Clarendon shrugged. "I think the injustice goes beyond sending starving boys to the chain gangs. In October 1847, and again last year, Irish priests wrote a memorial to me. Our government had just cut off the soup and ended all relief, and they pled for some kind of aid to prevent mass death. But they also wanted reforms and said that – as hallowed as the rights of property are – the right to life is more sacred. They wanted the laws which regulated landlords and tenants to be changed to reflect the golden rule of Christ. At the present time, a landlord can take a tenant's entire crop without paying him for his seed or his labor.[37] But from what I'm hearing, neither justice nor mercy is on your agenda."

Looking weary and resigned, Clarendon picked up his pouch. He knew his mission had failed, but good manners oiled the social tension. He focused on Trevelyan. "By the way, I understand that it is now *Sir* Trevelyan, and I congratulate you on your knighthood last April. Queen Victoria is grateful for your service to England with the Irish policy."

"Never in my life of public service have I worked so hard continuously,"[38] Trevelyan said.

At the door, Lord Clarendon turned. "Thank you for your audience, gentlemen . . . Good day." With a nod he departed.

Senior lit his pipe and blew out smoke in a series of short puffs. "Well, he's surely determined to promote some plan to contain or reduce the death toll. I understand Clarendon keeps writing letters to the Prime Minister, complaining about us and our policies."

Wood shook his head. "Don't be concerned. Since both Sir George Grey and I sit on the Prime Minister's divided cabinet, we can control the votes.[39] As Chancellor, I have more opportunity to steer Russell and the cabinet than Clarendon's letters from Ireland. Lord Russell vacillates on Irish relief – one day wanting to help the Irish and the next day, preaching economy. But whenever he feels inclined to endorse some generous plan, we've been able to discourage and stall him.[40] Besides, the public is behind us."[41]

Nassau Senior raised his brows. "But hasn't Lord Russell

threatened to resign if the emigration plan or some proposal for Irish relief does not get support?"[42]

"The Prime Minister won't resign and is too weak to get anything passed," Grey answered. "Trevelyan and I have a private understanding with the editor of the London *Times*.[43] His recent articles have stirred public opinion against Russell's emigration scheme."

Wood laughed. "Nassau, did you not recognize some familiar language in the articles?"[44] He winked knowingly at Trevelyan.

Senior smiled. "I say! Things are under control. Let's order a good bottle of French wine with lunch to toast Sir Trevelyan and his management of the press!"

Sir Wood leaned forward in his chair and put his hands on his knees. "Lunch in the dining room today is roast duck with orange sauce." As Senior followed his cohorts down the hall to the small dining room, their heels clicked on the polished floor. No one could challenge the direction of Irish policy, and few in England wanted to.

Meanwhile, in Ireland the worst human catastrophe of the nineteenth century continued unchecked. In County Mayo alone, 100,000 acres were vacant and empty of tenants.[45] According to Nobel laureate Amartya Sen, acclaimed scholar of famines, no other recorded famine in world history killed such a high percentage of a nation's people.[46]

Sen contends that almost always such famines can be prevented if the government in charge has the political will to act.[47] But, he says, that "will" is undermined when the rulers consider the starving subjects to be of an inferior status or are prejudiced against them.[48] Then the rulers develop a severe indifference to the fate of their subjects and are not motivated to come to their aid.

In Ireland the death toll rose into the millions. Scholars believe that the exact number who died will never be known because of inadequate record keeping and other factors. However, the 1841 Census put the population of Ireland at 8,175,124. By the next census in 1851, it had dropped to 6,552,385. According to the British Census Commissioners, the 1851 total would have been 9,018,799, had there been no famine. This meant that in these ten years Ireland had lost at least 2.5 million persons to death and emigration.[49]

However, this method of calculation ignores an important factor needed for accurate estimates, and that is the population growth that occurred between the 1841 Census and 1845 when the famine began. This growth can be estimated from the growth rate in Ireland for the previous 62 years. Based on the growth rate over this entire period, which has been calculated at 172%,[50] Ireland's population on the eve of the Famine would have been a little over nine million.[51] When this figure is compared with the census of 1851, an additional half million are missing.

Many believe both these estimates, however, are low because they are based on inaccurate and undercounted census reports, particularly in the South and West where poverty and death were highest.[52] The Irish distrusted British census takers and often hid from them. As the proverb warned, "It is better to exist unknown to the law,"[53] for once the government counted and identified them, it could confiscate their meager resources and force their sons into the army.

In fact, it was widely accepted that the 1841 census count was too low, and one enterprising relief officer in County Clare conducted a partial recount which showed the population to be one third greater than had been recorded.[54] If this were true in Clare, it would be even more likely in the wild areas of mountains, bogs, and glens in northwestern Ireland. Since far more people died than were able to leave, the death toll could be far higher than previously estimated.

Amartya Sen figures that between 1845-51, the famine killed at least one fifth of the Irish people.[55] Yet excess mortality extended beyond 1851.[56] In addition to deaths in Ireland, Sen calculates that another fifth emigrated.[57] But emigration was often but a prelude to death, and estimates of the number who perished at sea or shortly upon arrival vary between twenty to forty percent.[58] The emigrants were already weakened by hunger and disease, and conditions in steerage on the "coffin ships" were so horrific that only the slave ships of previous centuries were worse.[59]

Eviction and migration continued well after the time designated as the Irish Famine, with 900,000 departing Ireland in the five years after 1851.[60] What happened in the next twenty years was obscured when the census returns for 1861 and 1871 were deliberately destroyed by order of the British government.[61] Centuries of oppression followed by the Irish Starvation so scarred the people and the land that for more than a hundred years afterwards, a third to a half of each generation left Ireland.[62] Even in 2005 – one hundred and sixty years later – the population of the *entire* island was only around five million, slightly more than half the count at the time the famine began.[63] The remnants of stone cottages against a twilight sky and the mounds of mass graves still give witness to the time when the right to life was denied, and Ireland fell silent.

A NOTE FROM THE AUTHOR

Sir George Grey, Sir Charles Wood, Sir Charles Trevelyan, and Nassau Senior were some of the chief architects of Irish policy for the British government during the Irish Starvation years. They met and conferred regularly on issues and plans for Ireland. The commentary attributed to them in this meeting was taken from historical records and documentary evidence such as letters, reports, articles, private papers, etc. with the sources of these included in the footnotes. Whenever quotations were paraphrased for more modern language, every effort was made to remain faithful to the original meaning and attitudes.

ENDNOTES FOR CHAPTER 23

1. Donnelly, James S. Jr. *The Great Irish Potato Famine.* (United Kingdom: Sutton Publishing, 2001) p. 89. Hereafter referred to as Donnelly, *The Great Irish Potato Famine.*

2. Gray, Peter. *Famine, Land and Politics: British Government and Irish Society 1843-50.* (Dublin: Irish Academic Press, 1999) p. 311. Hereafter referred to as Gray, *Famine, Land and Politics.* (Although Prime Minister John Russell insisted the government continue their program of feeding school children in western Ireland, this program was terminated by October.)

3. Woodham-Smith, Cecil. *The Great Hunger: Ireland 1845-1849.* (New York: Old Town Books, 1962) p. 339. Hereafter referred to as Woodham-Smith, *The Great Hunger.*

4. *Ibid.*, pp. 375-376. Gallagher, Thomas. *Paddy's Lament: Ireland 1846-1847, Prelude to Hatred.* (New York: Harcourt Brace & Company, 1982) p. 85. Hereafter referred to as Gallagher, *Paddy's Lament.* Gray, Peter. "Shovelling Out Your Paupers: The British State and Irish Famine Migration 1846-50," in *Patterns of Prejudice*, vol. 33, no. 4, pp. 47-65, (London: Sage Publications, 1999) p. 54. Hereafter referred to as Gray, "Shovelling Out Your Paupers." (Senior to Lansdowne, Dec. 2, 1848 in NSP, C218; Nassau Senior, "The Relief of Irish Distress," *Edinburgh Review,* January 1849.)

5. Donnelly, *The Great Irish Potato Famine, p.* 116.

6. *Ibid.*, pp. 140, 178. (Almost a quarter of a million people were evicted between 1849 and 1854. These evictions included only those recorded by the constabulary.) Keneally, Thomas. *The Great Shame and The Triumph of the Irish in the English-Speaking World.* (New York: Doubleday, 1998) p. 293. Hereafter referred to as Keneally, *The Great Shame.* Gray, Peter. *The Irish Famine.* (New York: Harry N. Abrams, Inc., 1995) p. 68. Hereafter referred to as Gray, *The Irish Famine.*

7. Woodham-Smith, *The Great Hunger*, p. 370.

8. *Ibid.*, p. 373. (Clarendon to George Grey, Dec.7, 1848.)

9. *Ibid.,* p. 375. (Clarendon to Trevelyan, Dec. 27, 1848.)

10. *Ibid.*, p. 381. (Clarendon to Russell, Apr. 26, 1849.)

11. *Ibid.* (Clarendon to Russell, Apr. 26, 1849.)

12. Gray, *The Irish Famine,* p. 153. (Article by Trevelyan entitled *The Irish Crisis,* 1848.)

13. Kee, Robert. *Ireland: A History.* (Boston: Little, Brown, and Co.; 1982.) pp. 96 and 98. Hereafter referred to as Kee, *Ireland: A History.* Woodham-Smith, *The Great Hunger,* p. 374. Gallagher, *Paddy's Lament,* p. 86.

14. Woodham-Smith, *The Great Hunger*, p. 374. (Clarendon to George Grey, Dec. 7, 1848.)

15. Kissane, Noel. *The Irish Famine: A Documentary History.* (Syracuse: Syracuse University Press, 1997) p. 51. (Trevelyan to Monteagle, Oct. 9, 1846.)

16. *Ibid.* (Same letter as above). Gray, Peter, "Ideology and the Famine," in Cathal Porteir, ed. *The Great Irish Famine,* [Thomas Davis Lecture Series] RTE/Mercier, 1995, pp. 86-103, p. 93.

17. Woodham-Smith, *The Great Hunger,* p. 374.

18. *Ibid.,* pp. 373-374. (George Grey to Clarendon, Dec. 10, 1848 – replying to Clarendon's plea for aid.)

19. Kerr, Rev. Donal, "The Catholic Church and the Great Irish Famine," Lecture Series in Commemoration of the Great Irish Famine, March 7, 1997, The Vincentian Center for Church and Society, c. 2000. (July 20, 2004). See, www.vincenter.org/97/Kerr.html, p. 16 out of 19. Hereafter referred to as Kerr, "The Catholic Church and the Great Irish Famine."

20. Woodham-Smith, *The Great Hunger,* pp. 371, 372, 376.

21. *Ibid.,* p. 371. (Wood to Monteagle, Nov, 1848.) Gallagher, *Paddy's Lament,* p. 92.

22. Gray, Peter, "'Potatoes and Providence:' British Government Responses to the Great Famine," *Bullan: an Irish Studies Journal,* vol. 1, no. 1, (Spring 1994), pp. 75-90, p. 85. (Wood to Clarendon, July 23, 1847.)

23. Gray, *The Great Irish Famine,* pp. 88-89. Donnelly, *The Great Irish Potato Famine,* p. 159.

24. Woodham-Smith, *The Great Hunger,* p. 371. (Trevelyan to Twistleton, Sept. 14, 1848.)

25. Kinealy, Christine. *This Great Calamity: The Irish Famine 1845-1852.* (Ireland: Gill & Macmillan Ltd., 1994), pp. 161-162. Hereafter referred to as Kinealy, *This Great Calamity.*

26. Woodham-Smith, *The Great Hunger,* p. 156. (Trevelyan to Colonel Jones, Dec. 2, 1846.) (Trevelyan to Routh, Dec. 8, 1846.) Gallagher, *Paddy's Lament,* p. 86.

27. Kerr, "The Catholic Church and the Great Irish Famine," p. 17.

28. Gray, *Famine, Land and Politics,* p. 309. (Clarendon to Russell, Dec. 16 and 26, 1848.) (Clarendon to George Grey, Jan. 13, 1849.)

29. *Ibid.*, p. 310. (Russell to Clarendon, Feb. 8 and 11, 1849.)

30. *Ibid.*, p. 310. (Trevelyan to Wood, Aug. 31, 1849.) (Grey Diary, Feb. 8, 1849.)

31. *Ibid.*, p. 308.

32. *Ibid.*, p. 308. (Grey memo: "Remarks on Emigration, Poor Law, and Ireland," Dec. 18, 1848, Grey Papers.) Gray, "Shovelling Out Your Paupers," p. 64. (Grey to Clarendon, Dec. 4, 1847.)

33. *Ibid.*, p. 310.

34. Woodham-Smith, *The Great Hunger,* p. 380. (Clarendon to Russell, Mar. 12, 1849.) Gray, *The Irish Famine,* p. 87.

35. Woodham-Smith, *The Great Hunger,* p. 375. (Clarendon to Russell, Feb. 9, 1849.) More on solidarity of the committee's position p. 380.

36. *Ibid.*, p. 377. (George Grey to Clarendon, Feb. 5, 1849.)

37. Gray, *The Irish Famine,* pp. 158-159. (Memorial to his Excellency the Earl of Clarendon, Oct. 26, 1847, as reprinted in the *Freeman's Journal,* written by Catholic prelates of Ireland.)

38. Kee, *Ireland: A History,* p. 96.

39. Gray, "Shovelling Out Your Paupers," p. 65. Gray, *Famine, Land and Politics,* p. 309. (Russell to Clarendon, Feb. 5, 1849.)

40. Kinealy, *This Great Calamity,* p. 359. Donnelly, *The Great Irish Potato Famine,* pp. 28-29. Gray, *Famine, Land and Politics,* pp. 242-243, 312, 316-317.

41. Gray, *Famine, Land and Politics,* p. 312. (Russell to Clarendon, Dec. 8, 1848 – said a great obstacle facing them in helping the Irish was the prejudice deep in the breasts of the British people.) Woodham-Smith, *The Great Hunger,* p. 382.

42. Gray, *Famine, Land and Politics,* pp. 309, 312.

43. Gray, "Shovelling Out Your Paupers," p. 64.

44. Gray, *Famine, Land and Politics,* pp. 308, 309. *(Times,* Dec. 26, 1848), p. 313. (*Times,* Feb. 12, 1849.)

45. Woodham-Smith, Cecil. *The Reason Why.* (New York: McGraw-Hill, 1953), p. 122.

46. O'Grada, Carmac, "Ireland's Great Famine: An Overview," Working Paper Series, November, 2004, Center for Economic Research, University College, Dublin, p. 21. Kerr, "The Catholic Church and the Great Irish Famine," p. 3. Barsamian, David, "Reflections of an Economist," Alternative radio talks to Amartya Sen, India Together, September, 2001, p. 7 of 17. See, www.indiatogether.org/cgi-bin/tools/pfriend.cgi. Hereafter referred to as Barsamian, "Reflections of an Economist."

47. Barsamian, "Reflections of an Economist," p. 8. (Sen says that while undernourishment is difficult to prevent, mass death from starvation can be prevented "with half an effort, without difficulty.")

48. Barsamian, "Reflections of an Economist," p. 8. (Sen explains that elites or upper class do not suffer from famine and have less personal incentive to stop it. Likewise, colonial administrations such as existed in India and Ireland are not as politically motivated to act to prevent famine affecting subject peoples as would occur in a democracy.) Donnelly, Jim, "The Irish Famine," British Broadcasting Corporation, 01-01-2001. See, www.bbc.co.uk/history/state/nations/famine print. html p. 5. (Donnelly says that fully documented ethnic prejudices caused British politicians to treat the Irish Catholic as "less than fully human.") Kinealy, *This Great Calamity*, p. 359.

49. Woodham-Smith, *The Great Hunger*, pp. 411-412.

50. *Ibid.*, p. 29.

51. *Ibid.*, p. 31.

52. *Ibid.*, p. 412. Kinealy, *This Great Calamity*, pp. 167-168.

53. Iomaire, Liam Mac Con, *Ireland of the Proverb*. (Boulder, CO: Roberts Rinehart, 1995), p. 94.

54. Woodham-Smith, *The Great Hunger*, p. 31. If this degree of error were extrapolated to the rest of Ireland, the actual population in 1841 could have been over 10 million, and using the same growth rate, the population in 1845 could have been around 11 million.

55. Sen, Amartya. *Poverty and Famines: An Essay on Entitlement and Deprivation*. (Oxford: Clarendon Press, 1981), p. 39. Hereafter referred to as Sen, *Poverty and Famines*.

56. Kinealy, *This Great Calamity*, p. 168.

57. Sen, *Poverty and Famine*, p. 39.

58. Metress, Seamus, and Rajner, Richard. *The Great Starvation: An Irish Holocaust*. (Stoney Point, New York: American Ireland Educational Foundation, PEC. 1996) p.

102. Gallagher, Paul. "How British Free Trade Starved Millions During Ireland's Potato Famine," *The American Almanac,* (May 29, 1995), p. 9.

59. Kee, *Ireland: A History,* p. 97. (Report of Montreal Board of Health, Aug. 12, 1847.) Woodham-Smith, *The Reason Why,* p. 123. Gallagher, *Paddy's Lament,* p. 206.

60. Keneally, *The Great Shame,* p. 293. Donnelly, *The Great Irish Potato Famine,* p. 178. (900,000 departed Ireland in the five years after 1851.)

61. Central Statistics Office Ireland. See, www.cso.ie/census/Access_to_Records.htm.

62. Keneally, *The Great Shame,* p. 293.

63. Frankel, Glenn. "In Ireland, It's Commuters vs. Kings," *The Washington Post, (Jan. 22, 2005.)* See, www.msnbc.msn.com/id/6854465/print/1/displaymode/1098.

ACKNOWLEDGEMENTS

I am indebted to the many scholars whose meticulous research contributed authenticity and historical accuracy to this story. Cecil Woodham-Smith's *The Great Hunger: Ireland 1845-1849* was very significant. Her trailblazing research in the 1960's, relying heavily on documentary evidence, presented a new perspective. Thomas Gallagher's *Paddy's Lament: Ireland 1846-1847* provided vivid details about the culture of the American wake, emigration, and suffering of the Irish people. Peter Gray's *Famine, Land and Politics: British Government and Irish Society 1843-50* gave great insight into the politics and motives of British leaders during the Famine. In addition to these three, I am grateful to all the historians mentioned in the endnotes to Chapter 23, whose works I consulted on many aspects of this tragedy.

I also want to acknowledge and thank my family and friends for their guidance, advice, and encouragement which sustained me during the journey of research and writing. My husband Tom was an integral part of this project in all phases, and without his patience and enduring support, I could not have completed it. I appreciate my adult children's steadfast belief in the book and the valuable feedback they furnished. I would like to mention each of the many friends who generously gave of their time to read manuscript and offer vital suggestions, but in naming some, I fear that I may inadvertently omit others which would be unjust. You know who you are, and I hope you realize how very grateful I am. However, a special thank you is due Carolyn Tharp for her careful proofing before publication. I also want to express gratitude to Carolyn Wall and members of our writers group for their advice and direction.

Some Questions and Topics for Discussion

1. The Prologue: Was there anything in the prologue that surprised you or helped you to understand the Irish experience? If so, what was it and why?

2. What moment in the story was the most poignant and emotionally powerful for you and why?

3. Chapter 5: Why did the Irish call workhouses "the pathway to the dead?" The photographs below, taken in County Mayo, 2008, are of an abandoned workhouse which was surrounded by a ten-foot stone wall and secured by a tall iron gate with guards. Families were separated and food was eaten in silence. Why was the workhouse built like a prison with harsh conditions?

4. Chapter 7: The Reillys came upon a village smoldering in ruins. The British army and the landlord's officials had driven out the families and torched and destroyed their homes. An angry Liam spoke through clinched teeth: "Why do the powerful think they have a right to do this? Why?" How would you answer his question? How do powerful people excuse such actions even today?

5. Chapter 7: The Murphys did not recognize Maureen McGuinness, a woman evicted from Ballinglass and now in the last stages of starvation. There is a word in Irish that means both eviction and extermination. Why were these two concepts linked in this way?

continued on next page

6. Chapter 13: What did you think of the trials held in Castlebar and the fate of Tomas and the other men? Do you think giving rewards to witnesses compromised justice? What other factors in the way the empire was run compromised justice? Explain your reasons.

7. Chapter 23: In the meeting at 10 Downing Street, Lord Clarendon, the British leader in Ireland, pleaded with Trevelyan, Wood, and Grey to reconsider the emigration plan which he and Prime Minister Lord John Russell had proposed. It would transport hungry Irish in western Ireland to colonies such as New Zealand and British Canada as unpaid or cheap labor to harvest crops, build railroads, etc. They refused to approve the plan once again. Why? What might have happened if this emigration plan had been accepted? Do you think this would have made a difference or not? Why?

8. Chapter 23, Aftermath: Why do you think the Irish Census returns for 1861 and 1871 were destroyed by order of the British government?

9. Chapter 23, Aftermath: According to Amartya Sen, acclaimed scholar of famines, the British government could have prevented or at least mitigated the Great Irish Famine with such steps as curtailing exports of food, providing cheap maize, continuing the soup kitchens, undertaking reforms to give Irish tenants some rights to land, or donating money from the British treasury. Even though Trevelyan, Wood, and Grey did not want to help the Irish, the British Parliament and the public could have challenged their policies. Why do you think they did not?

10. Why do you think the starvation went on for seven years and was so severe? What things do you think caused the Great Irish Famine and why?